JOE'S LAW

JOE'S LAW

America's Toughest Sheriff
Takes on Illegal Immigration, Drugs, and
Everything Else That Threatens America

SHERIFF JOE ARPAIO
AND
LEN SHERMAN

AMACOM AMERICAN MANAGEMENT ASSOCIATION
NEW YORK ✻ ATLANTA ✻ BRUSSELS ✻ CHICAGO ✻ MEXICO CITY ✻ SAN FRANCISCO
SHANGHAI ✻ TOKYO ✻ TORONTO ✻ WASHINGTON, D.C.

Special discounts on bulk quantities of AMACOM books are available to corporations, professional associations, and other organizations. For details, contact Special Sales Department, AMACOM, a division of American Management Association, 1601 Broadway, New York, NY 10019. Tel: 212-903-8316. Fax: 212-903-8083.
E-mail: specialsls@amanet.org
Website: www.amacombooks.org/go/specialsales
To view all AMACOM titles go to: www.amacombooks.org

This publication is designed to provide accurate and authoritative information in regard to the subject matter covered. It is sold with the understanding that the publisher is not engaged in rendering legal, accounting, or other professional service. If legal advice or other expert assistance is required, the services of a competent professional person should be sought.

Library of Congress Cataloging-in-Publication Data

Arpaio, Joe, 1932-
   Joe's law : America's toughest sheriff takes on illegal immigration, drugs, and everything else that threatens America / Joe Arpaio and Len Sherman.
      p. cm.
   Includes index.
   ISBN-13: 978-0-8144-0199-6
   ISBN-10: 0-8144-0199-6
   1. Arpaio, Joe, 1932– 2. Sheriffs—Arizona—Maricopa County—Biography. 3. Police—United States—Biography. 4. Drug enforcement agents—United States—Biography. 5. Corrections—Arizona—Maricopa County. 6. Prisons—Arizona—Maricopa County. 7. Law enforcement—Arizona—Maricopa County. 8. Illegal aliens—United States. 9. Drug abuse—United States. I. Sherman, Len, 1956– II. Title.

HV7911.A77A3 2008
363.2092—dc22
[B]

                                                                     2008007007

Printing number
10 9 8 7 6 5 4 3 2 1

CONTENTS

INTRODUCTION

We quickly tire of our heroes, probably because they're not really heroes at all. They appear, they glitter, they are everywhere, and then we learn the truth that they are nothing but false fronts, Potemkin villages, hollow beings constructed for media absorption and public consumption out of slogans and hype and pictures, saying the correct things, supporting the accepted ideas, doing nothing in the end that benefits anyone but themselves and their backers. Politicians, corporate heads, actors, athletes, celebrities of every miscreant variety—they're all part of the same media world we inhabit—and they've all disappointed us so many times that poll after poll demonstrates that we no longer trust any of our leading institutions.

And so to Joe Arpaio.

For more than twelve years, I've seen them come and go. I've watched the reporters find their way to Phoenix for the big interview, for their moment in the sun, and as we all know, the sun here can get pretty hot. They sweat through their tour of the tents, they go out on patrol with the posse, they stare at the pink underwear, the chain gangs, the public adulation. And they act like Columbus discovering America, like they've found something their audience will not believe, and they go home and do their story, which is the same story, over and over, declaring, and sometimes decrying, the wonder of Sheriff Joe, as he is known far and wide, and the Maricopa County Sheriff's Office.

But of course they don't stay long enough to really understand what's going on, but that's the nature of the modern media—hit and run. They don't stay long enough to understand that the Sheriff is the real thing, that he actually means what he says and then acts on those heartfelt beliefs and ideas, and that's why he has commanded such overwhelming support from so many people for so many years.

Apparently, it is easy to dismiss the Sheriff as a media phenomenon, as a sideshow with some clever ideas to distract an easily distractible public. But if that is so, name another elected official, and especially a dynamic, controversial one, who has won four elections in a row, quickly heading into his fifth, with an uninterrupted approval rating always in the neighborhood of 80 percent—80 percent!—from the people.

Can you imagine how hard it must be to maintain that level of support? Even more, can you imagine how hard it must be to maintain that level of support and never lose sight of your values and goals?

That kind of unprecedented success does not happen by chance. Nor can it be sustained merely by press events and rousing speeches. It can only be earned by doing what is hard and right and good, and doing all of it openly and honestly.

Even if you agreed with every action that Sheriff Joe has taken (and, obviously, most voters in Maricopa County have agreed with most of his decisions), even that probably wouldn't be sufficient to maintain your interest, not on our sensation-saturated planet, not for more than fifteen years. Sheriff Joe not only survives but triumphs because he has somehow reached across the divide and connects with the people of his county and, indeed, the people of Arizona and across the United States, and even beyond, in some inexplicable, profoundly personal way.

Perhaps Sheriff Arpaio has forged this link because he is so conspicuously Everyman, with distinctly American manners, beliefs, and ideas, though with overtly more courage and purpose and dedication than most of his compatriots. He is one of us, accessible and comprehensible, in more vivid colors, his life overlaid with drama, consequence, and daring.

That is often the point of art, or at least entertainment, presenting a portrait of an individual, fundamentally no different from anyone in the audience in appearance, ability, and personality, an ordinary person who rises when the occasion demands it and performs heroically. Cops are frequently employed as the character in these scenarios, because cops are viewed as basically ordinary guys (in movies, though less in books, male cops are the chosen gender) facing extraordinary circumstances. Consider Bruce Willis in *Die Hard*, Al Pacino in *Serpico*, Steve McQueen in *Bullitt*, Clint Eastwood in *Dirty Harry*, Danny Glover in *Lethal Weapon* (Mel Gibson's the crazy one), or, to shift to TV, anybody from *Law and Order* or *NYPD Blue* or *Homicide: Life on the Streets* or *The Wire* or any one of a thousand other shows.

Sheriff Joe is a larger-than-life character wrapped in flesh and blood. You'll appreciate that even more after you read his book and come to know more about his career, his life, and his principles. You don't have to agree with everything he does to be drawn in and appreciate his appeal as an elected official and as a man. I'm a true-blue Democrat and disagree with the Sheriff on a number of issues, large and small, domestic and foreign. Regardless, none of that matters to me in this instance, because I've learned, as we all should have, that honor and honesty and intellect and conviction count for more than any policy or plan, whether we're talking about how a school board decides to educate our children or how the President chooses to protect the environment, promote energy independence, provide health care, and conduct war. From citizen to government, our disinterest in adequately funding public schools has left Arizona ranked at the bottom in national education ratings, and the Bush administration's dishonest and dishonorable behavior has had ruinous consequences at home and abroad.

With that in mind, we can appreciate that the Sheriff is a person to be respected and admired. In a world so difficult and dangerous, in a time so uncertain and confusing, that is saying quite a lot.

This is the second time I've written a book with the Sheriff, the previous effort entitled *America's Toughest Sheriff*. The first time we collaborated, Sheriff Joe had only been in office a couple of years and was just beginning to gain national attention, so it was imperative in that earlier book to review in detail each of the Sheriff's programs. Such a comprehensive methodology is no longer necessary, as word of these programs has spread far and wide. Instead, this book takes a different approach, more personality than programs, more commentary than statistics, more passion than recitation.

This book is also about issues, national issues that will determine not only what sort of country this is and will be, but also what sort of people we are, and what sort of people we want to be.

Sheriff Joe's constitutional authority is only that of a sheriff, responsible for the jails and law enforcement in Maricopa County, Arizona. That's it. But his personal authority, earned by dint of everything he has done, everything he has stood for, extends far beyond the county line. His is a voice unique on the American scene. His is a voice worth hearing.

I hope you enjoy the book.

Len Sherman

★ O N E ★

THE BOTTOM LINE

I DROVE OVER to the Maricopa County Sheriff's Office (MCSO) Training Center, located on the west side of town. It's a huge facility, necessary to accommodate our needs. I walked up to the second floor and down the hallway, past classrooms teaching new recruits the fine points of being a law enforcement officer, a Maricopa County deputy sheriff, or detention officer. Other classrooms were filled with not only deputies and detention officers but also cops from other departments, all going over changes and advances in every related aspect of serving and protecting. Other young men and women dressed in shirts and T-shirts, in-between exercise modules or self-defense classes, hurried through the halls, flattening themselves against the walls whenever a superior officer strode by.

Lisa Allen, my longtime, immensely capable, and absolutely essential director of public information, led the way. She had arranged what was about to happen. For once, I was just along for the ride.

I walked into the large room we used for meetings and other get-togethers and was greeted by a couple hundred people shouting "Happy Birthday!" in ragged unison. It was my seventy-fifth birthday, and Lisa had arranged a celebration with coworkers and friends and Italian food from Buca di Beppo. A very big cake was wheeled out. It not only had an excessive number of candles, but was also accompanied by two firefighters in full gear. Lisa's idea of a joke—and not a bad one, I had to admit.

After amateur Elvis impersonator and professional detention officer Bret Kaiser finished with his rendition of "Happy Birthday," Presley-style, and my chief deputy Dave Hendershott offered his own version, showing himself to be not only musical but also surprisingly nimble for a large fellow, it was my turn to say something. Noting the many law enforcement officers and officials in the room, mainly though not entirely from my own department, I stated that while the sheriff sets the policy, the office is only as good as its employees, and we were fortunate to have the best, from top to bottom. It's never smart to break up a winning team, and I wasn't about to break up ours, not as long as I held office, which I intended to do for at least another four years, come next November. And who knew, maybe another four years after that.

And so the party continued, with pasta and cake and a lot of storytelling. And then, after some more fun, lunch was over and it was time for the deputies and lieutenants and captains and chiefs to get back to work, and that included me, too.

And I knew something that most of the others, even in that room, did not know. That while my talk of four or even eight more years of service was heartfelt, it also contained maybe a touch of bravado, because there was a threat hanging over my head, a threat unlike any other I had faced in a career filled with threats and dangers and even bullets flying past my head. It was a threat that endangered not only myself but also my wife, my family, and anyone near me. It was a threat that crossed borders and was the result of my work, work that could not, would not, stop.

It was a threat that meant my pledge to serve for many more years, for any more years, could prove to be a hollow boast. I knew it, and a handful of my deputies and detectives knew it, and some cops and agents in other agencies involved in the case knew it, too. Apart from that relatively small group, we had kept our awareness of the conspiracy secret while we conducted our investigation.

It was a race against a threat that had begun for me on March 21, 2007. That was the day the Yuma Police Department contacted the Maricopa County Sheriff's Office to say it had uncovered a plot to assassinate me.

The idea that somebody wanted me dead hardly constituted cause for me to jump up and barricade the door. I've lived with a near constant round of threatening phone calls, letters, and e-mails since becoming sheriff. And, even so, all this unpleasantness has been small potatoes compared to my previous life as a fed: The drug business is a vicious business, with the criminal organizations and gangs in charge willing to kill anyone and everyone who interferes or could conceivably interfere with their profits. I worked undercover for decades, in country after country, always one misstep, one careless word, one betrayal away from exposure and a bullet between my eyes, a bomb under my car, a knife across my throat.

As sheriff, it's been different and still more of the same. The potential players and deadly scenarios take on their own special character in Maricopa County, far from the mountains of Turkey or the streets of Mexico City or the jungles of Panama. Back in my days as a fed, there was usually a very direct, very unadulterated quality about those threats, that danger—the bad guys versus me, face-to-face, frequently gun-to-gun.

That's not the way it is now. I run law enforcement for the county. I run the jails. I deal with policy and programs and, God help me, politicians. I don't go undercover and I don't walk a beat, so my relationship with those we investigate and arrest is, at best, one step removed. So while the threats are specific and personal, they're from criminals and degenerates and murderers I haven't had the up-close pleasure of busting.

In a funny way, it's almost more disconcerting than what was always hanging over my head in my federal career. Back then, at least I had a fair idea who would be interested in gunning for me and why. Now, I have no way of knowing which of the 1.5 million people who've spent time in my jails since I became sheriff might want me dead, not to mention all the others, whether lowlife or high-flying criminals, who might be more than a little annoyed with how my actions have interfered with their interests or otherwise offended their sensibilities.

So I've had a long list of would-be assassins appear on my metaphorical doorstep. The first was in the Madison Street Jail, bonding out his wife, when he threatened to shoot me. The second was on the other side of the bars at the same jail, in custody, when he somehow managed to get my home phone number and began calling me, announcing how he was planning a drive-by shooting with the aim of killing me. The third called my office and threatened me. The fourth stalked me and called numerous times with regard to my announced public appearances, when he wasn't leaving a message in a rap song that referred to killing me. The fifth sent harassing and threatening letters to both an ex-friend of his and to me. Investigators discovered a weapons cache in his possession. The sixth sent six threatening e-mails, in which he stated he possessed a knife and was going to kill me by either stabbing me in the heart or slitting my throat. Just to round it out, he also promised to rape and kill a local female news anchor. When he was picked up, he had a folding knife in his pocket. The seventh was a conspiracy among three jail inmates to murder both then-governor Jane Hull and myself.

All were arrested and convicted.

Still more cases haven't been resolved. One person obtained an MCSO radio frequency and called in, on fourteen occasions, to inform me, "I'm gonna put a bullet in your brain," or some such similar sentiment. Another called the Glendale PD to issue death threats against me, accompanied by several audible gunshots heard over the phone. Yet another shot up a mailbox in the parking lot of a shopping center in Anthem and wrote various menacing statements on the box, including this gem, bereft of punctuation: "Joe by the time you read this you will have heard the boom." And still another mailed me a spent bullet casing with a note that promised, "The next one will be for real and you better watch your back."

Some threats resolve themselves, and not usually in happy ways. In May 2002, a jail inmate loudly threatened to kill me. Soon thereafter, he hanged himself.

Seven people have been convicted of charges related to threatening me. Another six have charges pending. Another two are awaiting trial. Those are the ones we've identified, tracked, and caught. That's definitely not everybody.

And so, considering the history, you'll forgive me if I took this latest news with a dash of skepticism.

But then I heard the details and I had to pause and think again. After all, even though anyone can learn how to make a bomb (thanks to the Internet), that doesn't mean you can figure out a way to get it surreptitiously in position where it will do the most harm. This plot had the earmarks of people who not only understood how to do things, but also how to actually get them done.

The initial incident report didn't give away much in the way of details. The first line to fill in read "Incident/Crime," and the investigating detective had typed, "Threats to Commit Off." That was it.

Didn't sound like much. The incident was assigned a case number and a location, which was the Yuma PD's office.

There are a lot of categories, with a lot of little boxes to check off. Location of Offense? The choices start with Air/Bus/Train Terminal, then proceed alphabetically to Bar/Nightclub, Construction Site, Grocery/Supermarket, Lake/Water, Residence/Home, School/College, or Other/Unknown, with many more possibilities in-between. That last box, Other/Unknown, was checked, a theme that would continue throughout the report. *Suspect—unknown. Home address—unknown. Age—unknown. Height, weight, hair color, eyes, complexion, build, driver's license: unknown.*

The one line that that had a little more to say was under *Victim: Arpaio, Joseph.*

You haven't lived until you've seen your name on an incident report.

✴   ✴   ✴

IT BEGAN with a call from the Yuma Police Department. The caller wanted a meeting with a detective with whom he was familiar. This wasn't just any bum off the street, this was a confidential informant (CI), somebody who had worked with the local cops for a couple of years. Sure, the guy was known to be something a big talker, but he was a guy the Yuma PD judged to be reliable, a guy the cops were willing to listen to, within the reasonable bounds of trusting what a CI has to say and why he's saying it.

The detective and the snitch got together, and the CI stated he had learned of a conspiracy underway to assassinate the sheriff of Maricopa County, and that this conspiracy involved a lot of people, some of whom were very serious and very dangerous.

The CI had attended several meetings held in the town of San Luis, Mexico. On one side was a contingent of Mexicans, who were part of a drug cartel based in the region. On the other were a few

Americans, identified by the CI as members of the "Minutemen." The Minutemen have courted controversy since the group's formation in 2005. They are dedicated to monitoring the U.S.–Mexico border, dedicated to doing the job they contend the government isn't doing. Some call them patriotic and activist, others call them vigilantes and extremists. California Governor Arnold Schwarzenegger has praised the group as doing "a terrific job." The Anti-Defamation League has asserted that the Minuteman Project (the primary Minuteman organization) has links with neo-Nazi and white supremacist groups.

The assassination was the sole agenda for the meeting.

To the Yuma police, this threat sounded real, and it sounded in motion. Yuma PD called MCSO.

Maricopa County isn't on the border, and we haven't had much contact with the Minutemen. That alone made the whole story suspicious, not to mention the notion of this particular group of Americans meeting with this particular group of Mexicans. At first glance it didn't make sense, and I didn't jump.

I can't say the same for my staff, which was ready to park our U.S. Army tank (purchased with drug money) outside the building, its .50-caliber machine gun pointed down the street. Figuratively speaking, of course.

We waited. The CI returned to San Luis (more formally known as San Luis Río Colorado). The town is situated in the state of Sonora and sits on the border, adjacent to the city of the same name in Arizona, twenty miles from Yuma. It's the fourth-largest community in Sonora, with a population of some 140,000. Its rapid growth has been fueled by its proximity to the United States and the opportunities, primarily criminal opportunities, that its location provides.

On the other side of the border lies San Luis, Arizona, a much smaller city, with a population of about 22,000.

The snitch was gone, out of touch, out of communication. We continued to wait. We didn't have a choice. A week later, he surfaced.

My detectives were down in Yuma and ready to talk to the CI. And that's what they did, right at the Yuma PD office. And this time he had some details.

The CI had a story to tell. He said he knew a man by the name of Miguel Escalante, an administrator for the Meraz Drug Cartel headquartered in and around San Luis. He was also the contact with the Minutemen.

Escalante needed the CI at the meeting to translate.

The CI claimed that Escalante had a guy named Luis Figueroa in his employ. Figueroa's job was transportation, ferrying the players to and from the property where the meetings were held. The main house on the property was referred to as "the green house," owing to its exterior color. There was a guesthouse behind the main house, and both buildings sat on a large parcel of land surrounded by a six-foot black wall and two metal gates, one to accommodate vehicles, the other for pedestrians. The gates were controlled electronically by someone inside the house.

The property was owned by Escalante.

The first meeting took place the week before, on March 18. The participants were two Minutemen, their translator, Escalante, Figueroa, and the informant. The Minutemen had a straightforward request: They wanted me dead, and they wanted it to look like illegal immigrants had done it. Their plan was that my murder would so outrage the American people that they would take up my fallen cudgel and demand that the government do something about the illegals. In this way, not only would the cause win, but so would the Minutemen, as leaders of the cause.

Escalante wasn't interested in the Minutemen's motivation. He did want to know what the Americans were prepared to pay for this service.

The Minutemen offered a sum of $3 million, in cash.

Things got a little uncomfortable when one of the Americans asked Escalante if they could trust him to carry out the job. Even drug dealers and killers have their pride, and Escalante was overtly offended by this query. In fact, he told the Minutemen they could get up and get out and forget the meeting ever occurred. Calmer heads prevailed, and the situation was smoothed out.

In part to compensate for the insult, Escalante wanted half of the payment up-front, half upon completion. The Minutemen agreed and promised to return with $1.5 million.

One day later, the Minutemen were back at the green house. They carried two bags: a large suitcase and a briefcase. The Americans opened the briefcase first. Inside were photos of me, taken in different places around Phoenix and the county. Research material.

The Americans opened the suitcase. It contained wrapped bundles of $100 bills. The CI wasn't in the room when they counted the money, but he saw the Benjamin Franklins, and he saw an awful lot of them.

Escalante ordered Figueroa to take the money away. The stash safely out of the way, Escalante informed the clients he would have Los Zetas carry out the assignment. And they would do it in approximately three days.

Nobody in law enforcement, nobody in the know, hears Los Zetas and doesn't pay attention. Los Zetas is a shadowy outfit, the kind of frighteningly ruthless group that Hollywood would invent, except Los Zetas is all too real. The Zetas were started by the head of the formidable Gulf Drug Cartel. They were a band of enforcers and killers recruited from the ranks of Mexican Special Forces, some of whom received their advanced training at the School of the Americas, Fort Benning, Georgia, with regular Mexican military, police, and some common thugs thrown in as well.

The Zetas started with some fifty guns-for-hire concentrated along Mexico's border with Texas, doing the dirty work for the cartel. They were good at what they did, and they prospered and grew. Within five years, the group had morphed into a 2,000-strong paramilitary organization operating throughout Mexico and spreading into the American Southwest and beyond. Within those five years, Los Zetas had outgrown its original sponsor, the drug cartel, and began pursuing its own agenda, murdering hundreds of police officers, corrupting many more than that, taking control of entire police forces, and doing much of the same in the political arena, buying, intimidating, and killing their way to power. And that doesn't include the dozens, then hundreds, then thousands of drug couriers, dealers, and traffickers they've murdered, along with all the innocent civilians in the wrong place at the wrong time.

Confirmed reports have elements of the group working in cities from Atlanta to Los Angeles. In Dallas, for instance, the Justice Department believes that a police officer was murdered by a man with ties to the Zetas, and that the Zetas have been established in the city, and killing at will, for at least three years.

Military training has made them organized, disciplined, and deadly efficient. That efficiency, as well as the confusion inherent when dealing with informants and brutality and corruption, keeps Los Zetas in the shadows, and a lethal enemy. They are regarded as the foremost threat to the Mexican government, a threat to the very existence of the Mexican state.

However you add it up, the mention of Los Zetas in this equation did not reassure anyone.

Back at the green house, the Americans told Escalante that their boss, "the head honcho" of the Minutemen, wished to be involved in setting the fine points of how the assassination should unfold. The boss would be available for consultation in seven to ten days. Thus, they told Escalante to hold off on kicking the plot into motion.

The informant had one more detail for my detectives, and this was one detail that only made the tale that much more intriguing. In the middle of the meeting, a phone rang. It was a call for Escalante from Elias Bermudez. The CI knew it was Bermudez because Escalante answered the phone with the Spanish equivalent of, "Hey, what's up, Elias?"

The CI could easily match the first name to the last because, at the March 18 meeting, the Minutemen had said that Elias Bermudez had facilitated this get-together. Bermudez was and is the head of *Inmigrantes Sin Fronteras*, Immigrants Without Borders, an activist group that essentially wants amnesty for all illegals and open borders for the rest. And while he expresses his displeasure with my actions to anyone who'll stop and listen, especially anyone from the press, this was a kind of negative expression I wouldn't have anticipated.

But once his name was brought up, we had to consider it. A couple of facts about Bermudez deserved a second glance. First, Bermudez had once been the mayor of San Luis, Arizona. That could mean he was familiar to the CI just from the publicity that came with occupying that post. Perhaps. It definitely meant that Bermudez knew people in the area and, obviously, it was possible he knew some unsavory people.

The second fact that might have been pertinent was found in public court records. Bermudez had been convicted in 1996 and had served time on several charges, including conspiracy to manufacture, distribute, and possess with intent to distribute methamphetamine; laundering of monetary instruments (more commonly called money laundering); and conspiracy to launder monetary instruments. The CI identified Bermudez from an unmarked photograph.

Again, the Yuma police knew their CI, and they placed credence in what he had to say. Point: The CI had been providing the Yuma PD with what it regarded as solid information on the murder of six people in the area. Point worth respecting.

At this moment, enough information had been accumulated that, whether I liked it or not, I had to take this threat seriously. The first person I thought about was Ava. She was at home, which would be an obvious target to any would-be assassin, and a car was dispatched to get her. This wasn't her first time at the dance, so to speak, so she knew to pack a bag with everything she might need. The deputy standing in her front door was practically hopping from one foot to the other, urging her to get out now, but Ava remained calm and left when she was good and ready.

They took her to a safe place of her choosing. When I left the office, I didn't go home, nor did I head to where Ava was stashed, just in case somebody was following me. Instead, I moved into a hotel. For the next few weeks, I would stay in a hotel for a few days, then move to another hotel, so as not to be too predictable, too easy to track. I was constantly surrounded by a security team drawn from the ranks of MCSO deputies. It's an exhausting way to live, separated from your home, your things, your routine, and most of all, the person to whom you are closest.

After a few days, Ava insisted on joining me, despite the objections of my security detail. Her presence made it a little easier to bear the situation.

The investigation continued, and it all revolved around the confidential informant. The snitch was gone for another three days in the beginning of April. The cops were there when he returned from Mexico, eager to hear the latest installment.

The tale picked up with the Minutemen's "head honcho" flying to Yuma from Phoenix. His compatriots were idling with Escalante, Figueroa, and the informant in the green house, and he kept in touch with them via cell phone. Not quite an hour after midnight, the Minuteman boss called to say he had rented a car in Yuma and asked for directions to Escalante's house. The American was instructed to park his car in San Luis, Arizona, and walk across the border. Once in Mexico, he was to continue walking until he reached a store named OXXO. Figueroa would be waiting to drive him to his destination.

The meeting between the two bosses, Minuteman and drug trafficker, started around 2:00 a.m. The Minuetman was introduced to Escalante by the name of "Burklett" or "Barklett." The CI wasn't exactly sure how to either pronounce or spell it.

There was a hitch: The CI wasn't in the room when the pair confabbed, but he managed to listen anyway. He heard the Minuteman explain to Escalante why he wanted me dead, which was basically what the Mexican had heard before—namely, the Minutemen were losing their influence and standing, and the assassination of a prominent leader in the fight against illegal immigration, by illegal immigrants, as the evidence would indicate, would change the political landscape in their favor.

What the CI said next was both rich in detail and provocative in description. One of the Minutemen handed Escalante three identical strips of paper. Each strip was about seven inches long and one and a half inches wide, and contained the same information, separated into columns: three different names, one Anglo-Saxon (presumably American), two Spanish (presumably Mexican). Beside the Anglo-Saxon name was an e-mail address using the same moniker.

These strips of paper provided the means by which the Mexicans could communicate with the Americans in the future when necessary. Any e-mails were to be sent to the address attached to the American name, though addressed in the body of the e-mail to the first Mexican name, signed with the second Mexican name. The fairly elaborate code was the result of the Minutemen's belief that U.S. Customs monitored e-mails coming from America, but not into America, and not from Mexico.

The CI was somehow able to make off with one of these strips of paper and deliver it to the Yuma PD, which handed it over to MCSO.

The informant had a final fact to relate to the cops. Around 3:30 a.m., Escalante received another phone call from Elias Bermudez. No useful details of the conversation were provided.

Two hours later, the meeting ended. The plan was for the three Minutemen to be taken to the airport. The plan changed, and the two American underlings were going to wait for somebody who was heading down from Phoenix, while the boss departed. They were put up at the San Angel Hotel, in San Luis. The CI even had the room number—127. He knew this because he brought food to them during their stay.

You can find the San Angel on the Internet. One site that reviews hotels in Mexico gives it five stars. Another site lists the virtues of its ninety rooms and six suites: "Comfortable carpeted rooms with cable TV, telephone, coffeemaker, and safe-deposit box. Suites with jacuzzi, air-conditioning, and electronic-keyed entrance." The establishment's facilities are mentioned as well: "Restaurant, bar, lobby bar, room service, laundry service, fax, two convention rooms, swimming pool, kids [sic] pool, jacuzzi, spacious gardens, and parking." All that to be had for about one hundred bucks a night.

Not a bad place to hang out when you're setting up a murder.

Later the next night, the Americans were escorted back to the green house, where Escalante was waiting. Figueroa arrived, Bermudez in tow.

The meeting was held in another building behind the main house. The CI wasn't invited inside but watched through a large picture window. He could see the men talking and laughing.

This meeting lasted approximately two hours. Figueroa left the property with Bermudez. The informant thought Bermudez was being escorted to the airport.

The following day, Figueroa, two of Escalante's employees, and the CI drove to the ranch. According to the informant, the ranch belonged to Oegario Meraz, the presumed head of the Meraz Drug Cartel.

The CI and Escalante's employees were ordered to sort through a pile of clothing at the ranch and put the garments into six stacks by size and type, consistent with Figueroa's directions. The clothes ranged from suits to camouflage to western wear to designer shorts and T-shirts. When they were done, the CI noticed a brown van pull into the driveway. The van stopped and several men got out of the vehicle. The CI thought the men were members of Los Zetas. The men started going through the clothes.

That wasn't the end of it. When the CI and the others returned to the green house, the van had beat them to it; he saw it parked in the rear. When the informant went into the house, he saw a handful of AK-47s—semiautomatic rifles—that he believed were intended for Los Zetas.

On Friday, April 6, 2007, the CI agreed to be polygraphed by an MCSO examiner who had been dispatched to Yuma. The examiner went through his paces, which of course took some time. For our purposes, we'll cut to the relevant part of the examination:

Question: Were you at a meeting where it was discussed to kill Arpaio?

Answer: Yes.

Question: Did you translate for Escalante at a meeting to discuss killing Arpaio?

Answer: Yes.

Question: Did you see a large sum of money at a meeting between Minutemen and Escalante to kill Arpaio?

Answer: Yes.

The examiner's conclusion: "No deception indicated."

❋　　❋　　❋

THE INVESTIGATION continued. Life back in Phoenix wasn't getting any easier for Ava or me, or, for that matter, for the rest of my family. The situation wasn't scary, but rather tiresome. You can't live in a constant state of worry, let alone fear, not after so many years of dealing with a long line of very tough characters, of playing the odds, of testing the limits. You just can't be tense all the time. You have to know when to sit up and pay attention, and you have to know when it's okay to relax.

The confidential informant had earned the right to a hearing. Still, the question remained—did the involvement of this disparate cast of characters in an assassination plot make sense? In particular, did the leading role of the Minutemen sound right?

The immediate answer was no. Nothing in the Minutemen's history suggested any disposition toward committing such a despicable act. Nor did it seem conceivable that an organization famously and publicly strapped for cash possessed the millions of dollars required to pay the Mexicans.

Nonetheless, if we were going to all this trouble to take this threat seriously, then we had to look at the best possibilities. To my mind, four presented themselves, and I will explain them in ascending order of likelihood.

First, the funds to pay the Mexicans could have been acquired through a drug deal. Operating down at the border, it was possible that some of the Minutemen had become familiar with other Americans or Mexicans dealing and transporting and had decided to get involved in the business, and thus had the money to pay for the hit.

Second, it could also be that the illegal activities of those Minutemen had nothing to do with the organization itself, that they had gone off the reservation and gone into business for themselves, choosing to pursue this course on their own.

Third, the men so eager to kill me weren't Minutemen at all but were simply using the group as a cover to hide their tracks and were instead miscreants with whom I had previously tangled, or whose business I had hindered or halted. They could have been drug traffickers from any one of a dozen countries or a collection of deadbeat dads my deputies and posse members had busted last Mother's Day, when we had conducted our annual roundup of these bums.

Fourth, and the most probable explanation, to my mind, is that the Mexican drug cartel was well aware of the CI's reputation as a big talker, and they used him to spread the idea about the plan being initiated by and paid for by the American Minutemen. (They might have known he had a big mouth, but if they had known or even suspected he was a police informant, they would have summarily executed him.) In fact, they could have simply fed the snitch the details of the tale, maybe even paid him to talk it up, and set him loose. Maybe the part about the drug cartel was also a fraud, covering up for another gang with a grudge. A lot of people south of the border could have wanted me dead, including a lot of drug traffickers, going back to my days as a fed, and a lot of human smugglers, as they watched us crack down on their business. The Arizona Department of Public Safety estimated that the annual revenues derived from smuggling human beings into the state added up to an astonishing $1.7 billion, and that was a lot of money, spread among a lot of people who had a stake in not being hindered or halted. This whole game could have very easily been a combination of fact and fiction, the plotters looking to misdirect our investigation, both before and after the attack, and the Minuteman part of it would have been the most dramatic piece of that misdirection.

This was all speculation, no doubt about it, not enough for an arrest. Still, speculation was part of the package, part of the investigative process. We built our cases by following leads, finding evidence, putting the pieces together, trying to decipher where to look next, trying to anticipate what the bad guys were going to do next, trying to figure out how to get there in time to stop whatever was brewing, whatever was in store.

So speculating, that was how I sized up the Minuteman angle. Whatever the truth was regarding the border group, other organizations and people and factors had to be evaluated with a harsh eye, taking apart the claims of the informant as best we could, piece by piece, inch by inch.

And all the while, we had to follow the plot, because it was now in motion. The informant was being run around a bit by his employers, from border town to border town, Algodones to Sonoita to San Luis, renting hotel rooms, ferrying information, supplies, and food on behalf of the cartel and Los Zetas. He met with an ex-commandant of the Sonoita border checkpoint who was supposed to smooth the way for the CI and the killers to drive around Mexico and pass into the United States. He picked up the Mexican visas the Zeta team would need for their journey.

The CI was informed he would drive to Nogales, Arizona, meet up with the Zetas, and drive them north to Guadalupe. At this juncture, he would receive further instructions, including information from Elias Bermudez on how and where to find me.

On April 12, 2007, the CI joined up with five of the Zetas. Three of the killers climbed into a truck, with the CI behind the wheel, and the other two got into a car driven by the comandante. The small caravan drove for five hours to Nogales, Mexico. Following the comandante's direction, the CI stuck close behind him. The comandante sped through the Mexican inspection stations, clearly still a presence with the boys in uniform, and the CI followed suit.

During the long drive, the informant found himself in conversation with Mario, who appeared to be the leader of the team. Mario was about forty years old. He had graying black hair, stood maybe five foot eleven, and weighed in at a muscular 180 pounds.

Mario stated that the business of Los Zetas was killing, and thus that was his business as well. He claimed he had been inside the United States on three occasions, the last time a year ago in Laredo, Texas, pursuing his chosen line of work.

They passed the night in Nogales, Mexico. They were holed up in a house owned by one Mike Gallegos, who was described as a prominent owner of a trucking company, well-known in both Nogales, Mexico, and Nogales, Arizona.

In the morning, another Zeta member arrived at the house, a female called "Sergeant Rose." Rose was American, born in a small border town in New Mexico. Rose said she had spent four years in the U.S. Marine Corps and had served in Operation Desert Storm.

Sergeant Rose was a key figure. She briefed the other killers on the task ahead, and she was very specific. She displayed photos and videos of me, taken at different locations throughout Greater Phoenix. Rose played a video of me leaving the building where MCSO is headquartered and walking across the courtyard and into the attached parking garage. She stated the trip took me six minutes from start to finish, from one exit to the other.

Rose knew I sometimes ate at a restaurant named Los Olivos in Scottsdale. The videos she was showing the Zetas had been taken with a hidden camera, by someone who had followed me around. The CI had the definite impression that Rose had shot the videos herself.

The entire chapter with Sergeant Rose was particularly disturbing. The woman hadn't been speculating—she had facts and the video to back them up.

When she was finished, it was evident what would happen next. Los Zetas would head to Phoenix.

It wasn't time to let down our guard, not while the details of this entire story, the facts underlying this conspiracy, remained unclear and uncertain. The problem was, you never know how long this kind of story could stay unclear, uncertain, and most disturbing, unresolved. The bad guys weren't on your schedule. It was like contending with a professional car thief; he didn't have to take the first or fifth or fifteenth vehicle that passed by. If he wanted a red, two-door Ford Mustang and he was patient enough, he could wait until that exact car showed up. Same here: Unless the contract included a timetable (and that idea had been thrown out by the client), the Zetas could pick and choose whatever made the most sense to them. And they weren't suicide bombers, but pros, who worked solely for profit. That meant they wouldn't do anything, no matter what the contract said, that could put them in a position that would result in capture or death.

Well, we'd have to work this one out over time. If anyone doubted I was taking this matter seriously, all they had to check was my schedule. For obvious security reasons, I had to cancel most of my personal appearances and speeches, and that entailed a lot of cancellations. Anybody who knows anything about me knows that's one thing I would never do readily or lightly, short of pain of death, which was exactly what this case potentially entailed.

One unprecedented concession was about all I could take. Ava and I weren't prepared to live out our days in a random series of hotels. After so many weeks away, we were moving back home, drug dealers and vigilantes and killers be damned.

✳   ✳   ✳

PUTTING ASIDE the sheer entertainment value of a complex assassination plot, I wanted to open the book with this tale in order to highlight the one significant factor that rendered this plot all too likely, and that factor had nothing to do with any of the players potentially involved or the details of preparing and driving and planning. No, the most significant factor was how the plot was based around the relationship between illegal immigration and drugs and violence. Regardless of the outcome of this investigation, this much was already clear and certain: that the criminals involved, whether human smugglers or drug dealers or killers, as well as the accountants and other managers and support personnel and corrupted government officials and paid-off military officers and crooked cops, had no trouble moving among these different criminal enterprises, one illicit activity building upon another, all working together to make them all more powerful, and more destructive, to individuals and to society, on both sides of the border.

Keep that in mind when we delve into these issues, these many crimes. Too often, political types, with every kind of agenda other than the safety and betterment of the American people, will try to steer the conversation away from what's really going on and make it into a principle, a cause, or an ideology.

I don't have any conflicting loyalties or duties or interests. I'm going to give it to you straight, like always.

Understand that while we neatly isolate issues and problems and crimes into separate categories, that is not how the world actually works.

So let's talk about what's going on, in all its frequently messy, confusing, conflicting reality. Let's cut through the political rhetoric and media spin and the rest of the crap and let the truth out, whether we like what we see and hear and learn or not.

ILLEGAL IMMIGRATION

THE TOWN of Cave Creek is named after a small stream that flows from the hills to the northeast. Almost 5,000 people live within its boundaries, mainly scattered among the desert's cacti and coyotes. East of Phoenix and north of Scottsdale, with Interstate 17 eight miles to the west and the Carefree Highway two miles to the south, Cave Creek is well positioned for anyone looking to get anywhere from Las Vegas to Mexico to California.

The sheriff's substation is right along Cave Creek's main road, not far from the restaurants that line the town's main street. That's where the Human Smuggling Unit assembled for that night's detail.

The border is a sieve. Everybody knows that, everybody complains, and nobody does anything about it. The illegal immigrants enter through Texas, California, New Mexico, and Arizona—a lot through Arizona. Phoenix has emerged as both a final destination and an important way station, a transshipment point, for Mexicans and Guatemalans and Salvadorans and anyone else who treks north.

That's why the Human Smuggling Unit, also known as the MCSO's Triple I (Illegal Immigration Interdiction) Strike Team, exists. Its job is to stop this trafficking in men, women, and children. To stop it and enforce the law.

A lot of people like to think this traffic in human beings is a victimless crime, but they are wrong, dead wrong. For one, it is a business, a billion-dollar business, controlled by vicious gangs that have reached their tentacles from Latin America into the United States. It is a supremely well-organized business, with much of the personnel structure familiar to any corporation: executives, managers, accountants, lawyers, drivers, security, just for a start. And then there's the physical infrastructure, again exceedingly organized and maintained.

Border towns act as the central staging areas for people looking to come into the States. Recruiters are posted at the bus stops, advertising their services to those arriving in town, soliciting clients for their coyotes. The larger gangs own their own hotels, where, for a fee—always for a fee—the client can stay until departure time, when all the arrangements are made.

Different destinations have different charges. By the time the client leaves Mexico, the route has been arranged and the coyotes at all the way stations from Mexico to his ultimate destination are ready and waiting.

Not only do different destinations have different charges, but there are also different levels of service available. A story circulated through the ranks of the deputies about the big-time player who was caught driving a couple of illegals. Usually someone else acted as the driver, but this time he did the driving because he needed some fast cash. Once in the bag, he told the investigators about how some special clients paid a lot more for the higher grade of attention. Especially intriguing, not to mention worrisome, was his tale about some Middle Eastern types who paid $10,000 to $20,000, per person. For that fee they'd be provided with fake IDs, taught some Spanish phrases, and brought into America through the proverbial front door, driven across the border in a Mercedes, relaxing in the back seat while a chauffeur in a nice suit handled the vehicle.

Was there any substance to this tale? Not to my knowledge, though there are many who believe it, including a bunch of United States representatives. Either way, true or not, it did make for a nice story, and perhaps it serves as a useful cautionary tale, a warning to keep our eyes open and prepare for anything.

On the other hand, an FBI report surfaced near the end of 2007 warning that the Zetas and the Gulf Cartel had contracted to smuggle no fewer than 60 Afghan and Iraqi terrorists into the U.S. via tunnels under the border, along with a pair of Milan antitank missiles, Soviet surface-to-air missiles, grenade launchers, long guns, and handguns. The purpose of this invasion was to attack Fort Huachuca, the nation's largest intelligence training center, where 12,000 men and women, representing all four branches of the armed forces, worked.

The military took the alert seriously, and security was beefed up. Of course, nothing happened.

Still, it was another intriguing story.

Putting that elite terrorist transportation service aside, illegal immigration is so lucrative that drug gangs have not only gotten into the business, they have begun to dominate it. In addition, smuggling people is a lot safer than transporting drugs, at least for the criminals—the penalties are nothing compared to what the drug laws impose. Finally, those smuggled people, often smuggled families, are generally in search of work, not a fight. They are usually unarmed and helpless, ready prey, not about to joust with rival drug dealers.

The situation in Mexico has gotten so bad that some border towns are essentially wholly owned subsidiaries of the gangs.

In response, the strategy on our side for a long time has been to lock up the coyotes. They're the key to the problem: Catch them and convict them so that the growing business end of the trade will dry up, and take a bite out of the entire problem.

As we all know, that didn't work. In part, it hasn't worked because it's not always easy to tell the coyotes from the customers. The coyotes aren't going to talk, and the customers won't necessarily spill the beans because they could very well be afraid of retribution, most probably against their families back home.

Now let's look at the situation from another angle: Border Patrol has spent a lot of time picking up illegals marching through the desert and then sending them back. They send back so many people, so quickly, so often, that some enterprising illegals my deputies have arrested have made the trip *three times in five days.*

Three times in five days is not effective law enforcement, and it's not a working national strategy. Three times in five days is a roller coaster without the laughs.

So, clearly, the strategy of "catch and release" has been as futile as focusing exclusively on the coyotes.

I had another idea. A pretty simple idea, really, simple and straightforward. My idea was that you arrest everybody involved in the crime, coyotes and customers, conspirators and coconspirators. You wrap them all up and charge them all with a crime.

There are those who claim I did this for political reasons, to appeal to a citizenry disgusted with the illegal flood and ready to embrace any new idea. That's nonsense. I didn't know how it would play with the public, and frankly, I wasn't worried. I knew it was the tactical and strategic smart play, and I was willing to let the results speak for themselves.

✳   ✳   ✳

IT WAS JUST after 10 p.m. The unit, consisting of a lieutenant, two sergeants, four deputies, and two detention officers, was ready to go. Most of them had done this before; a few had been at the detail for more than a year. They knew what to expect. They knew where the Mexicans and other illegals hid out during the day, and they had a pretty good idea where they'd be going when night fell. And they knew they would capture their fair share of illegals, just as they did, with hardly ever a misstep, every time they went out on patrol.

On this night, however, instead of just heading out to the usual areas, the order was to spend an hour driving around Cave Creek. A church had taken the lead in providing a form of sanctuary to illegals. The Good Shepherd of the Hills Episcopal Church had organized a "day laborer center" to help the "undocumented workers" (as those supporting the alleged rights of the illegals liked to call them) who gathered each morning in town to seek jobs for the day, usually in the construction industry. Though the center had been in operation for six years, the increasing influx of people coming into Arizona had dramatically swelled the numbers of illegals, as well as potential employers, gathering outside the church. The situation was causing friction in Cave Creek between those who supported the church's effort and those who opposed breaking the law.

Tensions had risen to such a degree that the town council held a meeting only days before the patrol, in order to give the locals a chance to speak their minds. The meeting was standing room only, with both sides passionately, vocally represented. Here, at this small town assembly, you could see so many of the issues that bedevil the entire nation at work.

A priest about to take up his duties at the parish declared that it was his duty to minister to the poor and oppressed, meaning the illegals. It was, he said, ". . . a top issue in our country. It's a problem we're going to have to deal with somehow as a society." On the other side, many people held that we had to deal with this problem through the legal process, and breaking the law was counterproductive.

Those supporting the church contended that the illegals were going to come regardless, so the center alleviated some problems that could arise without any basic support for these people. Those opposed stated that the center did just the opposite, intensifying the problem by attracting illegals, who even paid $10 for a ride up from Phoenix to Cave Creek. The problem was then compounded because those who did not find a job for that day had no choice but to loiter in town until their scheduled rides back to Phoenix. Considering that the illegals were normally dropped off at six in the morning and not picked up again until nine that night, we're talking about a long time with nothing productive for them to do in town.

The economics of the issue also came under scrutiny. The common refrain we all hear is that *illegals do the jobs American citizens refuse to do*. While that might be true in some industries, it is hardly the case across the board, even in Cave Creek. One shop had to close its doors in town because it could not compete with the lower costs associated with the "imported low-wage workers," another laughable phrase preferred by supporters of illegal immigration. At the town assembly, another man stood up to say, "When Carter was president I made $13 an hour. That same job now pays $12." The opportunity to hire people who are not in a position to demand benefits or even decent treatment, and who unquestioningly accept lower salaries, has hurt many American workers.

The mayor of Cave Creek noted that he used to live in Mexico, which meant he had to have in his possession a passport, a visa, and a work permit if he chose to seek a job. As he stated, "One dynamic is law, the other is compassion." He also said he had no desire to "round up" the workers and take them away. The issue needed to be dealt with on a national level, he said, adding that "if Cave Creek can set the stage on this one, then wow."

The mayor was right in saying the issue needed to be dealt with. However, it is not the role of those elected to enforce the laws to wait for someone else to do what is right and legally mandated.

The town was deciding whether to implement a statute, passed by the Arizona legislature, giving cities and towns the authority to enforce an antiloitering ordinance, which of course would allow the town to arrest any illegals idling on its streets. The measure had not yet been adopted by the town council, revealing the division that existed not only in the public debate, but within the ranks of government as well.

Personally, I saw no need to wait to act. I possessed all the authority I required, under the law, to enforce the law. The Arizona legislature had already passed Arizona Statute 13-2319, precisely to take on this problem, defining the issue as such: "It is unlawful for a person to intentionally engage in the smuggling of human beings for profit or commercial purpose."

Section D-2 of the same statute got to the heart of the matter: "Smuggling of human beings means the transportation or procurement of transportation by a person or an entity that knows or has reason to know that the person or persons transported or to be transported are not United States citizens, permanent resident aliens, or persons otherwise lawfully in this state."

In other words, smuggling of human beings, which by definition included a commercial aspect, which was money changing hands to profit the smuggler, was a felony in the Grand Canyon State. The hitch, as far as the county attorney was concerned, was that the issue revolved around *transportation*. The legislature hadn't precisely stated its intentions in passing the law and had left those intentions open, whether intentionally or not, to interpretation. Considering the ambiguity of the letter of the law, the county attorney determined, at least initially, that the legislature had intended that the offender must be literally moving human beings from one place to another for our deputies to have the right to initiate an arrest. Thus, again, given the predicate probability for a stop, which included a wide range of violations—for example, a speeding car or a broken tail light—a deputy could pull that vehicle over and investigate. If, however, the deputy spotted a car already stopped by the side of the road with a group of men standing nearby, the prime element necessary to invoke the statute had not been met, and he could take no action.

Now that might seem ridiculous, and perhaps it was. You might wonder: If this is a crime, then what difference could it make whether the coyote and his charges were moving or not? Wasn't the very appearance of these people within our borders the essence of the crime? If you saw a different sort of criminal, a murderer, for instance, standing, walking, bungee jumping, or sleeping, you'd arrest him, wouldn't you?

All good questions—questions you should address to members of the Arizona legislature, which perhaps purposely declined to clarify its intent to any unmitigated, indisputable degree. (After all, a lot of them are lawyers, as is the governor who signed the bill, so they know something about legal clarification. Unfortunately, they're also politicians, so they know more than a little about dodging responsibility.) Regardless, this was the law the politicians had passed, and this was the law we all had to live under.

It took some effort, but eventually my office was able to work with County Attorney Andrew Thomas and arrive at a clear, firm definition of the law, which we agreed to translate as such: that transport meant not only witnessing the physical act, but the entire mechanism of transportation. That meant we could raid drop houses, where coyotes stashed their loads of illegals between rides, as well as pick up those men standing near a car stopped by the side of the road. And—most critically—we could arrest the coconspirators (those smuggled), as well as the smugglers—the coyotes.

Even with this expanded interpretation, our authority was not solely granted by the state of Arizona. Many of my deputies have federal authority as well. Section 287(g) of the Immigration and Nationality Act permitted, and I quote, "the performance of immigration officer functions by state officers and employees." This "cross-designation" between U.S. Immigration and Customs Enforcement (ICE), the largest investigative arm of the U.S. Department of Homeland Security, and local law enforcement was granted to police officers and sheriff deputies after they successfully completed an intensive five-week training course. This was not a symbolic or unimportant designation by any means; not only did it facilitate the cooperation between federal officers and MCSO, it added a key element to the crime that rendered our work that much more efficient and even doable.

Remember, the Arizona law addressed the issue of transporting illegals for profit. Let's say a deputy stopped a car and the occupants, as was par for the course, refused to admit they had paid for the ride. That meant an essential element of the crime under Arizona law— smuggling, rather than merely enjoying a sociable ride with pals— did not exist, and so the deputy had no power to effect an arrest. With the federal cross-designation, smuggling remained one basis for action, only now the fact of encountering an illegal constitutes another basis for an arrest. The deputy now had the same authority as a member of ICE, vastly increasing the ability of my deputies to fight illegal immigration.

Credit for first recognizing the value of 287(g) must be accorded to Chief Jerry Sheridan. As the man in charge of our jail system, he recognized that we were in perfect position to check on the legal status of those already in our custody. For that, we could use federal status, which meant 287(g) cross-designation. After a long career as a fed, I wasn't so enthused, not interested in having a U.S. government agency attempt to stomp into our jails and claim primary authority. However, I was quite enthused about an idea I had regarding cross-designation: gaining the federal stamp for detention officers and deputies. In this manner, we wouldn't just wait for illegals to show up in our jails, gathering up those who had already been gathered up for other offenses; rather, we would be doing what I always did in my career, going out and making cases.

Before we did anything, I had to negotiate with the feds. They liked the notion of giving cross-designation to detention officers and asserting their authority in this static location, but they weren't quite prepared to include deputies, especially not to the extent I was contemplating. So we negotiated, and I didn't make the deal until everybody agreed that the feds wouldn't even think of trying to big-foot all over our jails, and no fewer than 160 deputies went through the training.

As of this writing, those 160 deputies have completed the ICE course. Not only is this an impressive percentage of my total force, it is fully *one-half* of all the local or state law enforcement officers cross-trained in the nation. Now, with the door wide open, I do not profess to understand why other agencies have not taken advantage of this tool.

And it's certainly worth noting that the cross-designation has been a terrific success in the jails. Since starting the program, our detention officers have interviewed 5,650 inmates with regard to their citizenship and found an astounding 3,388 illegals among them.

* * *

MY DEPUTIES left the substation and drove onto Cave Creek Road. While keeping in radio contact, each car chose its own route. That's what being a deputy is all about, relying on your experience and knowledge and instincts to decide how to do your job. An officer in a municipal police department, whether Phoenix PD or Chicago or New York, is more much restricted in his actions. He has a sector to patrol, in a certain manner, and specific duties to perform, as determined daily by his command. That's not how a deputy operates. While both deputy sheriffs and police officers are equally and thoroughly law enforcement officers, with responsibilities and jobs that overlap in the most essential ways, their manner of performing their tasks is often quite dissimilar, which makes them very dissimilar types of law enforcement officers.

Part of this is practical—unlike a city, where the streets are laid out on a grid, the entire city occupying a very defined space where each police officer's area of responsibility is similarly defined, I have some 900 deputies deployed over an incredibly large and diverse region. Most deputies patrol alone, and backup can be an hour away. You can be deep in the desert, even out of range of phone or radio communication, and face situations and threats that no big-city cop will ever have to tackle. You have to be the type of individual who prefers that sort of challenge and independence.

It's an old cowboy concept, emblematic of the classic "rugged individualism" that won the American West. My deputies live that concept, deciding what to do and how to do it in service to the law and the community.

That's why a couple of cars quickly abandoned the Cave Creek patrol, deeming it pointless as the illegals were gone for the night and the town itself was off the usual smuggling route. They headed west, out toward I-17, which links Phoenix to Flagstaff. From I-17, they turned off on New River Road, south of the Tonto National Forest, and started roaming. The deputies were well into the desert now. The roads built through the sand and cacti are dark and lonely, not used this late by a lot of traffic, the only light provided by the moon and stars. For those who live back East or near any city, where the electricity is never turned off and illumination from storefronts and houses and apartments and streetlamps and vehicles always cuts through the dark, it might be hard to envision how bright a cloudless, starry night can be, or how absolutely black the same scene is on a moonless, overcast evening.

Tonight, the moon was almost full and the stars were out, and the deputies in their cars could drive with their own lights off, just in case they came upon any suspicious activity.

Before too long, the rest of the deputies had departed Cave Creek and headed west, ranging far and wide. The detention officers in their van also moved west, finding a spot to park outside a supermarket, near the highway, ready to pull out and go when a deputy made an arrest and transport the prisoners to the holding facility.

The deputies kept in loose contact, not needing to talk unless they encountered something unusual. Usually, the cell phones and radios stayed silent, and each deputy was alone with the night. One deputy passed another on a nothing lane off Lake Pleasant Road. They both had the same notion, to check out a known staging area for the coyotes, so they agreed to accompany one another. Before long (and only because they knew where to look), they had found the small, smoothed patch off the road that served as a parking lot and the entry into the desert.

The two deputies shut off their cars and quietly got out. Though they had no trouble picking their way through the loose rocks and small, thorny plants on the uneven terrain, they used small flashlights to check around their feet to make sure they didn't bump into any critters—snakes, scorpions, Gila monsters, and other night hunters—creeping and scrambling over the earth. Rattlesnakes don't necessarily go looking for trouble, but if you stepped on one, or even a little too near, they had a tendency to react badly, fangs bared.

The deputies reflexively touched their holsters. The level of violence was increasing exponentially in the smuggling business. Dead illegals were found bound and gagged in the desert. There were shoot-outs on the highways, gangs chasing down cars filled with what they believed to be Mexican or Latin nationals, battles between Border Patrol and other U.S. law enforcement officers and the criminals. Thankfully, none of my deputies had yet met with armed resistance in pursuing the coyotes, but given the escalating bloodshed, it only seemed a matter of time.

As the deputies pushed ahead, they saw evidence of human visitation: a red shoelace torn off by a sharp branch, the discarded wrapping of a candy bar, empty plastic water bottles tossed around the ground. Debris, but no people, the only living creature a sizable and furry tarantula that scurried back into his hole as soon as the flashlight highlighted him.

A hundred yards off the road, the deputies came upon the main camp. It was just a round, cleared-out space, the size of a large living room, where the illegals hid during the day. It was hard to imagine what it must be like: crossing the border on foot, walking mile after mile to get somewhere, thirsty beyond measure, beyond endurance, perhaps seeing some fellow travelers or even family members drop and die right there, in the middle of a desert nowhere, only to be shoved into the back of a stifling, crammed truck or car, then dumped here to lie in the dirt in one hundred ten plus heat, to sweat and suffer hour after hour, waiting, praying for the sun to finally go down so the awful journey could continue.

Whoever had been here was gone. There were scores of similar sites scattered around, and it was impossible to say when this one would be occupied again. The deputies returned to their vehicles and drove off. They went their separate ways, each following his nose.

One of the deputies headed over to Route 60, outside of Wickenburg. Travelers, legitimate and otherwise, used Route 60 to either keep going to Vegas or turned left for California. On any night, you could count on at least six illegal loads using this route. The deputy set up on a rise off the road, where he could watch traffic in both directions.

It was well past midnight, and the light traffic had thinned even more, with big rigs dominating the road, at least four to every single car that passed. Though the diminished traffic cut down on potential hits, it had its upside as well, because each possible vehicle received a thorough share of attention. It was a constant guessing game between the gangs and law enforcement; as the cops figured out where the bad guys were concentrating their efforts, which resulted in more stops and arrests, the bad guys adjusted accordingly, picking new times and new routes. As there were only so many major roads through Arizona, the coyotes ended up playing musical chairs, employing one highway until it got too hot and then eventually returning when the cops focused elsewhere.

Regardless, Wickenburg was prime hunting grounds, and it didn't take too long before a car worth looking at drove by, heading north. The deputy pulled onto the highway and followed.

You learned to spot which vehicles were most likely to be carrying illegals. Whether a sedan, SUV, van, or truck, the vehicles were usually weighed down, stuffed beyond capacity with human cargo. The tires would bulge, overburdened, unless they were using special commercial tires, which would also be noticeable. The windows were frequently covered with paper or painted over to obscure what was going on inside. Some of the more sophisticated, or least better-funded, coyotes had extra shocks or struts placed on their vehicles. The overwhelming majority of cars and vans were old, fairly beat up, and in need of a coat of paint.

The deputy followed the car. It was a small Toyota, and he could see several heads in the backseat, poking over a line of baseball caps arrayed on the back window ledge. He couldn't stop the vehicle just on the suspicion of ferrying illegals; some other violation had to first present itself. With a car in this kind of shape, a violation wasn't going to be terribly hard to find: If the registration tags weren't out of date, the left braking light would be broken or the right turning signal nonexistent.

The deputy didn't have to look for any of these things, as he had positioned himself at a spot where the speed limit abruptly dropped from sixty-five to forty-five, a drop that most drivers didn't respond to with any urgency. This car had made the same mistake, cruising much faster than legally permitted. And so the deputy flicked on the lightbar on the roof and pulled behind the Toyota, which took the red-and-blue flashing hint and pulled over.

Any traffic stop is fraught with potential danger, and every cop knows to approach cautiously. And so the deputy walked slowly forward, keeping an eye out for any movement inside the car. He had already called it in and expected backup to arrive within minutes. Regardless, he wasn't inclined to wait.

The five men in the car resembled deer caught in the headlights, and tired, dirty deer at that. They sat quietly in their seats, shoulders slumped, expressions defeated. The deputy spoke fluent Spanish, which was useful since nobody in the car spoke English. They all looked to be in their thirties. The driver did the talking. He claimed they were driving from Queen Creek in southeastern Maricopa County to Stockton, California. He claimed they were all friends. He didn't have much more to say.

Two more patrol cars arrived, and the deputies started taking the men out of the car, one by one, for interrogation. The second deputy was Hispanic, and he spoke Spanish as well.

Every one of the men had the story straight, right down the line. Yes, they were all friends, out for a friendly drive. No, the passengers did not pay the guy behind the wheel any money, they were—remember—friends.

The deputies walked each man ten feet from the car, onto the sand at the edge of the desert. They spoke to their charges in a casual manner, neither threatening nor badgering. The deputies didn't learn much and had each man kneel on the ground while they brought out more passengers.

The deputies found a cell phone on the front seat and put it aside. The phone could prove useful in uncovering more information and more leads.

It more than stretches the imagination, the idea that a group of four pals, none of whom carried any identification familiar to Americans—no driver's license, no Costco card, no Barnes & Noble membership—had prevailed upon a fifth man, another pal who also wasn't an American citizen, to drive a worn-out car, for no expressed reason, some 800 miles from one city in Arizona to another in California. Life doesn't work like that.

The detention van arrived. The men were loaded inside. Just then, another car drove past. The car wasn't speeding, the tires weren't spreading out, and the lights seemed to be working just fine. However, the deputy noted, the vehicle had gained ground on the truck slowly chugging along before it. In fact, the car was close behind the truck, very close, too close, precariously close. It was a situation practically crying for official intervention.

The deputy flipped on his lights. When he walked up to the driver's window, he saw an unusual sight: three grandmotherly types, easily in their seventies, two in the back and one in the passenger seat, primly attired, hair pinned in buns, hands in their laps. The driver was a young woman, maybe in her late twenties, probably one of the elderly women's granddaughters. The girl was the only one who spoke English, and her grasp on the language was comprehensible, though far from conversational.

The young woman was a bit flustered. She said that she was driving to Vegas from Nogales. Nogales is on the border with Mexico, and there are actually two towns of the same name, an American town of some 20,000 and a Mexican counterpart that's considerably larger, with perhaps a quarter-million residents. Federal Highway 15 runs through Mexico and ends at the border, where Interstate 19 begins, and then heads north for sixty-three miles, where it links into U.S. Interstate 10 outside of Tucson.

Why anyone would drive through the night from Nogales to Vegas was a mystery at best, an outright lie at worst. The deputy decided to leave it a mystery and forgo asking too many questions. Throwing grandmothers into jail wasn't exactly an appetizing proposition. Besides, he didn't have any information they were illegal, and he seriously doubted the young woman was working for any smuggling gang.

And there was always another van, driven by an authentic coyote, probably heading this way right now. And, lo and behold, so there was.

It was a minivan, chugging along, white smoke trailing from its exhaust pipe. Not counting the driver, six men were inside. One was actually curled up in the storage compartment in the rear. He was either so exhausted or such a deep sleeper that even stopping and having his fellow passengers interrogated by deputies didn't wake him. It took the back door opening and a deputy's hand gently shaking him to get him to his feet.

The men were dressed alike, in dirty jeans and wrinkled, button-down cowboy shirts. The story offered by the first couple of guys was the usual, as they stuck to the prepared script: They were all buddies, all out for a pleasant outing.

But then the cracks started to show. More often than not, that didn't happen until later, when the real interrogation began, indoors, along with the processing, assisted by computers, police records, and the Internet. That interrogation could continue for as long as it made sense, hour after hour after hour, often for eight or ten or twelve continuous hours. That's why the unit only went out with no breaks. It was an all-night event, followed by another day's work, then and there. The crew was on call 24/7, so when a deputy on patrol found himself knee-deep in coyotes and illegals, he called on the Human Smuggling Unit for assistance.

Anyway, this stop was taking a mildly intriguing turn. One of the men insisted he had been in Arizona for months, but a bus ticket from one Mexican town to another, travel completed two days ago, was pulled from his pants pocket. This contradiction had the deputies, who by now had arrived in force, pressing harder. The next guy, for some reason, veered from the script and stated that he and the driver were cousins. And that wasn't the end of it—he admitted he had paid the driver for the trip, despite their alleged familial tie.

The deputies had them, and they pushed, breaking down the fairy tale. The coyote knew he was cooked. He sat down on the ground, nothing to say. The detention officers handcuffed the lot and stuffed them into the van, which was now filled to capacity.

Another car went by, another candidate virtually demanding investigation, and one deputy took off. When he caught up with it, he found a scared husband and wife in the front, and three young children—one a baby—in the back. The baby was sleeping, and the other two children stared at the deputy wide-eyed. It was policy not to separate children from their parents unless circumstances left no other choice. And that baby—that baby tucked into a blanket was very small and very new, which meant the child could have very easily been American born, and hence an American citizen. And that opened up the issue of potentially sending the parents and maybe one or two of the kids back to Mexico, while the baby, and maybe one of his siblings, had the right to stay in the United States.

He let them go.

The night was running down. The detention van contained a nice haul, eleven in the back, and that translated into a long day ahead. In addition, the deputies had bagged another couple of vehicles, booty as part of a felony case. The unit had seized sixty vehicles for the county—so many vehicles that there was a backlog in servicing them and putting them back into the field as undercover or plainclothes vehicles, or selling them at auction.

The unit decided to wrap it up and get ready for the next phase of the operation. Just then, a cargo van came from the south and headed north. It was low to the ground, and the windows were blacked out.

The deputies looked at each other. They couldn't wrap it up, not just yet.

THREE

MORE WAYS TO TAKE ON IMMIGRATION, FROM THE POSSE TO ICE

THE POSSE was assembling in the Tent City parking lot.

The tactic was straightforward enough: Get as many bodies out there as possible, fan out throughout the desert, and catch as many smugglers and their customers as we could find. The tactic was also the strategy, because the more people on the other side of the border realized we were serious, the fewer would want to risk smacking into our patrols, and so simply showing the flag, so to speak, would help alleviate the problem.

We had done this before and it had worked like a charm, gaining enormous attention both in Arizona and throughout the country and beyond, in both the English and Spanish media. And more and more, evidence pointed to coyotes mapping out routes into America that bypassed Maricopa County.

It only made sense. My department was the only local law enforcement agency in the United States that was actively looking to search out and arrest not only coyotes but their customers, too. Why risk getting picked up when it was just as easy to map out another route, travel another highway—go round Maricopa County.

Coyotes might be low-life criminals, greedy and predatory and frequently vicious, trading on the desperate hopes of their fellow human beings, usually their fellow countrymen, but that doesn't mean they're stupid.

And so I called out the posse, and the posse responded, as always. More than a couple hundred trained citizens, ready to serve, gathered in the parking lot, in full gear, in the burning summer heat. They had brought some of their equipment, owned and maintained by individual members of the posse, including a reconditioned U.S. Army Humvee, a tricked-out dune buggy, and personal sedans painted and equipped to function as patrol vehicles. If it had been appropriate to the mission, they would have also brought their horses and motorcycles and boats and airplanes and bicycles, all at the disposal of the Maricopa County Sheriff's Office, all entirely paid for by the posse volunteers.

The TV cameras were there, as usual, and assorted other reporters, too. I explained what we were doing, that deputies and the posse were going to aggressively enforce the law. "They come across any illegals," I said as plainly as possible, "they're going to be locked up, and they're going to jail."

I made it clear this did not mean it was open season on every person on the road. "We have to have probable cause," I said. "Whether the person went through a red light, whether he had fake license plates—I can go on and on and on. We will pursue this type of activity when we have probable cause."

At the same time, we were inaugurating a new program, a hotline so the public could report any suspicious behavior. "I want them to call in for *any* illegal," I stressed. "It doesn't have to be a smuggler. Any illegal, they can call in and have evidence that they are illegal, and we'll pursue that."

To advertise the hotline, we were placing banners on the sides of the huge tractor-trailers MCSO used to ferry food from points across Arizona and all the way to San Diego, California, back to the jails. Each banner was highlighted by a big red stop sign with the message DO NOT ILLEGALLY ENTER etched across it. To the side was written "Help Maricopa County Sheriff Joe Arpaio Fight Illegal Immigration," along with a phone number to call.

Apart from our unconventional promotional methods, attaching the banners to the trucks, allowing for rolling and maximum visibility, hotlines were nothing new. Law enforcement agencies everywhere used hotlines to get information on murders, rape, toxic dumping, domestic abuse, corporate fraud, drug dealing—you name it. I had started an animal cruelty hotline and in no time had 400 calls from citizens relating stories about other citizens committing alleged outrages against pets and other creatures. We investigated those calls and proceeded when appropriate. I didn't receive any condemnation from anybody for that hotline.

A quick check of the local paper's archives showed, as expected, a long list of articles on the illegal immigrant hotline. Perhaps not as expected, in the midst of all those hot-button pieces was a brief article—a notice, really—about another hotline. It was entitled "Elderly Abuse Hotline," and the entire article read, "Anyone who suspects that an older person is being mistreated by someone should call Adult Protective Services," closing with a phone number. Apparently, no one objected to that hotline or worried that feuding family members, maybe fighting over control of the patriarch's estate, would call in false reports. While that might have been a possibility, the benefit to individuals and to society clearly outweighed the risks.

Using the same time-tested technique for illegal immigration, for this crime, only makes sense. However, for some reason, several of the reporters assembled before me couldn't gather that it was just as it appeared to be, law enforcement reaching out to the public for assistance. The truth is, and will always be, that law enforcement in every jurisdiction, at every level, depends upon leads and evidence generated by a curious and concerned public to solve every kind of case.

Still, this fact of Crime Stopping 101 seemed to elude a substantial percentage of the local media members standing before me. Did we want neighbors to inform on neighbors? Did we worry that people would use the hotline for their own petty, personal reasons? Were the deputies going to investigate people, arrest them, merely because of a phone call? How far was this going to go?

I explained, over and over, that they just didn't get it. It had nothing to do with abuse of civil liberties or enacting extraordinary police measures or picking on anybody. This was police work, simple and sound. And it worked: Since we had started the new effort to stop illegal immigration, we had already arrested some 460 illegals, of whom no less than seventy turned out to be smugglers.

I kept going over the same ground with the reporters, until Lisa Allen, in charge of the media, couldn't take any more. On behalf of the many posse members waiting in the heat, she stepped up to announce we had to get the operation going. While the posse headed toward their vehicles, I answered still more questions, but in the end, some of them got it, some didn't. You can only do so much with the press.

✳   ✳   ✳

CHIEF BRIAN Sands, as the indispensable head of Enforcement Support, was in charge of the two essential pillars of this endeavor—our illegal immigration effort and the entire posse—and he now ordered the operation to get moving. In no time, the deputies and posse members mounted their vehicles and headed out, onto the roads and into the desert.

I can't claim I originated this idea of overpowering force. It worked back in the day when men lined up with spears and ran at another group of men who were waiting on the other side of the field with their own spears. It worked then, and it would work now.

I had my own experience with this sort of thing when I was in charge of the government's operation along the border with Mexico. It goes back a few years—well, more than a few years—and it was quite a show.

It was called Operation Intercept, and it was intended to stop the importation of marijuana across the Mexican border into the United States. The operation began on September 21, 1969, and was heralded by the U.S. Bureau of Customs as an "unprecedented . . . historic effort."

Richard Nixon had assumed the presidency earlier that year, and he was determined to take on and win the fight against drugs. He had pledged during the campaign to do something about this scourge and ordered Attorney General John Mitchell to get cracking. In response, the AG placed Deputy Attorney General Richard Kleindienst and Assistant Secretary of the Treasury Eugene Rossides in charge of a twenty-two-member task force to come up with some solutions. The task force comprised individuals representing virtually every consequential department of government.

On June 6, 1969, the task force issued its report, which essentially called for a full-out assault on the drug traffic right on the border, stopping the bad guys before they could get into our country. Of course, stopping the bad guys meant stopping everybody else, at least for a time. And that made the whole thing very interesting.

At the time, I was based in Baltimore, serving as the deputy regional director of the Bureau of Narcotics and Dangerous Drugs (BNND), one of the several bureaucratic forerunners of the modern

Drug Enforcement Administration (DEA). The BNDD had been moved from its original home in the Treasury Department to the Justice Department, and thus my chain of command led directly to Deputy AG Kleindienst. Over the years, as a result of our long, working association, Kleindienst and I would become good friends.

I was assigned to represent the BNDD for the duration of this operation. And so, as Operation Intercept got underway, I found myself in a small plane flying up and down the border beside the Treasury Department representative, G. Gordon Liddy. Liddy, as you might recall, would emerge only a few years later as one of the prime conspirators in the Watergate scandal that would eventually bring down Nixon's presidency. In fact, the day after the 1972 Watergate break-in, Liddy informed Kleindienst, who was now attorney general, that the plot had originated in the White House, so Kleindienst had to arrange the release of the burglars. Though Kleindienst would refuse to interfere, he kept Liddy's confession to himself instead of reporting it and breaking the case wide open, then and there. This failure would force Kleindienst's resignation the next year. He was later convicted of a misdemeanor for perjury during his Senate testimony for his confirmation hearings, for which he was fined and given a suspended jail sentence.

For his part in the scandal, Liddy would earn himself a prison term. Upon his release, he followed a path of unexpected American innovation, taking disgrace and transforming it into celebrity. He was reincarnated as a radio talk show host and even occasional actor, with a memorable turn as a spook gone very bad on the 1980s hit series *Miami Vice*.

But that was all in the future. On this September day in 1969, I was watching from the sky as American policy transformed into practice.

The result was overwhelming and immediate. For 2,500 miles, from San Diego to Brownsville, Texas, the U.S. government threw the full weight of its force into the effort. The *New York Times* wrote:

Operation Intercept is being waged by nearly 2,000 agents of the Bureau of Customs and the Immigration and Naturalization Service. Working around the clock, from the Pacific to the Gulf, they stopped 2,384,079 citizens of the United States and Mexico at thirty-one border crossings in the drive's first week.

The operation completely altered how the American agents conducted their inspections. Again, to quote the *New York Times*, now four days into the action: "Before Operation Intercept went into effect at 2:30 p.m. Sunday, inspectors took less than a minute to process a vehicle and its passengers. Only one car in twenty was given the present three-minute treatment, including thorough scrutiny of the trunk and engine areas, under seats and behind cushions and door panels." The new policy "calls for a 100 percent inspection of all persons and vehicles crossing into the United States, and there are no exceptions."

Twenty-three days later, Operation Intercept abruptly ended. It was not only judged too harsh, too draconian, but it was also too visible, too public. It was an embarrassment to the Mexican people and the government, and it interfered with too many tourists and too much commerce. It couldn't go on, and it didn't, hastily replaced by Operation Cooperation, a severely watered-down version of the original, designed to be, quoting the head of the new program, ". . . less burdensome economically to those persons who are engaged in lawful commerce between the United States and Mexico."

The funny thing was, Operation Intercept had a real impact. Studies showed that the supply of drugs was interrupted, causing the price to jump, which was supposed to reduce usage across the board. Of course, really fighting the drug war required, and still requires, a much broader plan—but that is a story told later. The point is that massive focus and force does work, at least in its limited objectives. Choosing those objectives will ultimately make the difference between long-range success and crashing failure.

And so I do all that I am capable of doing, within the borders of Maricopa County, utilizing the resources of my office, relying on my experience and judgment. And as much as we are doing, as much as we are accomplishing, imagine what might be possible if other local and state law enforcement agencies in other states, and the entire government of the United States, actually did what the law and the people demand.

Again, I must state that I have compassion for the people trying to cross our border in search of better lives. My parents came to this country from Italy. But they came legally, just like millions of others who left their homes to find new opportunities, new freedoms, new futures.

There were other differences as well. My parents, like all other immigrants exclusive of those from Mexico, held to certain hopes and truths:

1. My parents left Italy and basically never expected to return, unlike the illegal Mexican immigrants. Because their country is contiguous to the United States, Mexican immigrants not only take their earnings and return home, going back and forth over the border, but they are encouraged to do exactly that by the Mexican government in order to help sustain Mexico's economy. And they did so to the tune of more than $20 billion last year.

2. My parents did not regard any inch of American soil as somehow belonging to Italy, so their arrival here never constituted a "reconquest" of that land. A growing movement among not only Mexican nationals but also some Mexican-Americans contends that the United States stole the territory that is now California, Arizona, and Texas, for a start, and that massive immigration over the border will speed and guarantee the *reconquista* of these lands, returning them to Mexico.

3. Previous immigrant groups, while congregating together, also dispersed throughout the country, accounting for the existence of a

"Little Italy" in city after city, for example. This is in stark contrast to the exceptional concentration of Mexicans in the Southwest. This practice has permitted second and third generations of Mexican immigrants to maintain identities, from language to customs to beliefs, separate from the American mainstream, as opposed to so many millions of immigrants from other places, who longed for their children to become assimilated into their new homeland instantly and thoroughly.

4. My parents came to America legally. That was the norm for our entire history. No other group except the Mexicans, and other Hispanics as well, has broken the immigration laws in such astonishing numbers.

5. The scale of the immigration is unprecedented. How many Mexicans are illegally in this country? Ten million? Fifteen million? Twenty million? No one really knows for sure.

6. Usually, specific groups immigrate for only a relatively short time. The potato famine brought the Irish in the 1840s and 1850s, ending during the Civil War. Large-scale Mexican immigration started in the 1960s, continues to this day, and promises to continue indefinitely—unless we do something.

I'm hardly the first to consider these factors. Many others, led by the scholar and author Samuel P. Huntington, have gone into these issues in far greater depth.

These issues do not mean that Mexicans are our enemies or that we have to cut off all Mexican (and other Hispanic) immigration. It does mean that we have to understand what is happening and what underlying facts are pushing people to act in certain ways, and we have to deal with all of this information intelligently and forcefully.

I've always enjoyed terrific support from the Hispanic community, without which I might not be sheriff, and I have always worked to serve and protect their homes and businesses and neighborhoods the same way my deputies serve and protect the homes and businesses and neighborhoods of everyone in Maricopa County. I do not expect my support to drop because I am enforcing the laws of Arizona and the United States. My many years in law enforcement, including four terms as sheriff, have evidently demonstrated to the majority of Maricopa County citizens, including the sizable number of Hispanic citizens within that population, that I deserve their support. Otherwise, denied their backing, I wouldn't have an approval rating of over 80 percent, a measure of support that I know no other elected official in Arizona can claim, and I doubt any significant elected official anywhere in the country can equal. I've enjoyed that measure of support, virtually without interruption, for the fifteen years I've been in office, because of the work I have done and the stands I have taken.

In fact, isn't it offensive to assume that Hispanics are somehow less interested in enforcing the laws of our country? Isn't it naive at best, racist at worst, to assume that Hispanic citizens are less concerned with the security of our borders and the consequences of unchecked, unregulated, uncontrolled illegal immigration, that they constitute some mindless bloc, reflexively ready to destroy the American future in favor of promoting Mexico or wherever else they once hailed from?

It's offensive and it's not true.

✳   ✳   ✳

WHILE THE posse was fanning out over the desert, from outside Phoenix to Gila Bend to Lake Pleasant, searching out illegal activity, it was important to recall that I already held some 2,000 illegal immigrants in my jails, many of them right there in Tent City. That's out of a total jail population of 10,000, understand. So there were 2,000 individuals who were *not* arrested, tried, and convicted because they are illegal, but because they committed some other crime.

Some months ago, I had started a program to teach those in my jail some basic English. It was a two-week course, two hours a day, in which they learned some useful phrases, such as "I need to talk to my lawyer," to help them communicate in the jails and when they traveled to court. They were also taught the words to "God Bless America," which I had them sing every morning. Hey, this is America, and they could honor that with a song.

The program is a success, and the program continues. No one is forced into the program. Every man in that classroom is a volunteer, and so many of them have volunteered that there is a waiting list. The program costs the county and the taxpayers nothing, because the money to maintain the classes come from the Inmates Fund, which collects revenue from collect calls made by the prisoners, and other sources.

Of course, there were always the critics, some of whom offered opinions tinged with their own personal ambitions and easily went way overboard. One Mexican-American radio host *insanely* declared—and I feel entirely justified in using the word *insanely*— that "it reminds me of the concentration camps. It reminds me of the political agenda of the people who were imprisoned because of war." Whatever that meant, and I wasn't the one to decipher that nonsense, it was intended to be outrageous, to stir controversy. It didn't happen, at least not in that instance, maybe because it was so ludicrous that even those who normally agreed with the radio host were insulted by his ridiculous claim.

My English program made the news across the country. The major news outlets all put a positive spin on the story. (Since you could count on reporters and producers putting some spin on virtually every significant story, one way or the other, my preference was for the optimistic evaluation.)

Lou Dobbs on CNN introduced me this way: "He calls himself the toughest sheriff in the country. And I have to tell you, I've never heard anyone argue with him about that."

After I explained the program, he asked with a grin, "And where in the world is the ACLU? I can't imagine that you haven't gotten a phone call yet."

"I wish they would," I replied, "My polls go up every time they zap me."

I gave John Gibson on Fox News a quick summary of my position. "They should never forget their own language, but when they're in jail, I set the policies," I said. "We have 3,000 Hispanics out of 10,000 [inmates]; 2,000 of the 3,000 are illegal, so they should be learning English in the jail. This is the United States of America, and they should be able to communicate with our officers in English, not training our officers in Spanish. It's very simple."

"How are the inmates taking to this?" Gibson asked.

"They're all volunteering," I said. "I have a waiting list. Isn't that good? So now when they go to court, they can speak English. And when they need help, for safety or health reasons, they speak English. They are in the United States, they understand that, and they understand what the language is in this country. It's helping them, and it's also helping our officers."

Gibson approved, and absolutely approved of what I said next.

"Everything we do in the jails makes common sense."

That's something my opponents manage to overlook in their criticism of everything we do. Everything makes sense. It either saves the taxpayers money, or it provides greater security for the public or my officers or the inmates, or it teaches the inmates something valuable, something they need to know, perhaps even adds a bit to their rehabilitation. Despite the "show" the media so enjoys, the show is only the gloss on intelligent, productive, well-considered programs.

Some might say that "common sense" stands in sharp contrast to some of the ideas presented by the federal government. In the case of making a dent in the steady flow of illegal immigration, the feds decided, with much fanfare, to build a fence between Mexico and America. Not the entire length of the border, but 370 miles of it, divided between Arizona, Texas, California, and New Mexico. (Texas gets the lion's share, with 153 miles, while poor New Mexico has the short end of the stick, with a paltry 12 miles.) As of this writing, the fence is priced at a cool $3 billion—and that's before the usual government overruns, courtesy of missed deadlines and $50 hammers. And if Halliburton gets involved in the deal and charges the government for Cadillac SUVs and five-star resorts and $48 six-packs of soda—in other words, the way it works the system in Iraq—then that $3 billion will constitute nothing more than a down payment.

In that same CNN interview, Lou Dobbs asked me what I thought of the fence. It had already been condemned far and wide by local and federal politicians on both sides of the border—the Mexican president called it "shameful" and compared it to the Berlin Wall—joined by environmentalists, agricultural groups, and water suppliers.

My opinion was based on my evaluation of whether the wall would work, and at what cost. And that evaluation came up with a pretty obvious answer. "I don't know if we'll just be selling more ladders and shovels," I said. "You know how to stop the problem? Lock them up as they come across. It's a federal violation. Why don't they put them in jail, right away, as they come across the border. Very simple."

"You have extensive experience," Lou said. "You're highly respected across this country. Maybe you can give us some insight? Why in the world is the federal government not enforcing the law? They're going to spend $3 billion on a fence? Can't they put up a few tents and put them in the tents for six months under the federal law?"

Lou ended the interview with a few words that I really appreciated. "We thank you for being here," he said, "and for leading the way in showing some folks how to innovate and be effective in law enforcement."

Innovate and be effective. That summed it up. And I wasn't kidding, or speaking off the cuff, when I talked to Lou Dobbs about putting up tents near the border. The catch-and-release formula the feds employed wasn't working and never would—the penalty for getting caught was minimal, the potential reward in successfully crossing over too great, for people to stop coming. That was what we were doing in Maricopa County, not simply arresting illegals but putting them in jail. By delaying their return to Mexico even a little, we were interfering with their ability to make money, interfering with their reason for coming to America.

That's what I wanted the federal government to do, to gather together as many old army tents as they could find, erect those tents along the border, arraign and try the illegals in courts set up close to those tents, and put those people convicted of illegally crossing the border into the United States into those tents for six months. In no time, and I mean very, very quickly, illegal immigration will dwindle to an astonishing extent.

Can it really be that simple? Yes. And even if you aren't convinced, I'd like to know why it doesn't make sense. What is its fatal flaw? And if you can't find a fatal flaw, on either a practical, economic, or political level, why not give it a try and see what happens?

Look, the problem began with us. For twenty years, nobody cared how many Mexicans and other Latins crossed the border. Nobody cared where they traveled or where they worked or what they did with their money or how they raised their families. We did care that our lawns got mowed and our trees got pruned and our babies' diapers got changed and our restaurants' dishes got washed. We created the problem because it suited our purposes, and also because we were too lazy to put the time and resources into stopping it.

We created a situation where, over many years, word spread through Latin America that the United States quietly if not overtly welcomed anyone willing to come and work. Not that there weren't always obstacles to their trek. As fervently as Mexican politicians like to complain about the "harsh" treatment meted out to their fellow citizens on our side of the border, for years Mexico has arrested, imprisoned, and mistreated all men, women, and children crossing Mexico's southern border, on their way north. Whether they hail from Honduras, Guatemala, or El Salvador, they are arrested, imprisoned, mistreated, and then summarily thrown back across Mexico's border. While the Mexican authorities maltreat citizens of fellow Latin nations, it encourages its own people to cross the American border, both to earn funds to send back to Mexico and to release some of the social and economic pressure building inside Mexico.

So, in a line, there's sufficient hypocrisy and blame to go around to include everybody.

But that's not an answer. That's not good enough. Facts are facts, the situation is what it is, and we have to deal with it. As far as I can see, I haven't heard anyone come up with a simpler, safer, more secure solution than tents on the border and actual prison terms. Cut off the incentive for coming to the United States—cut off access, stop the problem right there, at the border, block the routes and nab everyone—and maybe we'll have something substantial and real to show for it.

* * *

AS WITH many mistakes that we have made, and are still making, at least on the federal side, and as reluctant as we are to confront the problem head-on, we cannot think that our failure to act does not have consequences. I have received thousands of letters from across the country relating stories that speak to the problems that arise when the law is broken with impunity, and with the acquiescence of the government and the community.

Dear Sheriff Arpaio,
I am writing to you as a concerned resident of (a local apartment complex). I wish to remain anonymous. I have been a resident of (the

complex) since 2001. I have enjoyed living here up until now; I have seen this property deteriorate since we got a new manager. When someone moves out she moves in an illegal immigrant. . . . The property now has a number of illegals. I have both seen and heard them moving in and out during the night. . . . "The manager" went inside her office with a group of Mexicans, and the residents think she may be a coyote.

I think it is very sad when the police department will not enforce the law . . . as a concerned resident, I am hoping you will help in some way to clean up this property and look into the actions of the manager.

And why haven't they enforced the law? More than a few writers have known exactly where to place the blame. Simply put:

Dear Sheriff Arpaio,
Keep up the good work deporting illegals.
Too bad our elected Congress doesn't have the guts to enforce the law.

Other correspondents have taken a broader, more inclusive view of the problem, generously spreading the culpability—and with a horrific surprise at the end.

Dear Sheriff Arpaio,
I wanted to take a moment to send you a note of encouragement and "Thank You" for upholding the U.S. Constitution and enforcing the law of our land. Once again you have proven that you are an American Hero and a role model for us all. . . . I heard you on the airwaves today speaking about . . . your plan to check the immigration status of suspects and criminals. . . . You can do this because you are not beholden to a particular political entity or union members. It is because of these affiliations that other law enforcement leaders

and many politicians are failing their constituents. They are more interested in their power and positions than the betterment of their communities and their Nation. Your power is derived from the many Moms and Pops out there who are frustrated daily seeing their loved ones victimized and in many cases killed by these illegal aliens (as my daughter was). . . .

The more my office has delved into this illegal immigration issue, the more the letters have come. Tales, like the one above, have been sometimes disturbing, sometimes sad. They have asked for help, and they have offered encouragement. They have offered a portrait of a world that has been changing—changing before them, on their streets, in their neighborhoods—and not necessarily for the better.

Dear Sheriff Arpaio,
We here in New York are far removed from the Southern border . . . but nevertheless are affected by the invasion of illegal aliens who swarm across your borders in Arizona. The border crashers are transients in your county, but we receive thousands of them, who take up permanent residence here. We are extremely grateful to you for your patriotic efforts, on the first line of defense. . . .

And another New Yorker (albeit one from outside the city) wrote of his concern that what we faced in Arizona has been a foreshadowing for his own community.

Dear Sheriff Arpaio,
Please allow me to express my admiration for your stance on illegal immigration. Because I live in upper New York, I haven't experienced the onslaught of this invasion—yet—though I assume it's only a matter of time.
     The several times I saw you on TV, I couldn't help but be impressed with your determination, while at the same time experiencing a

growing anger over the coverage of protesters daring to challenge the U.S. laws. I have been following this illegal immigration issue for twenty years, and I am still astonished at the demands of these people who want to turn this country into a Northern Latin America, compliments of our government.

The public flaunting of U.S. law that we have witnessed in our streets and on TV, the idea that America must bend to the will of those illegally here and illegally demanding rights, as a matter of right, has proved perhaps the most infuriating aspect of the entire issue to the majority of Americans. Many people have written to me of their own experiences complying with the law of the land, and they feel it is entirely reasonable to expect others to do the same.

Dear Sheriff Arpaio,

Eight years ago I married a man from El Salvador, and he is now a permanent resident. Gaining his residency was a long, expensive process, full of immigration paperwork and appointments, but it was important to us that we follow the correct legal process for his citizenship.

Since our marriage, I have been immersed in the "Latino" community. Many of the people we run into are here illegally, so I see and hear firsthand their disrespect and contempt for our government and laws. They do not respect what America stands for. . . . They mock those of us who follow the rules. Constantly, my husband gets criticized and ridiculed for obeying and respecting the laws of our country. . . . They drive with false Mexican driver's licenses. They register cars the same way. They obtain fake Social Security numbers and any other identification they think is necessary.

We have called the immigration hotline many times, many times, but nothing seems to change. I have written to all of the U.S. senators twice to voice my disappointment in their leadership, or lack thereof. . . .

The details might be different, but the essence and the sentiment are the same from this writer:

> Dear Sheriff Arpaio,
> I am seventy-nine years old, and I was a legal immigrant from Canada in the 1960s. I went through an interview with the American consulate in Toronto, a police clearance, a medical clearance, and I had to prove I had sufficient financial assets to support myself so that I would not become a public charge. It grieves me to know that these illegals can cross our borders and almost immediately become eligible for medical benefits and other benefits at the expense of the American taxpayer.

And here's still more outrage and despair from another citizen, expressed in a handwritten letter, in the wake of a protest march of some 15,000 illegals and their cohorts, "an illegal march in support of illegal immigrants," as has been noted by others, conducted without a permit, closing down streets and businesses in downtown Phoenix.

> Dear Sheriff Arpaio,
> I can't see that they can protest in Phoenix the way they did. If we true Americans would do that, the police force would have been out and locked us up. My ancestors came through Ellis Island. My father fought in three wars for this country. I've seen what's happening here in Arizona for about the last ten years. When is it going to end?

Good question. And if it's up to me, it'll end here, in Arizona, and now. But the truth is, it's not up to me. It's up to law enforcement officers across America. It's up to fifty governors. It's up to Congress. It's up to the President.

It's also up to Mexico and the Mexican people. Many letters pointed out the corruption and poverty that has been eating away at

Mexico for generations. These same writers often mentioned that the sort of public scoffing of the law Americans witness on an ongoing basis, in interviews, rallies, marches, and protests, would never fly back in their home country.

> Dear Sheriff Arpaio,
> . . . The people that are walking the streets in protest marches need to head back across the border and protest the living conditions down there, and make their government provide relief for them. Of course, if they did that, they would most likely be shot.

Of all the correspondence I have received, and continue to receive on a daily basis, the ones that mean the most to me are the letters from our men and women serving in the military, and particularly from those serving in war zones.

> Dear Sheriff Arpaio,
> I am a member of the Kentucky National Guard. . . . I am now in Baghdad, and wish I could have met you, but I'll serve my country here, while you serve in Arizona. . . . I hope you keep the faith, do not let anyone say you're wrong. It takes strong people to protect, serve, and honor our country. . . . . You remind me of the young American soldiers here in Iraq, standing up and doing the job, regardless of what harm comes to them.

That soldier was wrong about one thing: My effort could not be compared to the sacrifices he and his fellow soldiers were making on behalf of our country. I was doing my job—he and his compatriots were the true American heroes.

★   ★   ★

BACK IN Arizona, the evidence was mounting as to the corrupting and dangerous impact of illegal immigration.

Example: Acting on a phoned-in tip, MCSO deputies discovered forty-nine people in a house in an unincorporated area outside the town of Litchfield Park, while ten more were in another house not far away. The public became aware of suspicious activity courtesy of gunfire emanating from the latter locale. One man was shot while three others were beaten. All fifty-nine people were arrested on suspicion of violating federal immigration laws. The more deputies we cross-trained in federal immigration enforcement, the more efficient we could be.

Of course, these drop houses were just two of many in Phoenix and Maricopa County. The economics of the smuggling industry explained why so many drop houses were scattered through my territory. Roughly calculating, we figure that each customer paid between $1,500 and $2,000 for the trip. Even discounting that a few of those picked up were coyotes, that would mean that in just two raids, the total bill the gang collected could have been more than $100,000. Each gang could have four or five such loads running at any given time, so multiply that hundred-plus accordingly.

And each load is over and done in just a few days, so they get to do it all over again and again and again.

A profitable business, indeed.

✳   ✳   ✳

THE EVIDENCE is contradictory and fundamentally irrelevant as to whether illegal immigrants commit more crimes than citizens. Overwhelmingly, of course, most illegals are here to work and build better lives. Regardless, that's not the issue. We already have more than enough crime in Maricopa County and throughout America, by virtue of the misdeeds of our native sons and daughters. With all that homegrown crime, we do not need the additional burden of contending with more imported crime.

And yet here it is, in so many forms. Remember my previous statement that 2,000 of the 10,000 inmates in my county jails are illegals who have committed a crime apart from entering and/or residing in the United States illegally.

Example: One of my deputies, an off-duty undercover narcotics officer, has encountered an increasingly common circumstance. He was driving away from the tents in the early evening, heading east on Durango Road, when he saw a guy driving erratically toss a beer bottle out of a car. In short order, the driver tossed a second bottle. By now, the deputy was following the car in his own vehicle, a Ford Expedition.

An entire six-pack of empty beer bottles flew out the car's window. A red light stopped the car, with the cop directly behind him. For whatever reason—maybe it was sheer paranoia, maybe the cop was too close—the driver panicked. He couldn't go forward because of the traffic heading north to south, so he slammed back into the cop's Expedition, hard. He smashed into the SUV over and over, then pulled alongside, managing to force the Expedition into oncoming traffic. A woman driving in the other direction hit the Expedition. The collision buckled the SUV's frame and severed the woman's leg. She would later die at the hospital.

The driver fled on foot but was apprehended about half a block from the scene. He was charged with aggravated assault and second-degree homicide. After a drug test, a cocaine charge was included.

It was quickly discovered he was an illegal immigrant. He had entered the United States illegally at least *five times*.

An aside: The illegal said he had learned his driving moves from American television. Hooray for Hollywood.

Could an American citizen have acted just as violently, just as stupidly, just as criminally? Absolutely. But that isn't the point. The point is that an illegal immigrant, a man who shouldn't have been in this country in the first place—a man who wouldn't have been in this country if the government had been dedicated to upholding the

law—was in a position to attack a sheriff's deputy and kill an innocent, forty-six-year-old woman.

Most crimes, especially serious crimes, perpetrated by illegal
immigrants are not committed against Americans, but rather against
one another. The desert is harsh and unforgiving, and too often, so
are the coyotes. They'll abandon their customers when it is con-
venient to do so, or simply rob or rape or murder them as part of
their plan. Seemingly every day, Border Patrol agents as well as my
own deputies find the bodies of those left behind by coyotes, if they
haven't collapsed of their own accord.

As noted previously, criminal gangs run much of the operation,
and make no mistake, criminal gangs are vicious enterprises. When
not seizing control of the human smuggling business simply as a
profit-making move, the gangs are using the illegals as human
decoys to divert the attention of American law enforcement away
from their drug shipments. New technology and increased manpower at the border have made a dent into drug, mainly cocaine,
shipments. To counter this development, the drug gangs are ordering coyotes and illegals to take certain paths and routes in order to
attract the Border Patrol and other cops, to clear out other paths
and routes for those directing the cocaine transportation. In particular, two Mexican cartels—the Sinaloa cartel, which controls the
Arizona border, and its main rival, the Gulf cartel, which dominates
along the Texas border—are prominent in this evolution of the
criminal industry.

It's a double win for the gangs. They get paid by the illegals,
whether they make it or not, and then they are paid for their drugs.
The gangs are not always waiting for their fellow Mexicans and
other Hispanics to sign up with their smuggling services; rather, they
set up teams of gunmen at many of the most popular crossing places
and roads and demand an extra fee from anyone passing through.
It's a form of "protection money," similar to the modus operandi of
the American Mafia.

On one occasion, heavily armed men stopped twelve vans, ferrying 200 illegals, on an isolated desert road just south of the border. Ordering everyone out of the vans, the men doused the vehicles with gasoline and set them on fire. The message was clear to anyone who passed by those charred metal skeletons—pay up while there's time.

On other occasions, illegals are held up at the border until the gang deems it most advantageous to send them across. They then flood the area and wait for the Border Patrol to respond. When and if law enforcement reacts, the gang dispatches its drug shipment.

As profitable as human smuggling can be, drugs still take the cake.

Of course, we can only do so much without the cooperation of the Mexican authorities. As corrupt as they are, especially near the border, where the gangs control not only what happens on the street but frequently what happens in the government, we have to appreciate the remarkable danger under which the Mexican authorities operate. Literally every day, sometimes a dozen or more bodies are discovered in alleys, in the desert, or in the fields. Many of them have been tortured, some decapitated. Giant cartels and individual gangs alike will not hesitate to kill anyone, cop or civilian, who dares get in their way.

The stakes are too high. Back in March 2007, to take only one example, Mexican police seized more than $200 million *in cash* inside a Mexico City mansion. It was the largest seizure of drug money in the world. The money was allegedly to be used to organize a methamphetamine factory that would have manufactured 3 million pills a day for the U.S. market.

Crime is about money, and as long as there is a buck to be made, smuggling of people, drugs, guns—you name it—won't stop of its own accord. And the corpses of the victims will continue to pile up, mainly because of the brutality employed not by Americans or American law enforcement, but by fellow Mexicans exploiting the illegals.

✳   ✳   ✳

TOGETHER, the deputies and the posse did themselves proud that night. Two cars were stopped near Wickenburg. The first was a Chevrolet van, pulled over on a lights violation. The van held eight people. One was arrested as a smuggler, along with six of his customers, who stated they had each paid between $1,000 and $1,800 for their trip into the States. A seventeen-year-old girl was detained and handed over to federal authorities for possible deportation. The van's destination was supposed to be Los Angeles.

Shortly thereafter, my guys nabbed a Nissan SUV for speeding. They snatched a smuggler and five customers, who paid from $500 to $3,000. Another seventeen-year-old girl was passed to the feds.

And that wasn't all the news. Our news hotline received a hundred calls in the first eighteen hours of operation, 152 calls by the next day. Seventeen callers offered information on drop houses, information we'd follow up, just as we'd follow up on tips regarding any other sort of crime.

Particularly intriguing were the forty-seven calls from individuals informing on members of their own family. We'd check on those, too, and carefully. After all, you never know what storms and personal grudges are brewing inside a family.

So the effort was a success, worth the hard work of putting together an operation of its size. And it promised more success, through the hotline, in the future. That's how law enforcement does its job, putting together evidence and responding to problems piece by piece, like a giant jigsaw puzzle that becomes clearer as you go on. Only it can never completely get done, because though the evidence and problems and crimes might shift and change, they never cease coming, and you never finish. You respond and help and protect and stop all sorts of bad guys doing all sorts of bad acts, and you win for the moment, and then you get up and do it all again tomorrow.

And so the fight goes on. Even though I pull out a few now and then, I know that statistics will tell you lots of different things and just about anything you want to believe. Statistics give the appearance of absolute certainty, which makes them so easy to manipulate and use to prove either side of almost any argument. Though I run for office every four years, I'm not a politician, definitely in any conventional mold, pandering to what I believe my constituency wants me to do, hiding behind data and studies and academic opinion for every action I take. I do what I know is right based on my evaluation of the situation, without looking for the cover of experts or statistics to defend my decision from criticism.

In other words, I lead from the front, not from the rear.

And so here we go again.

I was back at the training center, scene of my birthday party, although this time in the auditorium. I stood at the podium and welcomed the sixty-two Immigration and Customs Enforcement agents seated before me. As feds, they were all overwhelmingly dressed in predictable two-button blue suits, including the handful of women in the group. I was about to deputize them, giving these ICE agents, these feds, local and state authority to enforce Arizona laws.

"It's sort of a payback," I said, "because your SAC [Special Agent in Charge] made a promise to train 160 Maricopa County deputies, which we've done. So I'm going to swear in sixty-two federal agents. Under the Constitution, only the sheriff has the authority to deputize federal officers."

Just as 160 of my deputies had been granted federal authority after taking the course and becoming cross-designated, now I had done the same with the feds, granting them across-the-board law enforcement authority.

For some time, the sheriff's office and ICE did not see eye-to-eye, to put it nicely, on how to best fight illegal immigration. A lack of communication and cooperation had impeded our individual efforts to do our jobs, which naturally led to numerous discussions— loud, unhappy discussions on my part with the appropriate parties.

I lived through three reorganizations during my time with the federal government. Three times I got a new badge, under a renamed agency, from the Bureau of Narcotics, then the Bureau of Narcotics and Dangerous Drugs, and finally the Drug Enforcement Administration. Three reorganizations, and I tell you I learned one thing for sure: Every time the government reorganizes or restructures or rearranges, you lose two to three years, guaranteed. So you can be sure that when the government, in its infinite wisdom and equally infinite panic post-9/11, decided to create the Department of Homeland Security (it had to do something, anything, after all, at least for public consumption), two to three years lost was not only a given, but an optimistic prognosis. I have no doubt that much time was spent deciding what color the uniforms should be for the 150,000 employees of the new department. Four years after the DHS was thrust into existence, one-quarter of the cabinet department's top posts—138 out of 575—remained unfilled.

With that as background, is it any wonder that the cooperation between MCSO and ICE was so bad that the feds refused to take charge of the illegals we arrested, forcing me to get my own buses, march the illegals onto them, drive down to the border, and pass them to the Border Patrol (which enthusiastically accepted all)? It's kind of interesting that two organizations, both nestled within the bosom of Homeland Security, had very diametrically opposed ideas of interagency cooperation.

In any event, this increasingly unpleasant, highly inefficient situation had been remedied with the appointment within ICE of Special Agent-in-Charge Alonzo Peña, who not only understood what we were trying to accomplish, but also believed that it made sense. And that meant we could work together and accomplish terrific things.

"It is quite an honor to be here with the sheriff," SAC Peña said to the assembled. "I know when I got here, I had requests from many of you to have this cross-designation. It's another tool in our toolbox, to have not only federal authority but also state authority."

Even though I was the sheriff of Maricopa County, police authority was statewide, and so deputizing the ICE agents gave them authority across Arizona.

I returned to the podium to concur with what Peña had said. "We got the authority," I declared, "and we're going to use it, and I know there will be some great cases because of what we did today."

And right before I swore in his agents, I reminded Peña of one detail: "Any good cases you guys make are mine, right, special agent?"

FROM IMMIGRATION TO DRUGS

WE FACED an interesting situation here in Maricopa County a couple of years ago, interesting in the sense that the Chinese proverb employs the word as a curse. It all started with a racially motivated drive-by shooting in north Phoenix, a crime that went unsolved for months, until our Threats Unit broke the case. The two shooters were arrested and sentenced to eighteen years in prison.

As we will see time and time again, one crime often bleeds into another (sometimes literally), and so it was true here. This investigation led to another, the link provided by a teenage informant who was trying to get off heroin. By July 2004, my deputies were onto a pair of drug dealers, and an undercover detective, introduced to the dealers by the informant, purchased heroin from them on six occasions. The buys ranged from $40 to $60. So far, nothing out of the ordinary, as far as criminal activity goes.

The detectives running the case decided to delve a little deeper and set up surveillance on the dealers during the day. The dealers were singularly active, moving from south Scottsdale to north Scottsdale in the course of making ten to twenty deliveries a day. Scottsdale, which is adjacent to Phoenix, is no small town. It covers 185 largely affluent square miles (by comparison, Manhattan is twenty-three square miles), so the dealers were covering a lot of territory.

After watching this activity for three days, ten to sixteen hours each day, we decided to begin contacting the drug dealers' customers. At the same time, the surveillance would continue for another week and half.

The first person the detectives contacted was a seventeen-year-old girl. They watched from a secure location in north Scottsdale while she bought something wrapped in aluminum from one of the dealers. After the dealer departed, the young woman, seated in the car, heated the tin foil and commenced inhaling the fumes.

The detectives approached the teenager and she talked, admitting she had been purchasing heroin from the same dealer for about a year. She also said she was a high school student.

The detectives continued with this strategy of watching deals and then nabbing and interrogating the buyers, resulting in twenty-five arrests. It quickly became clear that a majority of these customers were of high school age. Operation Safe Schools was about to kick into high gear.

Weeks of surveillance and investigation resulted in the arrest of eight more dealers. Scottsdale PD added one to the list; not long before, its officers had arrested a guy for dealing heroin in a Scottsdale park. It turned out that the car this guy had been driving was also favored by one of the dealers my detective had snatched up. The car proved the link between the Scottsdale PD's dealer and the organization we were busting.

The conspiracy was quickly expanding.

Eleven of the young customers cooperated with our investigators, offering up with alacrity whatever information they had. It soon became clear that the dealers had targeted high school and even middle school students. And though the deals were consummated off campus, much of the drug use happened at school, with some of the more entrepreneurial kids deciding to go into business for themselves and negotiating their own deals with their fellow students.

The students said that cocaine and heroin were readily available and regularly used in the school bathrooms. Each of them knew other students, sometimes many other students, who made drug use a daily habit. One of the buyers told the detectives he had witnessed other students snorting cocaine and heroin while sitting in class and listening to lectures, concealing their actions behind the backpacks they placed on their desks.

The stories kept coming. One kid talked about watching members of the cheerleading squad down methamphetamines as a centerpiece of their diet regimen, while another of the apprehended customers related how football players were using steroids, although the sad truth is, in this day, neither of those situations could have legitimately surprised anyone.

The investigation continued for eight months. Eleven drug dealers were taken into custody and charged. Fairly early on, the detectives recognized that the dealers conducted their affairs in almost identical manner from one to the next: They employed the same type of cell phones, ditto for their vehicles, and likewise for the way in which they sold and delivered their product to their consumers.

And this was how it would happen: The customer called the dealer, who would set a meeting in a parking lot or shopping center after inquiring as to the buyer's location, a necessity in a town this spread out. After spotting the client at the meeting, the dealer would signal him to follow to another part of the lot. The deal was consummated in the dealer's vehicle, the happy customer would then get out, and the dealer would drive off.

Nice and neat.

The first two dealers we arrested generously consented to allow my deputies to use their cell phones and cars for investigatory purposes. Spanish-speaking detectives took over the phones and kept the drug business in business. And then the inevitable would occur: The buyers would show up, and the detectives would arrest them.

Those thwarted buyers, experienced in drugs but inexperienced with harsh legal consequences, provided both MCSO and Scottsdale PD with the names and phone numbers of other dealers. Still in undercover guise, we called them and ordered more cocaine and heroin, which nabbed eight more dealers. Now, with eleven dealers under lock and key, we subpoenaed their cell phone records. All together, for the duration of the investigation, no fewer than 160,000 calls were dialed to or from those cells. The next step was obvious: Making a very, very, *very* long list identifying the subscribers making or receiving those calls.

In short order, we focused our attention on 581 individuals who sent or received three or more calls to the dealers.

Before continuing, I need to point out one salient fact, pertinent beyond the details of this particular case: Those eleven men arrested and arraigned on drug trafficking charges were all Mexican citizens. Mexican citizens who were in this country illegally and quite overtly for the purpose of committing more crimes. Mexican citizens who should have been stopped at the border before they had the opportunity to commit more crimes.

Eighteen teens were arrested on drug charges; as noted, eleven cooperated with law enforcement, and the remaining seven faced charges of possession of narcotics.

As distressing as all that was, it was time for the more controversial component of the case, because simply rounding up the drug ring didn't wrap it up in any satisfying or satisfactory way. I knew we had an obligation to try to stop this operation before another drug ring popped up and more dealers took over for their incarcerated colleagues. The narcotics wouldn't stop coming; nor would the dealers who peddled them; nor, apparently, would the kids willing to buy and ingest them. We had to do something, and it involved going over the heads of the students and right to their bosses.

On Saturday, March 19, 2005, a fleet of MCSO deputies and posse members in unmarked cars headed out into the streets of Scottsdale and Phoenix to knock on hundreds of doors and alert parents that their children might be using drugs, based on their cell phone records. On Sunday, we hit the rest of the 581 households linked to those multiple phone calls to drug dealers.

And that wasn't all. We also contacted another 146 parents whose kids were picked out by informants as involved in drugs.

The mission was handled with precise instructions and tight supervision. Each team was led by a deputy who oversaw a handful of posse volunteers. The hundreds of addresses were divided among the teams.

Each posse volunteer was handed a written introduction, a script to be recited when someone opened the front door. The script started with the posse member stating his name and job, and explaining how he was assisting in the public notification of Operation Safe Schools. This mission wasn't about pursuing investigations or conducting interrogations or making cases, and we made certain the posse members announced that up-front, loud and clear, exactly as such:

We are only here to provide public awareness.

You are not under arrest, nor are charges being filed.

You are not the subject of a criminal investigation by the Maricopa County Sheriff's Office.

You will not be charged with any crimes in relation to Operation Safe Schools.

*Any information that you or your child provides will not be used
against you or your child in any way.*

The officers distributed pamphlets explaining the situation, along
with pictures of heroin, psychedelic mushrooms, steroids, methamphetamine, cocaine, crystal meth, and marijuana. The pamphlets
went on to list eleven warning signs for parents to look out for and
named nine treatment centers.

My people reported that the overwhelming majority of the parents were grateful for the information. One mother told a deputy
that even though her son had been arrested for marijuana possession two weeks before, it was only now, after speaking with the
deputy and reviewing the pamphlets, that she finally understood that
her son had a serious problem. Another mother said that after seeing the reports on the investigation on television, she had been
expecting a visit from the cops.

Of course, there were, as always, those few who did not appreciate this intrusion in their lives, who angrily rejected the proffered
information and basically shut the door in the faces of the officers,
intent on returning to their comfortable routines. Other critics
emerged as well, who felt I had overstepped my bounds. As you probably guessed, I didn't care. In my career, I had seen a wide variety of
drugs cause untold misery, so I had absolutely no doubt what mattered here, and complaints about tactics or protocol or whatever you
wanted to call it definitely ranked a distant second in importance.

Most people instantly grasped what was at stake, and it wasn't
protecting political correctness, but protecting our kids, and a lot of
them felt moved to write and tell me their stories.

Dear Joe,
The holidays are here and I have so much to be thankful for, even
though it is the first time I will be spending it without my son in
seventeen years. You see, on September 30, someone injected him

with heroin, by his own choosing, and he overdosed. The kids rushed him to the hospital and they were able to reverse the heroin and revive him. . . .

I am giving thanks for two things this holiday season. Thanks for such fine people like [the detectives] you have working for you, and thanks for having my son alive to have a second chance.

Other parents were not so fortunate. A few weeks after my deputies and posse members went door-to-door, a mother in Cave Creek found her fifteen-year-old son lying in his own vomit, next to a syringe and a portion of black tar Mexican heroin. The heroin was similar to that seized from the drug ring we had dismantled.

The boy was dead.

He might have heard about our bust and how we had warned parents about what was happening to their kids. He might have heard from his family, his friends, or his school that drugs can be lethal. He might have heard all or some of it, and he might have thought about it or laughed it off. It's also possible he had heard nothing. In the end it didn't matter, because he had gotten his hands on heroin and it had killed him.

That's why I wanted to make sure that the parents on that cell phone list heard about what was going on and that as many parents and kids throughout the county, on the list or not, were alerted. I released a video of an interrogation of a teenage girl from Scottsdale's Saguaro High School. We had arrested her when she tried to purchase $10 worth of heroin from an undercover agent. Though her face was obscured to protect her identity, it was chillingly clear just how young she was, from what she had to say and how casually she said it. Surely, part of the reason for her casual attitude was that she was hardly alone in her drug consumption, claiming that "tons" of her fellow students also used drugs during the day.

She was fourteen when she started with heroin.

Detective: Is that the first drug you ever used?

Girl: No.

Detective: What did you use prior to that?

Girl: Pot and alcohol and pills.

Detective: Where did you get those kinds of things?

Girl: My friends or my grandparents had a lot of alcohol always laying around the house.

Detective: Prescription medications?

Girl: Thirteen.

Eventually, they got to heroin. She hated the notion of sticking herself with a needle, so her boyfriend taught her to mix heroin in water and snort it. By the time she was sixteen, a friend was injecting her.

Detective: How long a time span was it that you were injecting yourself—or getting injections?

Girl: A month. Like for a month straight, I was getting injections, just like I had needles in my arm all day.

Detective: More than once a day.

Girl: Yeah, like three or four times. Sometimes more.

Detective: For a month?

Girl: Ah-huh.

Detective: Then what happened after that?

Girl: I overdosed and ended up in the hospital. So that kinda— I stopped using needles.

Detective: When you got out of the hospital, what was your drug use like then?

Girl: Nothing really changed. I was still using heroin for, like, it took about three days, and I was doing heroin again and anything else you would give me.

I released that interview to the media because people needed to know what was going on with their kids, without filters or interpretation. They needed to know the unvarnished truth.

I urged the Scottsdale school board to institute random drug testing. The testing would be done on a voluntary basis, with the parents' okay, and would not be used to kick anyone out of school, but to get that individual help. The school board rejected my proposal. Instead, the school superintendent announced he would ask the board for permission to have drug-sniffing dogs patrol the high school hallways.

That didn't make any sense to me. Dogs might be fine for sniffing out lockers, but how long would it take any students holding narcotics to figure out how to get around the dogs, to keep them out of their lockers and, for example, store them to their cars in the parking lot? In a fairly unusual event, the media expressed disdain that mirrored my own about the school board's idea. The plan was destined to fall apart of its own ill-conceived weight.

Life moved on—for students, their parents, and for the drug traffickers. Our fight remained the same—to serve and protect.

The drug war is not a fight we can win by segregating this offense from others, by neatly placing different criminal activity into orderly separate categories. In a phrase, drugs are not only about drugs. That's one of the lessons, one of the prime lessons, all of us have to acknowledge, and which this story demonstrated.

In a sentence: If you don't stop the crime at the source, you're not going to stop it. Isolate the problem at the root, or as close to that root as you can, and wrap it up before it spews out and spreads. Blow up the opium fields in Afghanistan, give the farmers incentive to raise alternative crops, stop the opium dead in its track right there, or else watch while it gets turned into heroin, shipped into the United States, and distributed to 10,000 dealers.

If you let it go that far—the product grown, processed, and distributed—how effective can your efforts to put that genie back in the bottle really hope to be?

Illegal immigration isn't only about who gets to vote or pay taxes or receive Social Security. Illegal immigration is the starting point of expanding criminal conspiracies, one rolling out into the next and into the next. That's why you need to understand (and it's really not too hard to understand) the link between illegal immigration and illegal drugs, and just how far the long, malevolent tentacles of the cartels reach. The cartels are taking over the routes for both businesses, and their increased opportunities to extract profit on both ends increases their power, as well as the suffering of every human being standing in their way.

The DEA in Arizona announced that cocaine and heroin seizures in 2007 were on track to double the previous year's yield, and 2006 was a record year. Marijuana seizures were up 25 percent, and the local DEA had already grabbed more weed than all of the previous year. The DEA contends that Mexican labs account for 80 percent of the methamphetamine in the United States, and those laboratories were put into operation after law enforcement closed down many of the stateside labs.

And that's not all. A brand-new danger has emerged on the streets. "Cheese heroin" is a blend of black tar Mexican heroin and crushed over-the-counter medications that contain diphenhydramine, an antihistamine found in products such as Tylenol PM. The combination of heroin and nighttime sleep aids results in a sedative mix that is startlingly deadly.

Cheese heroin seems the perfect drug to sell to student addicts.

A hit sells for as little as $2, making it within everyone's price range, making it completely accessible. How could anything so cheap and accessible be that dangerous? Even the name, "cheese," sounds benign, masking its potential lethality.

In Dallas, where cheese has really taken hold, twenty-one high school students have died from its use over the past two years. Again, our inability or unwillingness to control our border has led to the creation of yet another perilous problem.

In January 2006, the National Drug Intelligence Center within the Department of Justice warned that the Mexican drug cartels are moving in on their Colombian and Dominican counterparts as far from the border as Florida and New York. And the open border is not only used by Los Zetas and Mexican drug gangs, but by gangs from Central and South America, too. On February 16, 2005, FBI Director Robert Mueller testified before the Senate Select Committee on Intelligence that the Department of Justice estimates there are approximately 30,000 gangs with over 800,000 members in the United States. Many of those gangs and gang members are homegrown, while others hail from other countries. Whatever they do, whether it's human smuggling or narcotics or kidnapping or murder, they do so with horrific violence and extraordinary disregard for human life.

In Laredo, sheriff deputies found fifty-six illegals, including eleven women and two children, locked inside a refrigerator trailer, where they were on the verge of freezing to death. Here in Arizona, gangs have kidnapped scores of illegals transported into the country by rival groups, hiding them in stash houses in and around Phoenix until families paid a ransom. To encourage prompt payment, women have been raped, fingers cut off, and other equally brutal outrages perpetrated.

✳ ✳ ✳

GIVEN HOW difficult and seemingly unwinnable the war against drugs seems to be, I am sometimes asked if I think we should just give up and legalize at least some drugs. Of course, marijuana is always mentioned first because many people equate it with alcohol and cigarettes (the nicotine and tar kind).

More and more Americans support the legalization of marijuana. A 2006 Zogby poll found that nearly half of Americans back changing federal law to "let states legally regulate and tax marijuana the way they do liquor and gambling." The exact count: 46 percent in favor, 49 percent opposed, 5 percent undecided.

Especially interesting, especially to me: The highest level of support was out West, where yes-on-marijuana sentiment reached 55 percent.

I can understand why many Americans feel this way. As a nation, we embrace alcohol, despite the societal and human wreckage it causes every single day, in contrast to our official condemnation of pot. The hypocrisy can be (excuse the expression) hard to swallow. One example to demonstrate the position in favor of pot: Alcohol often causes drunk drivers to drive in a riskier, more aggressive fashion, whereas marijuana usually causes its users to proceed more cautiously.

On another front, some of the children of the sixties, who enthusiastically embraced marijuana, find it difficult to order their own kids to stay away from it. (Actually, many find it difficult to order their kids to do anything, but that's a different, albeit related, issue.)

Finally, many people ask: Why fight a losing battle? Instead, why don't we make reality work for us and go from prohibition to taxation, precisely as we did with alcohol? In many ways that's the most persuasive argument of all. They advocate robbing criminals of their profit and power, halting the imprisonment of otherwise-innocent Americans for getting caught up in what they regard as a "victimless crime," and adding billions of dollars to the government treasury instead of spending billions on law enforcement and incarceration.

While all of that sounds reasonable and well intentioned, I stand firmly against legalization of drugs. There can be no equivocation on this. That's the situation we're in right now, living with a patchwork of confusing laws that vary from city to city, state to state, making it illegal to buy marijuana but not possess it, legal to possess a small amount but not more than that, with criminal penalties attached here but not there, etc. Once an act has been decriminalized, when the most severe penalty is reduced to a monetary fine, the underpinning moral and legal rationale to obey that law rapidly disappears. We have to take a stand, one way or the other, and I stand with fighting drugs, no quarter offered.

Let me use pornography as an example to explain my position. Though it might be hard to imagine today, pornography was once illegal in the United States: No mainstream raunchy magazines, no explicit cable television shows, no triple-X films, and no Internet sex websites (no Internet, actually). The hottest tickets around were 8-millimeter stag movies, usually allegedly shipped from Denmark or Sweden or some other foreign land overrun by depraved purveyors of lascivious behavior.

Pornography's illegal status resulted in one undeniable fact—the vast majority of Americans would not buy the movies. Even if they could somehow find them, most Americans would not break the law. It was as certain and as simple as that.

With the elimination of statutory prohibition, moral and ethical prohibitions quickly vanished as well. Having swept away all inhibitions, porn is ostensibly everywhere, from bookstores to video stores, movie theaters to TV screens, corner newsstands to computer monitors. The customers are no longer just the usual suspects—college boys and dirty old men—but now everyone is welcomed to join in. The legitimization of porn has brought mothers and fathers, sons and daughters, friends, family, and coworkers into the fold. Porn is everywhere and for everyone because the law has granted it an implicit stamp of approval.

Put aside intellectual questions regarding the First Amendment or your own feelings about porn, pro or con, and focus, for purposes of this discussion, on the matter of cause and effect, which asks: Has widespread use and distribution changed pornography from something potentially harmful to something neutral or even positive, simply because retail outlets sell it, the citizenry buys it, and the state collects its slice of tax revenue?

Clearly, the answer is no. The acceptance and use and even enjoyment of something does not make it instantly sound, safe, or beneficial. At the very least, a lot of people who study this issue assert that pornography desensitizes the viewer to an entire spectrum of human emotions and distorts both those emotions and then the viewer's responses to other people. At the very worst, a lot of people maintain that pornography results in violence against women. Either way, I've never heard anybody say porn does anything good for anybody other than the guy making money off it.

It's all just idle talk now, because pornography is legal, and people can't get enough. Porn's the biggest moneymaker on the Internet, and it's fair to say that the Internet as we know it, a growing information and business entity, wouldn't exist without porn's underlying financial stimulus. Few people are worried about pornography's negative impact, because when the law declares it to be okay, then it's okay by them, and that's all they need to know. They're going to buy it and they're going to watch it, even if scientists knock down their doors and force them to hear proof beyond a shadow of a doubt that porn is harmful to their mental health and the mental health of their unborn descendants. They won't care, or more exactly, they won't worry about it, because it is legal.

You think that's an exaggeration? Ask Philip Morris or R. J. Reynolds what they have to say on the subject. The respectable status of the tobacco companies, despite the relentless efforts of scientists and doctors and activists to warn Americans and put them out of business, has trumped all other concerns, addicting millions of people and earning the tobacco companies billions of dollars every year. If tobacco were stumbled upon only yesterday and cigarettes invented today, and all the health risks were known from the start, tobacco would never have become legal.

The same questions and answers could be posed of alcohol. None of it matters now, for tobacco and alcohol are cats long out of the bag and gone. Narcotics must not be permitted to imitate their history.

Another issue to consider, and another entirely practical issue at that, is where legalization really will end. The vast majority of people who want marijuana legalized do not feel the same way about so-called harder drugs, and even fewer still would like the government to declare every drug made readily available to anyone on demand. The idea is to focus on marijuana, which is widely viewed as a relatively harmless drug that is certainly no worse than, if not a substantial improvement over, all forms of liquor, from whiskey to wine.

But that position is manifestly simplistic and ultimately unworkable. To begin, today's marijuana is not necessarily the same as that consumed by the aforementioned children of the sixties. Some of it is two to three times more powerful than anything available thirty years ago. Other studies have shown that a certain percentage is ten to twenty times more potent. Additionally, two studies demonstrate disturbing similarities between marijuana's effects on the brain and those effects produced by highly addictive narcotics such as cocaine and heroin, not to mention alcohol and nicotine. In the first study, a team from the Scripps Research Institute in La Jolla, California, and Complutense University of Madrid, Spain, linked the anxiety and stress caused by marijuana withdrawal to the same brain chemical—a peptide called corticotropin-releasing factor, or CRF—associated with emotional distress experienced during alcohol, cocaine, and opiate withdrawal. The second study hailed from the University of Cagliari in Italy, where researchers discovered that THC, a cannabinoid that is the active ingredient in pot, causes a release of dopamine in the brain, resulting in the biochemical rush that reinforces drug dependence, just as it does in other drugs, including, once again, nicotine and heroin.

As worrisome as that might be, there's more to be said, for if pot is getting more powerful and the government does legalize and regulate marijuana, how long will it be before an enterprising criminal starts producing substantially stronger pot, outdoing the legal variety? Will the government respond by moving the goalposts of legality, or will there then be legal marijuana and illegal marijuana? Will some additives be permitted and not others? Will that just create another illicit market or, more likely, build irresistible pressure to keep opening up more and more drugs to the public? Where will it stop? Put another way, once the brakes are released, how can they ever be applied?

Again, the legal prohibition against drugs keeps millions of Americans from using them. For that reason alone, drugs cannot be legalized. Nor should they be decriminalized. Does it make any sense that it's illegal to sell marijuana but not to own it—or the other way around? Of course not. We have to be consistent, and we have to be logical. If we are ever going to seriously impede the flow and use of drugs, we have to devise a sane, dependable, unfailing, and unbending national policy that the states can enthusiastically embrace and enforce. We have to be united in this, and we have to stop them across the board—stop them cold.

It has been calculated in years past that 70 percent of all crime in America begins with drugs, in one form or another. Today, that figure has to be changed, because in many cases the precedent crime to drugs is illegal immigration.

Just as illegal immigration is the gateway to the drug business, so drugs are tied into other crime, directly or indirectly. That 70 percent figure already mentioned? Guns, prostitution, burglary, robbery, assault, murder—put any of those offenses, or choose one of your own, next to the word *drugs*, and it'll be an appropriate fit, a clear match.

Now, with the intensifying role of illegal immigration as the source of criminality, the same reality applies to that illicit act. Illegal immigration is a perfect complement to most other crimes.

For now, let's return to the role of illegal immigration in the origin of drug crime. Tighten up the borders, and you stop the traffickers and mules from bringing the drugs into the country. Tighten up the borders, and you leave the meth labs without a market, so the labs wither and die. Tighten up the borders, and you starve the cartels. Tighten up the borders, and you stop the murders and kidnappings and other crimes committed by drug cartels in furtherance of their interests.

The problem isn't only about law enforcement. If we want to eliminate or at least control drugs, we must not only arrest the trafficker and the pusher, but help the addict and user as well. Many venues for reaching them are available—hospitals, treatment centers, and support groups. My venue is the jail, and I take full advantage of my time with those trapped by drugs and caught by the law. I instituted the first random drug-testing program in any jail system in the country. I also run an extensive drug treatment program, which I will describe in some detail in Chapter Five.

Stopping a crime isn't always about only stopping the crime. It can also be about fixing the problem, about showing compassion, about changing people's lives for the better, about providing hope and opportunity. It can be a beautiful thing.

As long as you don't forget to first stop the crime.

FIVE

THINKING OUTSIDE THE BOX

BY THIS point in these pages, I've mentioned more than once, sometimes in passing, our more famed innovations in the law enforcement business, because they are so integral to everything we do. Famed though they may be, I should take a few moments to review them for those of you not so familiar with some of these programs.

Necessity is the mother of invention, and few endeavors demand flexibility and resourcefulness more than dealing with crime. Crime is a moving target. New forms and mechanisms arise—witness the explosion in Internet-related crime—and criminals hurry to exploit whatever they can, like water rushing to fill any gap, seeking out the smallest crack. We will never completely, forever end crime unless human nature changes, and that's a concept beyond my job description to promote or initiate. Instead, crime is something we contain, a fact we prevent, stop, and punish.

Crime is not something that exists only within the bounds of law enforcement. In other words, crime is not only a matter of criminology, but also of economics, sociology, psychology, politics, history, on and on—factors far outside the ability of any cop to influence, let alone control. Still, we soldier on, working our side of the street. In doing so, the more aggressive and inventive among us figure out how to surmount obstacles and accomplish our goals.

So let's get to some of the ways I've surmounted obstacles and accomplished my goals. I'll begin with perhaps the most significant innovation, in terms of not just efficiently utilizing resources, but also sending a message first to the community regarding respecting taxpayer funds and then to criminals regarding our department's, and our county's, approach to punishment.

✳ ✳ ✳

THE TENT City Jail emerged from the dismal reality I encountered upon taking office. I discovered that the Maricopa County jail system, intended to incarcerate about 3,000 inmates, had swollen to more than 5,000 prisoners. The result was predictable: Rats and people react alike to dangerous overcrowding—that is, with stress, anger, and ultimately, violence. Prisoners fought prisoners, and prisoners fought guards.

The problem wasn't Maricopa County's alone. The year 1992, as statistically compiled by the Bureau of Justice Statistics (BJS), appropriately located within the U.S. Department of Justice, demonstrated that the state and federal prison populations totaled 850,566 inmates, while local jails held another 444,584 men and women. (Note: Men overwhelmingly outnumbered women—of those 800,000-plus state and federal inmates, 789,700 were male.)

And matters have not gotten better with time. The gross numbers have risen: As of December, 31, 2005, 1,446,269 prisoners were being held in state or federal prison, and 747,529 were in jails, for a total of 2,193,798 inmates. Including those on probation or parole, the total adult correctional population in the United States totaled more than 7 million individuals for the first time in our history. Three percent of the U.S. adult population, or one in every thirty-one adults, or 491 men and women for every 100,000 U.S. residents, were incarcerated. Figure the number any way you'd like, it is enormous and stunning.

The numbers keep rising. Six months later, the latest figures from BJS revealed that 2,245,189 Americans were being held in local jails and state and federal prisons, an increase of 2.8 percent from 2005, slightly less than the average annual growth of 3.4 percent since 1995.

And now there were 497 prison inmates per 100,000 U.S. residents.

All these statistics must be understood within the context of broader crime trends.

On the positive front, serious violent crime—homicide, rape, robbery, assault, and the involvement of juveniles in such crime— has declined since 1993. Property crimes, including burglary, theft, and motor vehicle theft, have been in decline since 1973. One example: The number of victimizations per 1,000 households regarding total property crime fell from 519.9 in 1973 to 154 in 2005.

Nonfatal firearm-related crime has plummeted since 1994, though it began to rise again in 2005.

Back to the negative side: Drug arrests for adults (those eighteen years of age and older) have been on the rise since 1970, though the same rates for juveniles have stabilized. Of all the cases handled through the federal courts since 1989, drug cases have increased at the fastest pace.

And for more bad news: According to the FBI's Uniform Crime Report, some of those happier trends started to reverse in 2005.

Violent crime climbed for two straight years, marking the first continual escalation in homicides, robberies, and other serious offenses since the early 1990s. The report, released in June 2007, showed a 1.3 percent increase in violent crime in 2006, including a 6 percent rise in robberies and a slight upsurge in homicides. This followed a 2.3 percent increase in violent crime in 2005, the first significant growth in fifteen years.

While this increase was found across the board and around the country, much of it was concentrated in medium-size cities, including Washington, D.C., Cleveland, Indianapolis, and Milwaukee, and a handful of the largest cities, including Houston and Phoenix. Different theories account for this intensification, from the growth in the juvenile population, to escalating numbers of inmates getting released from prison and jail, to the spread of violent gangs to more cities, to the decreased federal government spending on law enforcement—in part because of budget cuts, in part because money has been diverted to antiterrorism efforts.

Phoenix and its neighboring cities have a couple of unique problems: One, Maricopa County has experienced phenomenal population growth, and second, we're within figurative spitting distance of the border (Phoenix is a mere 187 miles to Nogales, Mexico), rendering our megalopolis a prime transshipment point for drugs and illegals. In addition, the issue of the rising juvenile population is particularly difficult and accounted for most of the ferocious skyrocketing in homicides from 1970s to the mid-1990s. Homicides peaked at 10.2 per 100,000 people in 1980 (not incidentally coinciding with the crack cocaine explosion), quite a contrast from the 4.0 rate in 1957 or the 5.5 rate in 2004.

There's a saying that goes, *There are no old heroin dealers.* The underlying theme is that you either get killed by a rival drug dealer, or you kill yourself by ingesting your product, or you reach an age when you realize you're not immortal and get out before you get killed. The point is that young people, juveniles, are more prone than their elders—even those barely their elders—to think they are invulnerable. Given their egocentric point of view, they are also more prepared to think that other people don't count, that an insult is adequate cause to commit murder, that a business dispute is reason to commit murder, that a cloudy day is justification to commit murder. When the juvenile population bubbles, problems ensue, problems that will dissipate when the bubble dissipates.

So the situation is both mixed and, despite the advances in many areas, not good enough. Too many Americans and U.S. residents are locked up, constituting the highest inmate-to-population percentage in the Western world.

But I've veered somewhat off the point, and so back to the dangerous congestion I found in the Maricopa County jails upon taking over the Sheriff's Office in 1993. Something had to be done, and the options did not include releasing inmates to free up space or turning away law enforcement officers who brought in prisoners. While other jurisdictions have done exactly that, they do not earn even my slightest consideration. You do not solve a problem by pretending it doesn't exist, by sweeping it under the rug or out the door.

The obvious solution was to build another jail, or maybe two or three. The obvious solution wasn't going to work. The Board of Supervisors, which controls the budget for the county, including my organization, not only wasn't going to hand over the required monies, it was busy slashing my funding. And those cuts weren't chicken feed, but $10 million out of $92 million. For those counting at home, that's more than 10 percent of my budget—a potentially devastating amount.

I won't go into the petty politics that prompted the board to damage county law enforcement, and thus the public safety, but suffice to say I fought the Man (yes, in this instance, I was not the Man), and eventually, after a year, the politicos began restoring the funding.

But I couldn't wait for the money, and besides, I didn't want to use the money, that hard-earned taxpayer money, to build more jails. I had already had the idea of using tents when I was running for office, and my idea had nothing to do with budgets or over-crowding. Rather, I wanted to put more people in jail, people who deserved to be in jail, and I didn't intend to spend one dime more of the public treasury than was necessary. (Yes, even though I already enumerated the incredibly huge numbers of Americans in jail, that is a societal issue to cure, not a law enforcement problem to ignore.)

I was ready to get started, and I knew where to go. I was aware that the military was contracting, downsizing, and throwing away a lot of equipment, a lot of it obsolete and a lot not. I was interested in some of the obsolete gear, specifically, the old tents.

The army was prepared to part with these aged tents free of charge. Before we could accept delivery of the equipment, MCSO had to get the Pentagon to grant a special rule change allowing local governments to obtain federal matériel for the price, or lack of a price, we had agreed upon.

The fact was, free made sense, because the tents, most of which were fit for twenty beds, with a few forty-bed behemoths in the bunch, weren't worth much, if anything, on the open market. Many of them had seen duty during the Korean War, which had ended a good forty years before, while a handful had actually served in the First World War, circa 1918, and had continued their service through the Persian Gulf War. Sure, some had holes, others were fraying, but that was to be expected—age did that to canvas.

I was doing the army a favor, and the army was returning the compliment. A deal all around.

So we poured the concrete foundations, we built fences, and we installed electricity and plumbing, evaporative coolers, and heating units. But before we commenced with any of that, the very first thing we did was plant the flagpole, from which flew both the American flag and the Maricopa County Sheriff's Office standard, high above the desert.

The tents opened on August 2, 1993, at high noon. We had a ceremony, and I made a speech, and my message was singularly laconic.

"Did anybody see that movie, *Field of Dreams?*" I asked the assembled. "They said, 'Build it and they will come.' Well, I built it and they will come!"

It was not long before a thousand inmates, all convicted and sentenced, resided in the tents.

Not surprisingly, not everyone was thrilled. New York's *Village Voice* declared the tents "concentration camp-like," which begs the question, What actually is the difference between concentration camp-like and an actual concentration camp? Is that similar to the difference between taking the Pirates of the Caribbean ride at Disneyland or being captured by real pirates, who actually pillage, plunder, defile, and murder you and your loved ones? Something like that? The newspaper's comment would have been funny if it weren't flat-out demented. In addition, note that the once-esteemed newspaper's reference to the Nazis would not be the final reference to the Third Reich employed by more distinguished members of the media.

Hey, nobody ever went broke accusing the media of being gracefully (never mind ethically) restrained.

My short answer to the critics—scattered, offensive, and ineffective though they may be—has always been the same: *You should never live better in jail than you do on the outside.*

To my mind, you don't need to say anything more. You shouldn't have to, because that single sentence encompasses the obvious essence of the matter. Jail is intended to be punishment, and making jail as unpleasant an experience as possible, without stepping over any moral or legal lines, can only serve as a deterrent to anyone considering a career in crime.

And, of course, these are tents we acquired from the military, tents used by our servicemen and women, tents exactly like those being used today in Iraq. So the bottom line is pretty straightforward: If tents are good enough for our troops faithfully serving our country, in a place that is more miserable, infinitely more danger-ous, and yes, even hotter than Maricopa County (despite temperatures that can approach 140 degrees inside the tents), then why aren't the tents more than adequate for inmates?

And let's not forget the long-suffering taxpayers. A new hard facility to house 1,000 prisoners can cost $100 million, $200 million, or more. Sure, you're not going to place serial killers and drug lords and Mafia bosses in tents; you need maximum security prisons with thick walls and every kind of surveillance and everything else you can think up to protect society from these monsters. But most criminals do not fit those desperate categories. They're not criminal masterminds or mass murderers. Tents and fences and barbed wire and guards are sufficient to keep them where the justice system has decided they should be. Why should money that could be better spent on schools or hospitals or road improvements, or whatever the people and the government deem important, be spent on prisoners when other, unbelievably less expensive avenues exist?

Currently, some 10,000 inmates occupy beds and cells and tents within the Maricopa County jail system. It's the second largest county population in the country, ranked only behind Los Angeles, and 2,000 of those inmates, male and female, are in the tents. The monetary savings have been enormous, the problems minimal.

Tent City Jail has been an unalloyed success. By the time you read this, we will have added more tents, capable of housing another 500 inmates, before we put up more tents to hold another 500.

I have no illusions that one day another sheriff will dismantle or neglect some of my programs, and they will fade into oblivion. He (or she) will do so because it will be politically expedient, or because his personal insecurities will demand that he differentiate himself from me, or because of some other pressure or enticement. Whatever. That is the way the world works. However, the one program I will wager that no sheriff will dare end, will dare tear down, not as long as he must face the electorate every four years, is Tent

City Jail. Can you imagine having to explain why the taxpayers are going to have to ante up hundreds of millions of dollars, or more, to replace a program that has existed without any compelling problems like riots or widespread violence, despite the disapproval of the ACLU, the *New York Times*, or similar "experts" in crime and punishment? I promise you, it's not going to happen anytime soon.

On the other hand, you don't see tents going up in Miami or Atlanta or Houston. You've probably heard all about jail overcrowding in Los Angeles, courtesy of the Paris Hilton debacle (a subject we'll get into in more detail in Chapter 10, where we focus our attention on the media, good and bad). In California, Governor Schwarzenegger and state legislators agreed to spend $7.8 *billion* to build 53,000 more prison and jail cells. As if that wasn't enough, California was also looking to transfer 8,000 inmates to prisons in other states.

So do the math: Assume my tents cost the county, with structural and other issues to be addressed, $100,000 per unit to erect for every 1,000 inmates. Multiply that cost by fifty-three, and you arrive at a price of $5.3 million. That figure would surely be reduced by the gross scale of the project, but whether I'm spending $4 million or $5.3 million, stack that up against $7.8 billion. You want to spend those extra billions on building jails and prisons, or on helping children and seniors and the sick and working men and women? As a taxpayer, which means of incarceration makes more sense to you?

(By the way, to further compound the nonsense, a wrench was thrown into California's plan by two federal judges, who ruled that the state was incapable of hiring enough guards and medical professionals to provide appropriate care and oversight to the prisoners on hand, let alone the thousands more who might be added to the rolls as a result of the building program. To quote U.S. District Court Judge Lawrence Karlton of Sacramento, "From all that presently appears, new beds will not alleviate this problem but will aggravate it." As far as I could gather, the argument was that, one, it's better not to build more prisons, because you might end up with more prisoners, and two, don't build more prisons, because the prisoners might not be treated with appropriate loving care—okay just appropriately. The judge seemed to be saying that instead of aggressively moving to cure this unacceptable situation, you might have to just let the bad guys go in the name of justice, which might be construed as caring more for the criminals than for the public. California's appealing the decision and pressing ahead with its building program in the meantime.)

Still, while a couple of small jurisdictions have put up their own tents, no major city or county has followed suit. I don't know why. I can't even begin to guess. It just doesn't make any sense. Nonetheless, I will reluctantly offer my opinion that it will be difficult to find a mayor or governor or police chief or sheriff who wants to be seen embracing and copying a program he can't claim as his own creation. Once again, it's human nature at work, a matter of jealousy and resentment. Many would presume that such small emotions have nothing to do with these politically, socially, and financially consequential decisions, but after many years of dealing with politicians and other government types overrun by ego, I can assure you that petty and selfish imperatives know no bounds.

It's not like the tents have been a secret. Through all the years, literally thousands of cops, politicians, and other assorted officials have toured the tents. They have complimented the facility, admired the way we run it, praised the programs we have for the inmates—they have loved it all. And then they have gone home and gone back to business as usual. If you see the logic there, drop me a note.

✳   ✳   ✳

TENT CITY Jail doesn't end with the tents. I inaugurated a male chain gang, followed by the world's first female chain gang (no one can accuse me of discriminating against women), followed by another first, the juvenile chain gang. The crews, consisting entirely of volunteers, clean the streets, paint over graffiti, and most dramatically, bury the bodies of the indigent in the county cemetery.

That last duty is a sight to behold. The female chain gang, fifteen in all, assembles at six in the morning. Padlocked together at the ankle, they are driven by van to a county cemetery, a modern potter's field, about thirty minutes out of town and into the desert. A priest is waiting. So are the caskets, ordinarily more than one, often half a dozen or more, containing the corpses of those who have died on the street or in emergency rooms or homeless shelters, unknown and unmourned. Smaller coffins hold the bodies of children or babies. Some of the women, particularly those who are mothers themselves, cry as the priest offers a prayer and the unadorned casket is lowered into the ground. The women then fill in the hole, and that corpse, that person, is consigned to oblivion.

It is, to say the least, a sobering experience, and hopefully a worthwhile one, as the women witness how sad life can be and how sadly life can end. If burying a forgotten infant abandoned by its mother, bereft of any love, does not compel a person to take stock of one's own path, one's own life, then I cannot imagine what would.

Again, everyone on the chain gang, male or female, is a volunteer. Some volunteer to give themselves something to do, others maybe feel they could use a dose of constructive discipline. I can't claim to know each person's motivation. I will tell you that for some of them, it is literally the first time in their lives they completed a task they had started and fulfilled a commitment they had made. They receive diplomas for their efforts, and you might be surprised at the pride they take in their accomplishments. It is the pride of someone who has never been pushed in any constructive manner or positive direction, someone who has never been expected to do anything with his or her life, someone who has never received encouragement or praise, not from a parent or friend or teacher.

These are not people who need television or movies or coffee or cigarettes or pornographic magazines or weight-lifting equipment, despite the livid cries from the usual suspects that prisoners are being abused by eliminating these distractions. No, these are people who need to focus on what's important, on lessons and actions that will teach them about themselves. We teach them by testing them, by forcing them to demand a little more and a little better from themselves. Political agendas and fund-raising opportunities aside (which is surely the primary concern of most of the people who most vociferously oppose my jail reforms), my aim is getting the inmates to understand that they will only have a decent future if they demand better from themselves and demand everything they are capable of giving and achieving.

The chain gangs, like the tents, have had a lot of people upset from day one. And that has attracted a lot of attention, not only from the Department of Justice, which routinely investigates jails and prisons across the land and has certainly spent its fair share of time with us, but from just who you would expect—namely, the American Civil Liberties Union (ACLU), Amnesty International, and the like. And while they sometimes gnash their teeth, ready and eager to complain, they always go home empty-handed (apart from the money they eagerly and expertly raise from fellow travelers)—and I'm still here. Do you think for one second that any of these investigative groups, from the feds to the media to the politically committed, would let me get away with abusing the prisoners? Do you realize how thrilled they would be to hang my scalp on their walls, how much they would love to catch me in wrongdoing, *any* wrongdoing, and end my career?

It hasn't happened because we do things tough, but we do them right. When we banned smoking, coffee, movies, porn magazines, and most television, we were tough but we were right. When we stopped serving salt and pepper with our meals and saved the taxpayers a cool $20,000 a year, we were tough, but we were right.

When we had the chain gang work in the streets and contributed thousands of dollars of free labor to the community, we were tough but we were right. When we dyed the underwear pink to make them easier to spot and stop the inmates from stealing the white boxers, which they were doing to the remarkable tune of $40,000 a year, we were tough but we were right. (No denying, there was the matter of embarrassing the prisoners, but stealing underwear? Really? I mean, how low can you go?) When we did the same with the handcuffs, which were also disappearing, we were tough but we were right. When we turned everything pink in the jail—sheets, towels, socks— but went back to the old-style black-and-white striped uniforms, we were tough but we were right. When we spent more on the meals for the dogs we rescued and sheltered than we did on the meals for the prisoners, noting that the animals were victims, not criminals, we were tough but we were right.

We have been tough but we have been right over and over, despite all the obstacles and skeptics and the often vicious political dirty fighting, and we keep going, keep working, keep moving forward.

(Note: I would have cut off all television, but we discovered, to our general amazement, that there is a federal law on the books that *requires* cable TV in jails. So I put back the Disney Channel and the Weather Channel. I was ready when a reporter asked me why the Weather Channel: "So they will know how hot it's gonna be while they are working on my chain gangs.")

It's almost embarrassing to admit, but when I first ran for office, I stated that the sheriff should be an appointed, not elected, position. It didn't take a month in office before I realized that that might have been the stupidest thing I've ever said (at least in public), because it wouldn't have taken a month for my boss, be that a mayor or board of supervisors or governor, to fire me and get rid of a headache before it started to pound away at his undoubtedly grander plans and ambitions. But, thankfully, I'm not appointed, I'm elected, and I answer directly not to one boss but to 4 million bosses—namely, the 4 million citizens of Maricopa County. And where the one boss, the political boss, will surely have a laundry list a mile long of reasons, both overt and secret, for evaluating anything I propose or do, my 4 million bosses generally rely on one criterion: common sense. Does it better serve the community? Does it protect the community? Is it socially responsible and financially responsible? Is it, when all is said and done, in the best interests of the people?

✸　✸　✸

THE JAILS, tents, and hard facilities aren't only about punishment and physically tough lessons. While I've already described my English classes for illegals, we have other, more extensive educational programs.

I want to start this section by mentioning another type of hard facility, one of which I am very proud. It's a thirty-year-old jail at First Avenue and Madison Street in downtown Phoenix. It was closed for repairs back in 1999, then I put in air-conditioning and had the cells fixed up. Did we do all this for male inmates? Female inmates? No and no. We did this to care for our animals. I call it MASH, short for the MCSO Animal Safe Hospice, and it's a no-kill shelter intended to care for animals that have been neglected or abused by their owners and thankfully rescued by the Animal Cruelty Investigative Unit. These animals are in legal limbo until their owners' cruelty cases are decided in court; after that, hopefully, they will be adopted into decent, loving homes. MASH also houses, for up to sixty days, the pets of individuals who have been forced to take refuge in domestic violence shelters that do not accept pets.

While the MASH program is designed to care for the animals, it has a powerful effect on some of the inmates as well. You see, as part of the MASH unit, inmates are allowed the opportunity to care for the abused animals, to groom, feed, exercise, train, and nurse them. The point of this considerable effort is to create a bond between the inmates and the pets, to have the inmates not only take responsibility for the well-being of another living creature, but also feel compassion for something (if not exactly someone) other than themselves.

It works, more often than not. Once you unlock the human heart, once you provide another perspective on life, once you prove there can be another way, people can begin to change, slowly, hesitantly, perhaps even reluctantly, but change nonetheless.

* * *

THE MASH unit is part of my Adult Inmate Programs section that works in so many ways, often in conjunction with community groups or other criminal justice agencies, to give the prisoners a new lease on life. Just because you're in jail doesn't mean your sentence has to be wasted time. The choice is up to the inmates. No one is forced to gain a high school diploma or to improve himself in any manner. Those who choose to give themselves a shot at a real future have a range of classes and programs at their disposal.

For many, not surprisingly, a lack of education is the beginning of the end. The Bureau of Justice Statistics has calculated that over 40 percent of all jail inmates in the United States have less than a ninth-grade education. It will shock no one that studies have demonstrated recidivism (the number of individuals who are rearrested and returned to jail) dramatically drops when inmates are involved in a corrections educational program. In fact, some studies have shown that recidivism rates dive from almost 60 percent to 25 percent for those who've earned a high school diploma or GED. In addition, these sorts of programs decrease incidents of violence in detention facilities.

Some of the programs are probably the kind you'd expect to see in jail: Alcoholics, Cocaine, and Narcotics Anonymous (AA, CA, and

NA) are active, with over 600 inmates attending these programs each week. Mothers Against Drunk Driving (MADD) conducts weekly meetings designed to foster education and awareness on this pressing concern, including a firm grasp on the impact on victims.

We have an anger management course, tailored to domestic violence offenders and other inmates involved in violent crime and substance abuse. About forty-five inmates attend each week. We have a program that helps prostitutes recognize and change their self-destructive behavior, averaging eighteen in attendance each week. We provide literacy tutoring for those who wish to raise their reading skills in anticipation of the GED class, along with a learning lab that uses computers to help inmates who have not been successful in traditional classroom settings in their GED preparation. We offer a program that provides health education and HIV awareness for about 125 inmates each month.

We are the only jail in the country where female inmates get the chance to participate in their daughters' Girl Scout troops. Girl Scouts Beyond Bars is sponsored by the Arizona Cactus-Pine Scout Council in order to cultivate and strengthen the bond between mother and daughter and break the generational cycle of crime. At the Estrella Jail, four inmate mothers and eight daughters attend each week.

Yet another program instructs inmates on all aspects of getting a job, from research to application to interview. The seventy-five or so who attend each week are also taught how to keep a job when they get one.

Another program discusses the consequences of being a victim of child sexual abuse, in the hope that the fifteen inmates who show up each week will be able to halt this pattern of criminality and abuse.

STRIPES—Sheriff Turning Regular Inmate Prisoners into Election Savings—was the first program of its kind that employed volunteer inmates to prepare blank ballots and instructional voting sheets for those requesting mail-in ballots. The first time STRIPES was put into practice, during the 1998 general election, the public saved over $70,000. Since then, the computerization of the voting process has put STRIPES out of business.

The GED program demands that inmates gain proficiency in five subjects: reading, writing, mathematics, social studies, and science. Classes are held four or five times a week, with some 160 prisoners in attendance.

But that's not the only high school program. Hard Knocks High School presents a modified curriculum to juveniles charged with serious offenses in the adult criminal justice system. Approximately 200 inmates participate every week in the only accredited high school in the United States under the control of a sheriff in his jail.

The Alpha Program is my outpatient drug and alcohol abuse treatment program licensed by the Arizona Department of Health. It is only open to sentenced inmates who go through a rigorous screening process, including individual interviews to determine their motivation and background checks to ensure they do not constitute risks to the general jail population.

Since Alpha began in February 1996, over 4,000 inmates have successfully graduated. You'll recall that the overall recidivism rate is 60 percent, and graduating with a GED or high school diploma can reduce it to 25 percent. As terrific as that is, the recidivism rate for Alpha Program graduates is an outstanding 14 percent. Think of the millions of dollars saved that would otherwise have to be spent on police work, prosecution, and incarceration. Think of the lives saved, both of the former predators and their potential victims.

Treat them now, or jail them again.

Let's put in hard numbers. Alpha participants, averaging 130 per program, meet four or five times a week. That 14 percent recidivism rate translates to more than ninety inmates not returning to jail. That counts for something. That counts for a lot.

Same as with the other programs in our system, Alpha is not easy. Just to stay in the program, inmates involved must maintain perfect disciplinary records. They must enroll in related jail programs, including anger management, job preparedness, computer learning lab, and the GED course, and they must complete them, beginning to end.

Those in charge do not kid around. Individuals are tossed from the program when their actions warrant it and to protect those who are truly trying to heal and build a meaningful future. That's not an idle threat: On three occasions in the past few years, the supervisors determined that the entire class had to be disbanded and everyone in that group returned to the general prison population. One such situation involved a gangbanger who joined the class the night before it was to begin. Everyone from the seventy-five-person class resides together in a dorm setting in order to build cooperation and a sense of belonging. However, this individual's presence irritated others in the group, members of a different gang, who proceeded to beat the new guy quite severely for some time. About ten people participated in the actual beating, while others stood on the lookout for guards. That left a lot of people who did nothing. And even though they were not directly culpable, one of the key tenets of the Alpha Program is to accept responsibility not only for your actions but for the actions of those around you. This was a case where no one acted properly, no one did the right thing. The ugly incident showed that these individuals were not ready to take up the challenge of Alpha, and it had set the group down the wrong road even before the program had formally begun. The class was completely scratched.

Alpha runs six months long, and it is intense, incorporating psychological and practical, as well as educational, challenges. Group therapy, work programs, random drug testing—the point is to address a wide range of behavior and responses, impressions, and ideas. That includes cognitive restructuring, where the goal is to give the inmates the tools to redesign and implement new thinking patterns that are necessary to truly commit to change.

We all know how much damage, how much ruination drug and alcohol abuse cause both those addicted and our entire society. Alpha makes a difference.

✳ ✳ ✳

THE LOWER Buckeye Jail is an enormous structure only a couple of blocks from the Tent City Jail. However, while the tent facility and its inmates are open to the elements, LBJ is a more traditional jail building, erected in 2004, solid and somber. The visitor enters through heavy steel-and-glass doors and approaches one of three windows, the glass thick and darkened, so it's hard to see the detention officer sitting inside. You talk into a microphone to relay your request, which is usually to see one of the prisoners, who might be a relative or friend or, if you're a lawyer, a client. Each inmate is allowed three visits per week, each visit lasting half an hour.

Assuming no problems, you pass through the metal detector and head inside. Everywhere you walk inside the jail, you hear the clanging of huge metal doors sliding open and then firmly shutting.

Fifteen young men—boys, really—file into the room. They sit in plastic chairs with attached desktops, in a circle around the rectangular room. They range in age from eighteen to twenty-two. They are mainly white, and all have close-cropped hair, as jail regulations stipulate. They have all used a variety of drugs, sometimes starting with marijuana, sometimes jumping right into cocaine or crack or crystal meth or heroin. Even so, they are not all in jail because of a drug conviction. Their youth and their drug use have given several of them bad skin and scars. A couple of the young men have elaborate, multicolored tattoos running up and down their arms, while another has a teardrop tattooed beneath his eye. The teardrop was once a statement that the person had killed someone, but that meaning has been diluted in recent years and it has become something of a fashion accessory, especially for gang members.

Most of the young men were introduced to drugs by their parents. This introduction came about in a few forms: They either watched their parents (or whoever functioned as their primary caregiver) ingest drugs or sell them. Some were even given drugs to use by their mothers or fathers, or both. Some were brought into the drug business, learning from the ground up, working as couriers or in some other low-level jobs. Many of them started smoking pot by the age of thirteen.

While it is a sad reality in virtually every jail that drug users manage to get their hands on drugs, even behind bars, these boys are now clean. But getting off drugs in an isolated setting like jail is not the same as staying clean once released—especially when they are released back into the same home, the same neighborhood, and the same socioeconomic circumstances. The best shot these inmates have is to change their internal lives in every manner—from how they think, to how they act, to what they hope for the future and whom they associate with—because the correctional system is not equipped to transport them to another place, city, or state.

Drugs aren't the sole issue for these boys. Thirteen out of fifteen of the boys are fathers, some with two or more children. None are married to the mothers of their kids. Some have virtually no relationship to the mothers. All claim to love their children. One hasn't seen his baby yet; she was conceived just before he was arrested and sent away. He doesn't have a picture of her, by his own choice, saying it would make him too sad to look at the child he couldn't stay with and couldn't take care of.

And so on to today's lesson.

The young men are at the end of their Alpha Program. This is the last week, and many of them are getting out of jail within the month. Their assignment is to make a "vision board," to take the magazines and catalogs the counselor has brought and cut out pictures that represent, in the counselor's words, "what we really want out of life."

And so the young men distribute the scissors (plastic children's scissors, to avoid accidents, intentional or not) and start leafing through the magazines and catalogs. They carefully remove the photos that symbolize a bright future, in which they have what they believe they want or need. They scan and scrutinize and clip with enthusiasm, pointing out to the others their favorite pictures, kidding one another with good humor. They enjoy the work and seem open and happy, and very young and innocent, much too young and innocent to have done the things that have gotten them here.

One inmate nudges the young man next to him. "How do you say that?" he asks, pointing to a word in capital letters in a periodical.

"Credibility," the neighbor replies.

"Credibility," the first man repeats. "I like that." He cuts the word out and pastes it on his page.

Another fellow chooses several photos of smiling families, a pretty mother and handsome father posing with their two adorable progeny, everyone clean-cut and overflowing with gleaming white teeth. The pictures have made him smile as well.

"I'm having a good day," he tells the counselor.

"Are you going to speak to your mother?" she inquires.

"I'm going to call her Thursday at six," he responds.

"Will she answer the phone this time?"

The query neither surprises nor upsets the fellow. "Hope so."

"How long as it been since you two spoke?"

"I haven't talked to her in two weeks."

"Will you go live with her when you get out?"

"Hell no," he laughs. "I'm going to live with a friend."

"A clean friend?"

"Yeah," he says. "He lives with his girlfriend and baby, and I can stay there."

"Okay," she says. "Good."

After some forty-five minutes, they put down the magazines and catalogs and plastic scissors and, at the counselor's direction, hold up their creations. One by one, each boy explains what his vision board represents.

A few themes appear over and over, practically without fail. Cars are a constant, from hyperexpensive sports cars to shiny, gilded sedans to huge trucks covered with chrome. Big wheels and silver rims are almost as enticing as the cars. One fellow has seven cars in a row down his page, all vintage convertibles, each a different color, allowing him to coordinate his orange clothes with his orange vehicle, blue outfit with blue car, so on.

Every boy has a picture of a house. A few are modest structures, but they are a distinct minority in a sea of mansions and beachfront villas.

And the girls. The girls are certainly out in force. Very pretty girls in bathing suits and high-fashion frocks.

Several of the boys have cropped photos of rap stars, including Tupac and Biggie Smalls, because rap star is the preferred future occupation of most of the inmates. The counselor points out that both those artists died violent deaths, both killed by gunfire, both victims of rap's excesses. This fact does not faze the young men in the slightest.

One young man has spread a picture of a blue sky across the top of his paper. He says it represents freedom. The counselor asks what freedom means to him.

"It means being free and going where you want and getting whatever you want to eat out of your own refrigerator," he says. The others mumble agreement and have a brief discussion on how the peanut butter served in jail is so unappealing, before returning to the topic of freedom.

"Freedom means different things," one boy says. "It means traveling. I plan on traveling around the world."

"Freedom is having choices to do what you want," someone else offers. "I want to grow old." He holds up his vision board to show he has stuck a photo of an old man on it. "That means I've lived a long time, had a good life, had kids, a house."

"I just want my kid," says another. "And I want to have more kids, lots of them. I want to take them to the snow, and the ocean."

"You've never seen either, have you?" the counselor says.

"No," he replies. "I want to."

God, the U.S. Army, diamond-encrusted watches—they all have their place in the vision boards.

They can't wait to get out. They can't wait to start fresh, to start their real lives, not the mistake they've been living. They will get jobs, maybe even become rap stars. They will have terrific homes, wonderful homes, and they will take care of their many beautiful, smart children.

And everyone will be so very happy.

They are twenty years old, going on fourteen. The challenge for Alpha is to ensure that when they are forty years old, they won't be acting like they are twenty.

You look at these young men, these boys, and you'd be excused for thinking that, despite their best intentions, they're doomed. But they're not. The program works. Most of these young men will not return to jail. They might not become rap stars, but they will get on with their lives. They will find jobs. They will have homes. They already have children, and hopefully they will build real families, which will most likely ensure that those children will not follow their fathers into the prison system.

And that means Alpha is a success not once, but twice or more.

We can't save everyone. Truth is, not everyone wants to be saved. So we save who we can and deal with the rest, as harshly as is required. End up in our jails, and you can find yourself on one path or the other. As you choose.

THE POSSE

EVERYBODY'S heard of the posse. And I mean everybody, not just in Arizona, not just in the United States, but around the world, just as everybody has heard of the sheriff and cowboys and Indians and the rest of our Western lore. And that's as it should be, because every nation needs unifying myths to rally around, and our myths are those of rugged individualism, of one man standing up, alone if necessary, for what is right. It is a noble myth, and like all enduring myths, it is based both on history as well as our sometimes-gauzy interpretation of that history.

So it is with the posse, an institution rich in both fact and fable. In the movies (usually an old black-and-white one), who hasn't seen the sheriff round up the posse, get on their horses, track through the desert and over the mountains, and corral the outlaws? As entertaining as that might be, it's also fundamentally true, and that's why the posse has not only survived from the 1800s to this very day with reputation intact, but has continued to attract volunteers, willing to do what it takes to join up, ready to serve.

The posse embodies something fundamental and essential in the American experience. It is the realization of the community working in accord, of men and women banding together to protect their streets, their neighborhoods, their towns, their counties, their country. Volunteerism is a vital part of America's heritage, and we volunteer to help one another, to build and sometimes rebuild America, through so many organizations, large and small. No fewer than 45 million Americans participate in volunteer activities, a figure that only counts those working with identified organizations. Countless millions more are involved with ad hoc or individual efforts that garner neither press nor outside attention. Think about a few people raising a few dollars to assist a neighbor in distress. A woman preparing meals for the housebound. A man offering to fix the roof after a storm for a single mom who can't afford to pay to have it done. High school kids having a car wash on behalf of someone in need of medical care, a person they don't even know but saw on television. Forty-five million Americans plus—that's a remarkable testament to the American spirit.

After so many years in law enforcement, at home and abroad, it has long been evident to me that the police are ordinarily underfunded and underrepresented on the streets, and that is the way it will always be. Not that the prudent patriot would think of that as a bad thing. I was stationed overseas long enough to know that Americans don't want to live in a country where there's a cop on every corner, watching every citizen, intruding on our every word and deed.

Still, when I became sheriff, I recognized that my office, responsible for covering so much territory and occupied with so many duties, could benefit from coordinating with whomever could help.

And since I already knew I couldn't expect too much support, political or financial, from our government overlords, the most obvious alternative was the public. And the answer on how to utilize the public was the natural result of what I learned while serving overseas, combined with what was already a proud tradition. And that answer turned out to be a better choice than any inducement, political or financial, the government could have offered.

It all started with the fact that I possessed no police powers while serving in my first foreign posting, working for the Bureau of Narcotics in Turkey, a subject we will discuss in more detail in Chapter Eight. I might have been representing the American government, but that didn't cut much ice with the local authorities, and it certainly didn't garner me any legal status under Turkish laws. In other words, I didn't have the right to arrest anyone, but had to rely upon Turkish cops and officials to help me accomplish what I needed to accomplish. I had to work hand in hand with anyone who would help, from the cops all the way up to the president, along with the army and judges and everyone else in a position to make things happen. I was a sort of "proto-posseman," bringing my ability and experience to the table, but having no authority to use them unless I was accompanying a member in good standing of Turkish officialdom. Working with a cop or investigator or soldier, I was de facto deputized and able to do my job.

In Arizona, as the newly elected sheriff, I faced a formidable number of challenges and goals, and I quickly determined that the resources available to me, in personnel and matériel, were inadequate to handle all of these issues and needs. I had to call upon outside assets and assistance, and I turned to a tried-and-true answer: the posse.

✳   ✳   ✳

WHILE POSSES were organized on a temporary basis for generations, as specific needs arose, Maricopa County formalized a permanent structure in 1941. Though the posse existed for a long time before I arrived on the scene, it remained a small unit, limited both in size and scope. I determined to change it in dramatic fashion.

I went on a recruiting binge, calling upon the citizens to take up the most basic and critical of volunteerism and the first responsibility of government: protecting the people and property of our community.

I enlarged the training of new posse members and the areas in which they could operate. I made the posse a centerpiece of the Maricopa County Sheriff's Office and integrated its members, whenever possible, in almost all areas of our work.

A posse member can choose from a wide range of options—and it is each posse member's choice to do as much or as little as suits that member's interests, abilities, and time. An individual can be detailed to an office and work the phones and help with the filing, or go all the way, including putting on a uniform, strapping on a gun, and riding beside a deputy in a patrol car. It all depends on the level of training the individual undertakes and successfully completes.

A posse member can aim to work with our most sensitive, classified bureau, the Special Investigations Unit, and deal with such matters as homicide, organized crime, terrorism, and intelligence, assuming the member passes a stringent security check and has skills useful to the unit. Often, though not always, posse members who decide to sign up for such duty are retired law enforcement officers, from the FBI or DEA or a police department, or they are ex-military and eager to keep their hands in the game.

At the same time, the posse member who ferries a patrol car to maintenance, or works an extradition detail, or does traffic control at an event or emergency, or drives the van to transport prisoners to intake is just as valuable as any other posse member, because that person is freeing up deputies from those jobs, allowing them to stay in the field.

We have fifty-five separate posse units, with a total membership of over 3,000 women and men. Posses are bound together by different imperatives and capabilities, from location to mission to equipment. For instance, various communities, from Fountain Hills to Rio Verde to Desert Foothills to Sun Lakes to White Tanks to Wickenburg, on and on, have posses dedicated to protecting their areas. Other posses attract members who own certain equipment and actually want to employ that equipment in a constructive manner, such as the Motorcycle Posse, the Divers Posse, the Helicopter Posse, the Air Posse, the Jeep Posse, and the many, many mounted posses, from Buckeye to Chandler to Maricopa to Mesa Southside to Queen Creek, and more. And yet other posses are constructed around skill sets, including Medical Rescue, K-9, Cyber, and Search and Rescue (SAR). SAR is sufficiently in demand in this enormous county that it has localized units, from Scottsdale to Gilbert to New River and beyond.

The underlying point is that as long as a posse member receives the proper training, there's virtually no mission he can't apply for—and as long as he has the gear that fits the mission, assuming he needs gear for that particular job. That's an important point to grasp: The posse costs the county nothing. Nothing. The volunteers pay for everything they wear, every tool they employ. And it's not cheap. Shirt, pants, boots, baseball cap, badge, belt, belt keepers, chemical spray, flashlight, flashlight holder, name tag, whistle, whistle lanyard—it adds up fast. If you complete the whole training course and become QAP, a qualified armed posseman, ready to patrol beside a sworn deputy (and we have almost a thousand QAPs), then you can add in the price of a handgun, duty holster, ammunition pouch, three magazines, cleaning kit—everything except bullets. We provide the bullets.

You go that route and we're talking expenses ranging from $1,500 to $2,000. And that doesn't include body armor (highly recommended if you're going to carry a gun), maybe a leather jacket for winter (it gets colder on a winter desert night than you might imagine), and on and on.

And those horses and helicopters and jeeps and motorcycles and airplanes I mentioned? Those are owned and maintained by the posse members who use them on behalf of the sheriff's office. Think about all the people (okay, mainly men) who purchase vehicles, whether designed for travel through the air, on the ground, or in the water, and who never get to use these expensive toys in anything close to the manner for which they are intended. Four-wheel-drive trucks aren't meant only to lumber down residential streets on the way to the supermarket and the office. Join Search and Rescue and take those monsters off-road and into the desert on real missions.

As well trained and as dedicated as the posse is, no posse member, under any circumstances, can work for the sheriff's office unless that member is under the direction of a sworn deputy sheriff. Long story short, let's say a posse member is motoring along on a Saturday night, going out to dinner and a movie with his wife, and he suddenly decides to pull out his badge, play cop, and chase after a speeding car that cuts in front of him. On rare occasion, that has happened, and the offending member has been immediately removed from the posse rolls and had to deal with whatever criminal and civil penalties might be attached to his action.

A posse member is only a fully deputized posse member, working on behalf of the MCSO, when under the supervision of a full-time MCSO employee. Remember, even in those movies about the Old West, the sheriff didn't send out the posse alone; the sheriff always led the group. We always know what the posse is doing, and we are always in charge.

Not everybody appreciates the posse, and I'll bet you can guess who. Yes, the local ACLU has complained, more than once, that the posse is some kind of vigilante squad—that it is tied to antigovernment militias roaming the countryside, or even the shock troops of a budding police state. It is insulting to everyone involved, from the deputies who work with the posse, to the volunteers who train them, and to the posse members themselves, who give their time and effort. The ACLU has done more than its fair share of valuable work over the years, but it is also saddled with an inborn and overwhelming streak of sheer idiocy, an utter lack of faith in the common sense of the American people, and a bewildering inability (or, more likely, unwillingness) to comprehend the basic decency and virtue of the American nation.

Apart from its regular activities and responsibilities, the posse is involved in too many jobs to enumerate all of them here. The mall program targets the parking lots of our major shopping centers during the Christmas season, when the stores are jammed and people are rushing about, distracted and easy targets for thieves. The program began in November 1993, when a couple of mall carjackings caused a public outcry and the governor reacted by phoning the accountable law enforcement agencies, from the Phoenix Police Department to the Department of Public Safety to MCSO, asking for help. All the agencies already had their hands full, and even a gubernatorial request did not make more cops and more money magically appear. And that applied to the sheriff's office, too.

Regardless, two days after I received that phone call, the sheriff's office had flooded the malls with uniformed personnel. The call had gone out to the posse, and more than 700 women and men responded, patrolling on foot, on horseback, and in cars, from November 20 to December 31, 1993.

The program was an instant success. Compare mall crime statistics for Christmas 1993 to those of Christmas 1992:

* Auto theft down 88 percent

* Burglaries from auto down 87 percent

* Vandalism down 75 percent

* Assaults down 72 percent

Additionally, deputies and posse members assigned to the malls participated in thirty-six arrests, 315 assists to other law enforcement agencies, 434 investigative stops, and 443 motorist assists.

Those 700-plus posse members worked 12,448 hours. Calculating the basic pay rate for deputies, those hours would have cost the county just about a quarter-million dollars.

As you can imagine, we've been doing the mall patrol ever since.

We serve warrants on deadbeat parents during the week of Mother's Day. We regularly sweep the length of Van Buren Street, Phoenix's own red-light district. We've had programs to stake out locations where graffiti has become a blight and arrest those we catch marking up buildings and walls. And now, of course, we're concentrating resources on tracking illegals. The posse is a flexible instrument, able to react and adapt, as per our needs.

✳ ✳ ✳

NO FINER example of capability and flexibility, of outstanding dedication and exemplary volunteerism, can be found than that embodied by the Mountain Rescue Posse. The team was originally formed in 1948, independent of the sheriff's office, by climbers who had returned home to Arizona from World War II. As Maricopa County grew, so the team grew in numbers and expertise, and it was increasingly called upon to respond to emergencies. By the seventies, MCSO asked the team to be the official technical rescue unit for the sheriff's office. This appointment immediately expanded the team's reach and support system, and the Mountain Rescue Posse was officially in business. And business has been good, which means a lot of people end up in bad situations: on the tops of mountains, on the bottoms of caves, and just about everywhere between.

It begins like this: Somebody calls 911 to report a small plane overdue in the wild, a hiker missing in the national forest, or a climber who has a broken leg and is precariously hanging off a cliff at the end of a rope. MCSO Dispatch recognizes such matters as being more in the line of rescue than law enforcement and contacts the MCSO Search and Rescue (SAR) coordinator, who alerts the posse's operation chief on duty. The SAR coordinator relays all the information in his possession, and the operation chief calls out the team. Of the forty-five active members, whoever is available replies so the operation chief can take a head count, and then everyone available responds. The mission is underway.

The mission can revolve around virtually any problem, any condition, anytime. Maricopa County is not only large, it also encompasses all sorts of terrain, from desert to mountains to forests to rivers to snowy peaks. The state of Arizona is substantially larger, with more of the same terrain, plus it has 300,000 caves and mainly abandoned mines. The heart of the team's work deals with technical rope rescue, and with a core membership consisting of climbers and mountaineers, the team is singularly adept at finding and extricating injured hikers, fallen climbers, trapped passengers in vehicles that have dropped over cliffs, and lost cavers. Once team members reach a victim, they can treat the individual on the scene, for counted among members are physicians, paramedics, registered nurses, physician assistants, and EMTs. Finally, each member must be sufficiently physically fit to transport the victim out of the area, even if that means carrying the person on your back.

While high-angle technical rope rescue is a particular specialty of the posse, it is far from its only job. Team members must be skilled at Wilderness Search, which means they must be self-sufficient for thirty-six hours in the field, proficient with map and compass, radio and GPS equipped, and familiar with conditions that can include working at night, in rough terrain, in inclement weather, and in the high heat of the summer desert—all at the same time. They must be adept at Alpine Rescue, even in Maricopa County, where the land can rise to 7,700 feet and be inundated by snowstorms. More than ten members have alpine expedition experience, and all members undergo thirty-two hours training each year in alpine conditions and snow and ice environments, equipped with state-of-the-art gear. They train in Swiftwater Rescue, for the dry desert can take even small rainstorms and gather them into dangerous flash floods, as the water races down steep rises and across hard-packed land. Fifteen members are certified swiftwater technicians, with more than eighty hours training, and all team members must acquire swiftwater first-responder status, capable of working with the posse's fourteen-foot inflatable rescue boat in rivers, canals, and flash floods. They perform Cave and Abandoned Mine Rescue, with each team member training for a minimum of thirty-hours per year, with appropriate underground communications and air-monitoring equipment. They work with Helicopter Operations, training with local and state aircraft, including MCSO's helicopter and the team's own helicopter. In addition, there's a twenty-five-member Helicopter Emergency Response Team (HERT), each member having over a hundred hours of Advanced Heli-Rescue training. The list of capabilities goes on and on, including Wilderness Medical Rescue, Wildland Fire Rescue, and Technical Animal Rescue, with QAP posse members assisting deputies in direct law enforcement actions.

The training, as you might imagine, is intense, and the time commitment even more so. A new member must first join the MCSO posse and complete its basic requirements. There's the MCSO Law and Legal course, the CPR/First Aid class, the Traffic course, and a background check and interview to pass. Those classes are requirements for everybody joining the posse. After that, it's on to Mountain Rescue's first physical test, a must-win trial called the "Mrs. Pat," which stands for Mountain Rescue Specific Physical Aptitude Test. It is a cut-and-dried exercise: While wearing a thirty-five-pound pack and laden with a hundred ounces of water, each applicant must climb and descend a mountain at least 1,000 feet in elevation. Along the way, you have to carry additional gear, tie rescue knots, and correctly identity UTM (Universal

Transverse Mercator) coordinates on a topographical map—all within a time limit.

Do that and you get to keep moving forward in the application and training process. No surprise, it doesn't get easier. The basic training class is eighteen months long, consuming the third Thursday evening and third weekend of each month, and full attendance is required. Not only do the instructors look for skilled and determined applicants, eager to learn, but for men and women who can sublimate their own egos and become part of the posse, wholly and without hesitation, because lives depend on teamwork, and teamwork depends on trust.

Same as with every posse, Mountain Rescue is financially self-sufficient. Though the team receives donations from both corporate and private sources, each new member can expect to spend at least $2,500 on personal equipment. Between training and missions, the applicant should anticipate dedicating at least 500 hours with the posse each year.

Of the forty-nine applicants in the 2006 recruit class, only ten remain in the training program.

Those 500 hours just noted constitute a bare minimum. Even so, that works out to about ten hours each week, and many posse members spend double that or even more on posse work. That kind of time expenditure leaves scant room for hobbies or holidays, and it certainly has an impact on one's profession and on one's family. Obviously, without the strong support of employer, partner, or employees, and even stronger support of spouse, children, or other loved ones, participation simply wouldn't be possible. In fact, a few members have managed to combine their personal and volunteer lives even more than they already were. Prime example: Team Commander David Bremson found love within the ranks and married Susan Klemmer, a rescue technician and EMT.

What this posse of volunteers and teammates has accomplished is just incredible. In 2006, the posse conducted fifteen search missions, fifteen technical rescues, one cave rescue, one technical animal rescue, four aircraft recoveries, two swiftwater rescues, and seventy-three HERT operations. To recap, that's in a single, typical year.

Practically, what would it cost our department in terms of personnel, effort, and money to get up to speed to perform half as well? How many hundreds of thousands of dollars (not including the purchase of another helicopter to replace the one the team has on call, courtesy of Doug Fulton, one of its members) are we talking about? What other services and responsibilities would be shortchanged by having to divert our attention?

A brief, dry recitation of Mountain Rescue accomplishments does not begin to tell the tale. It doesn't give a sense of what it's like to clamber up the side of a mountain and patch up a climber to a degree adequate to get him safely down, or how it feels to descend a few hundred feet down an utterly black shaft to recover what remains of a human body after a climber takes a wrong step and falls into nothingness.

✳   ✳   ✳

HURRICANE Katrina was a uniquely horrific event in American history, the greatest natural disaster our nation has ever experienced. Though the federal government failed in its most essential duty—to protect the public before the hurricane struck—and failed again in its aftermath, many Americans rose up and reached out to help our fellow Americans.

The Maricopa County Sheriff's Office was proud to be among those Americans. Though I was far away, too far away, on a rare trip outside of Maricopa County, spreading the word for a week and giving speeches and interviews throughout England (a program sponsored by the BBC), I immediately contacted the Federal Emergency Management Agency (FEMA), offered our assistance, and then called out the troops. Chief Larry Black quickly put together a force of sixty deputies assembled from the ranks of SWAT, Special Response Team (SRT), lake patrol deputies, and assorted emergency personnel, and forty posse members pulled from Enforcement Support, Communications, Mountain Rescue, and others. We figured we'd have to be self-sufficient for however long we were in Louisiana, so we put together a convoy. We got a gas truck to fuel our vehicles; a refrigerated tractor-trailer filled with ice and food, including 9,000 MREs (meals ready to eat); an armored car, in the event we ran into some real trouble; and vehicles towing boats and ATVs, in case we needed to get on the water or over rough terrain.

Nobody really knew what was happening in New Orleans. The only news getting out was on CNN and on the Internet, and those reports were scattered and incomplete. The local government had apparently effectively vanished under the storm's onslaught, and the federal government seemed to be living in a fantasy world of press releases and wishful thinking. The people needed help of every sort, in every way, and we were ready to provide whatever we could.

Word was New Orleans was sealed off, so Chief Black and Captain Joel Fox headed out first, driving in his four-by-four from Phoenix across New Mexico and Texas and down to Gulfport, Mississippi. Black had heard that the Louisiana State Police had blocked off many of the roads leading into southern Louisiana, even, astonishingly, denying access to police and other rescue personnel. The best route into New Orleans, he realized, maybe the only way, was through Mississippi. It added more than a few miles to their drive, but the men didn't have any options. They left Arizona three in the afternoon, drove all day and then all night, and well into the next day, before reaching Mississippi. And when they reached Gulfport, a beachfront city right on the Gulf of Mexico and the second largest in the state, they found nothing but confusion. Katrina had banged into Gulfport and flooded or destroyed much of the city. What remained was in disarray. The gas stations were either sucked dry or, inexplicably, locked up. The phone lines were down, and cops and emergency services from across the country were bumping into one another, all crowded into the city with no one to direct them where they might be needed.

Black and Fox hadn't traveled this far to be denied. They found a road into Louisiana and drove south, then north, maybe a little east and west, ending up in a parish that was well outside the disaster zone, apparently boxed in and stuck. The police, as unfathomable as it might be, were still turning back assistance. Was this just petty politics, the state's politicians afraid of letting anyone in who might not be directly under their authority? Or was this some reflexive form of xenophobia, a bizarrely misguided belief that outsiders would somehow make this awful situation worse? Whatever it was, it just didn't make sense, and now wasn't the time to stop and reflect.

Meanwhile, Chief Brian Sands had gotten his convoy in order and was driving toward Louisiana.

Black and Fox had been driving around for a few days, and enough was enough. They were locked down in Gonzales, a town south of Baton Rouge and north of New Orleans, along with other emergency types who had managed to get this far. But this looked like the end of the line. There just didn't seem any way to travel farther south and get inside the city. The Louisiana authorities weren't interested in cooperating, and that came straight from the top—not just from the local sheriff, but from the sheriff who was the head of the state's sheriff's association.

But then this übersheriff turned around, took a look, and turned back to Black and Fox.

"You guys got a helicopter?" he asked.

The overlord sheriff was referring to a chopper idling in a field just behind them. He explained that he could benefit from the services of such a craft. He wanted to get in the air so he could check out the scene from above. He was eager to visit some places not so readily available by car.

The man needed a helicopter, and lo and behold, the Maricopa County Sheriff's Office had brought one to Louisiana. More specifically, Doug Fulton, president of Fulton Homes Sales Corporation, and copilot Jeff Nadreau, executive VP of the same company, both members of the Mountain Rescue posse, had flown the company Bell 407 jet helicopter to help in the relief effort.

Doug Fulton loved flying. He did so three days a week, starting at seven in the morning so it didn't interfere with running his home-building company, one of the largest in Arizona. He had joined the posse four years ago and spent considerable time training and working with Mountain Rescue. He had carried climbers to precarious peaks to work their way down, and he had touched down to cart survivors out of danger. He had searched for those lost in the woods or in the mountains, and he found some alive and some dead.

And while Mountain Rescue was the focus of his volunteer work, it wasn't all he did with the sheriff's office. He also served on the Advisory Posse. He helped with the Memorial Fund, which raised money for the families of fallen deputies, and with the school-based STARS (Sheriffs Teaching Abuse Resistance to Students) program. With all that to his credit, it was no surprise he was named MCSO's Volunteer of the Year in 2005.

Giving back to the community was nothing new to the Fultons. His father, Ira Fulton, along with his mother, Mary Lou, were ranked thirty-six on *BusinessWeek*'s 2006 list of "The 50 Most Generous Philanthropists." They've given away some $265 million, approximately 60 percent of their net worth, including, most dramatically, $160 million to Arizona State University, which named two recipients of those gifts—the Ira A. Fulton School of Engineering and Technology, and the Mary Lou Fulton College of Education—in their honor.

Between his love of flying and adventure, and his family's spectacular legacy of giving, it was no surprise that Doug Fulton ended up in a field in Gonzales, Louisiana.

And now this Louisiana sheriff of local sheriffs wanted a ride on his helicopter.

Larry Black had his answer at the ready, and it was a simple trade, *quid pro quo*, as the lawyers like to say: You get the helicopter, and I get my deputies into New Orleans.

The deal was done on the spot.

Brian Sands gave Fulton the news that he was temporarily seconded to southern Louisiana's high command. Fulton had no problem with that; he had come here to help, and any way he could do that was fine by him.

The Louisiana sheriff assigned a man to lead the MCSO troop into New Orleans. They proceeded down back roads, avoiding roadblocks whenever possible. In Louisiana, not unlike a certain county in Arizona, the sheriffs rule their roosts, and nobody, not even the sheriff of sheriffs, tells them who to let in and who to keep out.

They zigged left and zagged right, and eventually made it to Algiers, seven days after they had commenced their journey from Phoenix. A ten-minute ferry ride from the French Quarter, Algiers sits on the west bank of the Mississippi River. Part of the Orleans Parish, it is a community within the city, architecturally and spiritually even more nineteenth century than the rest of New Orleans. It was also the only dry land around.

The police captain in charge of the Algiers precinct normally had eighty cops under his command. Now he was down to twenty-five, and they had been working nonstop. Most of their equipment, from vehicles to weapons to food, had either been lost or ruined in the flood. Grasping the desperate nature of his position, the captain had taken the initiative and directed his officers to march into supermarkets and Wal-Mart and Home Depot stores, anyplace they could get the supplies they required to do their jobs, and take what they needed. They'd total up the bill and the city would make good on it later.

Our deputies entered what looked like the aftermath of a war zone. Power, water, phones were gone. The flood had destroyed everything in its path, filling the streets with wood beams, floor tiles, chunks of concrete, furniture, clothes, garbage, sewage—the skeletal remains of a city. The waters had also brought inland from the Gulf snakes and rats and even crocodiles. Dead bodies littered the streets; since most of the government had collapsed, there was no one to collect them, so they just lay where they had expired, decomposing.

The only people left in New Orleans fell into four categories: those who had stayed behind to safeguard their property, however meager; those who had stayed behind because they had no way to get out; those who were there to protect the city; and those who were there to plunder the city.

There were certainly more people ready to plunder than on duty to protect. And that's where our deputies entered the picture.

We were the first relief the Algiers police had seen since the disaster struck, and their reactions started with disbelief and briskly shifted to deep gratitude. One New Orleans cop summarized the situation for his new best friends from Arizona, at least from his exhausted, embattled point of view: "You see those sons of bitches over there? We're feeding them during the day, and they're shooting at us at night."

Whether that was exactly so, I can't say. But the situation at night was like something out of a third world country, maybe a fourth world one. Without electricity, darkness ruled. Without a real government in place, criminals and criminally inclined opportunists ruled. The nights were filled with gunfire, a fair amount of it directed at the cops by looters and other miscreants.

MCSO deputies immediately began to patrol with the locals, trying to restore law and order.

At the same time, Fulton and Nadreau were busy in the sky. They flew mission after mission, ferrying not only the high sheriff and other parish sheriffs, but also other government officials and doctors and medical supplies as well. They landed outside the Superdome, the scene of so much misery, a symbol of the government's profound failure, transporting the arena's management team to survey the damage. They had to wear surgical masks and gloves to try to hold off the stench. The masks and gloves weren't enough.

Flying a helicopter is not a casual affair. The New Orleans mission constituted the second-largest rotorcraft airlift in U.S. history, second only to the Vietnam War. Helicopters were everywhere, military craft, police and rescue, Chinooks, Black Hawks, Seahawks, Hueys, and Dolphins, all crowding the sky. A Coast Guard AWACS circled overhead, attempting to direct traffic, but it wasn't possible to keep track of so many birds at once, moving in so many directions, operating independently or under the command of different agencies.

Transmission lines and telephone poles and church spires constituted a separate menace. You spent a lot of time looking up to avoid helicopters and looking down to miss getting tangled in some wire.

SWAT officers traveled on the flights with Fulton and Nadreau to ensure the safety of both the crew and the aircraft. Other pilots had guns shoved in their faces upon landing in a high school football field or on a city block, the helicopter ransacked for whatever it held, the pilots robbed, even physically assaulted.

Back on the ground, the MCSO deputies and posse members kept up the patrols, checking houses to see if they were abandoned or if a corpse was inside, providing aid and assistance to those they found alive and in distress, forcing the packs of looters who freely roamed the streets back into their holes.

When things straightened out a bit, and the waters began receding and the federal government finally began to get it together and help slowly began arriving, the time had come to head back to Arizona. And so the convoy packed up and headed home, deputies and posse members together. Only Fulton and Nadreau stayed a couple more days, at the request of the Louisiana sheriffs, before they too flew back to Arizona.

Over 100 deputies and posse together performed with courage and dedication. Not enough can be said in admiration of the leadership and skill of our deputies, and it is hard to imagine a finer instance of effective volunteer effort—until less than a month later, when Hurricane Rita struck the ravaged Gulf Coast. Once again, I dispatched over 100 deputies and posse personnel to support the relief effort. Once again, the posse proved its mettle and its worth.

* * *

ONE FINAL thought. I've had some visitors tell me that the posse might be okay for Arizona, out here in the Wild West, where there's open range and desert and cacti and exurbia, but it couldn't work in the big cities back East or in any other densely populated place. Too many people, too close together, too many problems requiring quicker reactions, no time for amateurs. New York City doesn't have a posse, but it does have an unarmed auxiliary force. The city's auxiliary police officers do not carry guns as they assist at parades and other public events, as well as patrolling in certain areas and providing "eyes and ears" for reporting crimes but not responding.

I'm sure the program works just fine, but it doesn't make sense to me to employ such a halfway measure. Ignoring the geocentric arrogance that different locales demand different solutions, the ultimate answer is pretty simple: It all depends on training. Provide the right training, along with the right leadership and direction, and your people, volunteers or paid, can accomplish anything.

Hey, from the start, my critics guaranteed that the posse would be a disaster. They said its members would run off and shoot up the town, surely killing somebody, and undoubtedly sooner rather than later. It hasn't happened. Flash: No posse member's ever shot any citizen, innocent or otherwise.

Not that it would matter, because I pledged from the beginning that even if a mistake, a bad mistake, was made by a posse member, I wouldn't panic or disown the organization or shut it down. Mistakes do happen, and they happen to police forces everywhere, as well as to everybody else. As careful as you can be, as prepared and as well intentioned, things go wrong. You fix them and get better and move on.

The posse works anywhere if those in charge have the foresight and the fortitude to see it through, come what may.

In other words, I don't think we'll be seeing the posse idea spreading from sea to shining sea anytime soon.

A LIFETIME IN LAW ENFORCEMENT

I KNOW WHAT it's like out there. I'd be willing to bet I know better than any other sheriff or chief or any cop running a department what it's like to be on your own, with no backup, nor any real hope of backup, forced to rely on your own wits and sometimes your own fists, or even your own weapon, to survive and accomplish your mission.

The Korean War started on June 25, 1950. I had just turned eighteen and just graduated from high school. I had grown up in Springfield, Massachusetts. My mother died in childbirth, and my father was busy day and night building one grocery store into two. He needed help raising his infant son, so I bounced from family to family until my father remarried when I was twelve and returned to his house, overlooking the town cemetery.

So now I was eighteen and free, and looking to get on with my life and get out of my hometown. The path seemed obvious: North Korea attacked South Korea with 135,000 soldiers across the thirty-eighth parallel, and I joined the army that same day.

I reached the rank of sergeant in my three years in the service. For whatever reason, even though I had volunteered, I wasn't dispatched to Korea. Instead, I spent most of my time in France. Not a bad alternative, most would probably say, even if I wasn't in Paris but further east, in Metz, relatively near the German border, but I was bored and ready to get out.

I wanted out not only because I had had enough, but also because I wanted to start my career in law enforcement. Since I was a boy, I had longed to join the FBI and be a real G-man. I still wanted to be a fed, though now I wasn't exclusively focused on the FBI, and so, to reach my goal, I took every civil service exam the federal government offered, including the tests for the Border Patrol and the Metropolitan Police Department in Washington, D.C.

I joined the D.C. police in 1954, a proud day for this rookie cop. My first beat was in the northern part of the city, near Walter Reed Hospital, close to the Montgomery County, Maryland, border. It was a nice neighborhood, which was good for the people living there, but not so good for an aggressive, twenty-one-year-old policeman looking to root out and arrest bad guys. I didn't cool my heels too long, maybe six months, before asking for a transfer to a tougher beat. And in Washington, a tough beat wasn't (and still isn't) hard to find. I was dispatched to Fourteenth Street, near the old stadium where the now deceased Washington Senators baseball team used to play.

I had gotten my wish. Fourteenth Street was more than tough enough. It was a poor, black neighborhood, and I spent about two and half years walking up and down its streets. It was a terrific training ground for a rookie, and I gained knowledge that has served me well throughout my entire career. I learned that successful law enforcement isn't only about watching and tracking and catching the bad guys; it's also about knowing the good guys. The most effective cop knows as much about his beat, his neighborhood, his community as possible. The most effective cop knows that most people on any block in any town are decent, hardworking, law-abiding citizens who not only appreciate the efforts of their local police, but are also, when called upon, willing to help.

There's a trust between the community and the police in a democracy that is a natural result of the community's inherent supremacy over the government. That trust can be broken should the police abuse their power, mistreat those who deserve their compassion and assistance, and take on the hostile appearance and attitude of an occupying force. Once that basic trust has been broken, every police officer in that precinct immediately discovers his job is that much more difficult and infinitely more dangerous.

Back when I was walking that Fourteenth Street beat, back in 1954, the public's trust in the police was pretty much a given. At least that's the way I remember it, though I don't deny I might be remembering those days through a soft gauze granted by the passage of time. Even making allowances, the police, just like the government, the press, corporations, and just about every other important institution in this country, were regarded with more affection and respect than they are today.

And so I walked my beat. I knew every shop owner on the street, every kid on the corner, every guy who liked to lurk in the alley. More than just the neighborhood patrolman, I was a familiar, welcoming face. I made myself part of that neighborhood, a constant, reliable, physical presence. I was the boss where I walked—in a way, maybe it was my first take on being sheriff, the lone lawman striding down main street at high noon, taking on all comers.

Not that everybody was glad to see me. Given my gung-ho disposition, I didn't wait for somebody else to let me know a crime was being committed. I did my own footwork, my own investigating, and

I took matters into my own hands. Not for nothing did I "win" the title of Most Assaulted Cop in D.C. in 1957, with a grand total of eighteen serious encounters—not a little pushing and shoving, not a couple of taps and it was over, but full-out battles. (Yeah, they actually kept track of that sort of thing, and earning that exalted status was considered something of an accomplishment because it meant you were out front and confronting the bad guys head-on.)

To demonstrate exactly how policemen were expected to deal with trouble, we were issued a .38 revolver, as well as a nightstick and a blackjack. Also known as a sap, the blackjack is a small, leather-wrapped lead weight attached to a strap, allowing the user to carry it concealed and swing it with maximum force. It can be a devastating weapon, effective in crushing bone and tissue, and it was widely employed by the police for many years. Our modern sensibility (on the positive side, better-educated officers and more enlightened leadership, and their negative counterweights, the timidity of political correctness and the fear of lawsuits) has caused the blackjack to be replaced by the baton, not to mention pepper spray, Tasers, and other defensive tools.

But back then, I had my blackjack and my nightstick, and I used both without hesitation and whenever necessary, which was often.

I'll call upon one story to sum up what it was like back on Fourteenth Street. Near the end of my Washington stint, when I was already a veteran at the ripe old age of twenty-five, I was patrolling with a police trainee, even younger than I. We came upon a fellow who was unmistakably, boorishly drunk. Public intoxication was a crime and one not as acceptable as it seems to be these days, and so we approached the offender. The brother of the drunk fellow was also on the scene. Not untouched by alcohol himself, he took exception to our interference with both his brother and their afternoon stroll. One thing led to another, and soon both men were exhibiting what it is technically called "disorderly conduct," culminating when one of the brothers jumped me.

Joe and Dad.

First Communion.

The young sergeant.

The rookie cop in DC.

Joe, Ava, and Rocco.

880-pound opium haul in Turkey.

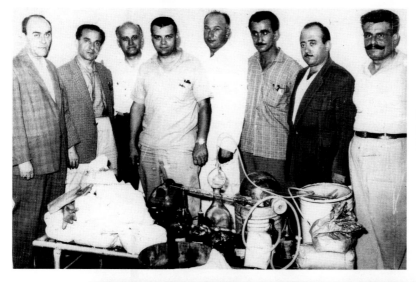

Busting an opium drug lab in Turkey.

One bullet hole of many in red Cadillac when Joe was nearly murdered near Vienna, VA.

Tent City Jail.

Pink handcuffs used in Maricopa County jails, complementing the pink boxers.

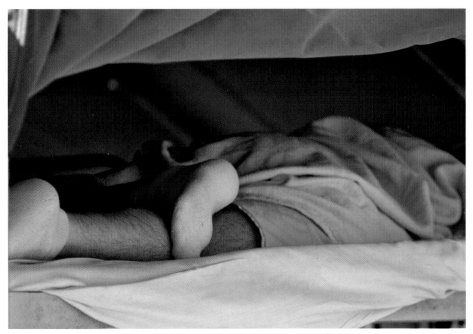

The pink theme highlighted as one inmate at Tent City Jail lounges.

Prisoners marched from an old jail to a new facility.

Joe's tank, purchased from the U.S. Army with seized drug money, ready for action.

One more tool in getting the public to join in the fight against illegal immigration.

An MCSO helicopter.

Sheriff Joe and Ava parade on Veteran's Day.

Joe addressing the Special Assignments Unit.

Joe helping a young inmate in the Alpha Program learn one small skill as he prepares for a new start on the outside.

Joe with two of his non-voting constituents, safe now in his MASH unit.

The old soldier on Veteran's Day.

Joe introduces "Elvis," a/k/a detention officer Bret Kaiser, at a fundraiser at the Improv in Tempe to benefit his MCSO Animal Safe Hospice (MASH) unit.

John Walsh of *America's Most Wanted* swears in Joe for his fourth term as Sheriff of Maricopa County as Ava watches.

Joe Arpaio and Bill O'Reilly.

Joe with George Bush.

Sheriff Joe.

The fight was on, no holds barred on either side. A crowd quickly formed, and before long it numbered over a hundred onlookers. Like any crowd, most people were there to watch the scene, just spectators, slowing down to take in the car crash but not wanting or intending to get involved. However, one voice in the group made his feelings known, yelling, "Kill the cop, kill the cop!" He shouted it over and over.

The crowd didn't react to his chant, but I did. The trainee and I beat down the drunks, and then, bleeding and hurt, I rushed in and cuffed the bastard trying to incite a riot.

Never back down, that was my motto. You back down, just once, whether facing two inebriated idiots or a gang of a hundred or more citizens, and you're finished. You're finished because nobody will respect you, nobody will count on you, and nobody, not to be too subtle about it, nobody will fear you.

The loudmouth ended up in jail, as did the brothers, after a trip to the emergency room. I wound up in the hospital as well, with head injuries. Notch up another assault for the titleholder.

✳   ✳   ✳

I SHARED rooms with my partner at the Woodner Hotel, a really nice apartment/hotel. It was a little above our pay grade, but we were able to afford it by splitting the expenses.

My partner introduced me to Ava. She had moved to Washington from Harrisonburg, Virginia, in the heart of the Shenandoah Valley, for a job as a bookkeeper/stenographer, and she was also staying at the Woodner. I couldn't know it at that moment, but marrying Ava would turn out to be the best decision of my life, the luckiest and the smartest move I would ever make. As my story goes on, you'll understand why.

My career took a turn in 1956, courtesy of Dwight Eisenhower's second presidential inauguration. We, meaning the metro police, were lining up to start off the grand parade, when the chief approached me. "You were in the army, right, officer?" he asked me, eyeing the American Legion hat I was wearing for the occasion. "So you know how to carry a flag?"

I said I guess I did, so I was handed a big flag and ordered to the front, and all of a sudden I was leading the entire procession down Pennsylvania Avenue, leading the marching bands and drill teams and military units and the President of the United States.

My unexpected starring role brought me to the attention of the sheriff of Clark County, Nevada, who was there to participate with a handful of deputies and horses. For some reason, he took a liking to me and instantly asked me to come out west. His department wasn't hiring, but the city of Vegas, which was located within Clark County, was, and he offered to introduce me to the chief.

I'd been with the D.C. police for almost four years. I wanted to be a detective, but the promotion rolls were backed up, which meant it could take a while . . . not to mention I was pretty constantly aching somewhere on my body, from one encounter or another, which made a change of venue sound like a not-so-bad idea.

I was a warrant officer in the Army Reserve, so I was able to hitch a ride for free on a military plane heading west. It was the first plane ride of my life.

I took the test, was offered the job, and accepted.

Las Vegas was a relatively small town, and the Vegas PD was similarly small, with only two squad cars out on patrol at any one time. Still, it was an interesting job, thanks to the casinos and big spenders and loose money that attracted a fascinating assortment of thieves, con men, and fugitives. In fact, Las Vegas was a magnet for reprobates and felons on the run from every state, seeking to grab some money and hide out. I nabbed one of those losers literally almost every day.

In addition to the usual lowlifes, I had one run-in with a celebrity. I was in my patrol car when a motorcycle went screaming past. All I saw was a beautiful blonde holding onto some guy as man and machine broke the law. I caught up and pulled them over. I approached the vehicle with the usual care every cop uses when making a traffic stop. One hand on my gun, I reached the driver, who turned and grinned. It was Elvis Presley. He was already a star and on the verge of becoming a very, very big star.

Elvis apologized for speeding. He was charming, in a simple, sweet way. Maybe because I was young (as was Presley), I let him talk me out of giving him a ticket. But also probably because I was young, I took him in. Well, I suppose it would be more accurate to say I half-ordered, half-asked if he would follow me. He readily agreed, and I brought him to the station. I watched with a big smile as my fellow cops crowded around, introducing themselves, getting Elvis's autograph.

In the midst of this once-in-a-lifetime performance, Elvis turned to me and asked if I'd mind having a mechanic in our garage take a look at his bike. Evidently, it was in need of a little tuning. Considering I had sort of hauled him to the station, and he had played along without complaint, entertaining the troops with genuine good humor, I was more than ready to return the favor. His motorcycle was given a first-rate checkup.

Later on, Presley was known as a friend of law enforcement. Rather dramatically, he handed out about twelve Cadillacs to police officers he met in the course of his travels. Personally, I like to think that one impetus for his fondness for the police was our brief encounter in Las Vegas back in 1957, when he was young.

I always thought I should have gotten one of those Caddys, but that's the way it goes.

✳   ✳   ✳

WHILE I was riding the range out in Nevada, my old roommate and partner from the Woodner Hotel in Washington had also left the D.C. police and joined the Bureau of Narcotics. He gave me a call from Chicago, where he was posted, and said the bureau had an opening. I should apply, he said, assuming I was interested.

I had only worked in Vegas for six months, but I was ready to move on. Besides, I had never abandoned my dream of becoming a federal agent. This sounded like my opportunity.

I knew the agent-in-charge in Washington, who was close to the commissioner, who sent me over to the deputy commissioner, who interviewed me. The deputy commissioner gave me the once-over and got down to brass tacks.

"You're Italian, right?" he asked. "You mind busting Italians, undercover?"

"No," I replied. "I can do that." That sealed the deal. I got the job.

The Bureau of Narcotics (BN) only had 250 agents, supported by a paltry yearly budget of $6 million, probably what today's Drug Enforcement Administration spends on those snazzy department baseball caps.

I received a special appointment to the Bureau of Narcotics and was dispatched to Chicago, just like my old partner. The appointment, formally under the government's Schedule A, was the fastest way into the agency and allowed me to skip taking another civil service exam. The benefit to the government was that while you were a regular agent, you weren't technically civil service, which saved the poorly funded bureau some money and some benefits, at my expense. In fact, the BN was so strapped it had me take the oath of office in Chicago instead of flying me to D.C. for a proper ceremony. I didn't care. I was a fed.

Ava, who had stayed behind in Vegas while I tried out the new job, joined me in Chicago, where we were married.

The bureau had hired me because I was Italian, and it needed Italian agents to hit the Italian neighborhoods and penetrate the mob. I had never done any undercover work, nor did I have any training. It didn't matter. I was willing to learn, and I was ready to learn on the job.

I didn't know much about drugs. Back in the D.C. police academy, we had spent maybe a week getting a primer on illegal drugs and the drug business. Additionally, I was supposed to attend a special Treasury school to get indoctrinated into the ways and means of my new job, but there wasn't time now, so it was put off indefinitely. I would soon be making so many cases and be so busy between investigating and testifying that I would never get the chance to go to the Treasury school. All around, I was going to learn on the run.

I took to my new job like a duck to water. I found I liked working undercover, playing a role, getting inside a bad guy's head, inside a crooked scheme, a criminal conspiracy, and rolling up the whole show. I found I could outthink them, outtalk them, outfox them, and bust them.

I had the knack.

I played a hundred roles, with a thousand stories to accompany them. I flipped through my always-expanding cast of characters, picked the appropriate one, and ventured into neighborhood after neighborhood, buying drugs from dealer after dealer. I traveled throughout Chicago, north to south, east to west, anywhere I thought I could find narcotics. With only 250 narcotics agents scattered throughout the country and just a few in Chicago, I was pretty much on my own and worked according to my own wits and instincts.

A great deal of police work is the result of tales told by informants. How a cop uses his informants is up to his individual judgment and depends on the circumstance. You can let the informant initiate the contact with the bad guy, then let him make the introductions, then let him negotiate on your behalf, and then, if it makes sense, complete the transaction. Or you can step in at any point in the game and take over the deal.

I used my informants in the most effective manner possible, according to the demands of each case. When I didn't have an informant, I developed my own information and made my own deals. There are a million ways to cut the drug deal, so to speak, and I used every one.

I was in constant motion. I did so many undercover deals, I made so many undercover buys, that I couldn't believe I wasn't recognized the minute I came into view, even with phony glasses or a fake mustache. I wasn't even recognized in the black or Puerto Rican neighborhoods, where I was something of an anomaly. After all, the normal MO for an agent who worked up a case through an informant in a neighborhood with an ethnicity other than his own was to seek out a more "suitable" agent to make the buy. In other words, an Italian agent for an Italian street, an Irish agent for an Irish street, a black agent for a black street.

That didn't cut any ice with me. I walked in, told my tale—whatever it happened to be that day—did my deal, and made my bust.

I worked the little guys hard, working my way up the ladder to the bigger guys. That was the mission: Clean up the trash on the streets, and shut down the operation at the top. Work it bottom to top, and back down again.

I made so many busts I acquired the nickname "Nickel-Bag Joe," referring to my ability to start with a measly five-dollar bag of heroin deal and build on it and follow the trail higher up the food chain.

Those were busy days. Busy and interesting. Every deal was different from the one before and the one after. A few cases will give you a sense of what it was like.

On a Chicago afternoon, in the Melrose Park area, I walked into an ice cream parlor to make a phone call to somebody about a drug investigation. I wasn't undercover that day and wasn't dressed to play any particular part. Even so, I struck up a conversation with a guy in the shop, who turned out to be a serious drug dealer. In short order, we were negotiating a heroin purchase.

While we were getting into it, the dealer was on his guard. I could tell by the way he focused on my shoes in a most derisive manner. They were, I had to admit, typical of the kind of shoes cops wore: cheap, unstylish, and scuffed. He mockingly called me, of all things, a "fed." I really didn't have any other choice but to agree with him, sarcasm on full, that yes, he had found me out. I was a cop, and a fed to boot. This little taste of reverse psychology had the desired effect, and the dealer was sufficiently reassured, a situation that would have turned 180 degrees if he had gotten a peek under my coat and spied my badge, handcuffs, and gun.

We quickly concluded our transaction, which added up to a small sample bag of heroin. I didn't care that it was small, because it was only the opening bid, the first deal. Before long, we met again and made a larger deal. Before long, we arrested three major drug dealers and seized two kilos of pure heroin.

My new pal, the shoe-snob criminal, received a life sentence for his misdeeds.

And the other investigation, the one that prompted me to stop in the ice cream parlor to use the phone when this all started? It proceeded on course and concluded with its own list of arrests.

✸　✸　✸

A LATIN American organization was operating out of Chicago, and I had managed to get inside and arrange to purchase a large shipment of marijuana. Details agreed upon, I got in my car and followed the suspects, as per their instructions, to pick up the merchandise. I soon discovered we were heading out of state.

That was all right with me. I was cruising along in my Cadillac, my preferred mode of transportation, driving down the Indiana Turnpike. Trailing from a safe distance were no fewer than ten vehicles carrying officers from the Michigan State Police and agents from the Bureau of Narcotics.

Everything was proceeding as planned, until I noticed something, or to be more precise, smelled something, rapidly followed by my seeing something.

My Cadillac was on fire.

I veered off the road, the car ablaze. The bad guys ahead spotted what had occurred and also pulled off and stopped. They leaped from their vehicle and extinguished the fire. They had risked their lives to save mine.

Even though my car couldn't, I kept my cool. I didn't break cover. I maintained my undercover pose and called my backup, addressing them as though they were part of my gang, instructing them to deliver another car to me. They got what I was saying and dropped off the car. I got in and the journey continued.

We finally stopped when we reached a farmhouse in Fennville, Michigan. Ten Mexican-Americans and 150 pounds of marijuana were waiting in the farmhouse.

The bust was carried out without complication. The seizure constituted a Michigan record at the time.

✸　✸　✸

The plot that opened this book was far from the first murderous threat I've faced. The drug business attracts the most vile and violent types, as epitomized by the two gentlemen I went to see at their pizza shop, two gentlemen with whom I made a deal for a large quantity of heroin. When they delivered the two pounds of junk, they were promptly arrested.

I appeared in court to testify against them. A brother of one of the defendants was in the audience, and in rather dramatic fashion, he made a motion, directed at me, that was the Mafia sign for death—a thumb, palm up, placed under the jaw, and then thrust aggressively forward. Just in case I didn't get it, he announced loud enough for me to hear that he was going to "kill Agent Arpaio."

That made it easy. I arrested the dumb son of a bitch on the spot. For threatening a federal officer, he was convicted and got two years' probation.

I can't say you ever get completely used to being threatened, but you do get a sense of what's just talk and what's more tangible, and more dangerous. You learn to live with it. You really don't have a choice.

*   *   *

IT'S NO secret that the money in the drug business is huge, sometimes unimaginably huge. There's so much that it can prove irresistible even to people who should know better. People like cops.

I got wind of a Chicago police officer who had joined the bad guys. In my undercover capacity, I arranged a meeting. He was happy to sell me heroin. He was the brazen sort, even having me call him at his police station, selling me the heroin right in his squad car on three occasions. He was shameless, but he wasn't stupid. He would flip the switch on his lights and sirens and speed through the city streets while we exchanged money for drugs, effectively prohibiting any surveillance.

Of course, his ploy didn't halt the investigation, and I was eventually able to identity the entire gang. It was time to wrap it up.

I set up another buy with the cop. I also arranged for Chicago PD to radio their man and order him back to police headquarters. I was sitting in his car when he arrived, and they arrested him and confiscated the drugs. The cops barely had to take more than three steps out their door to chalk one up.

He wasn't the only corrupt law enforcement officer I put behind bars. It's a cliché television cops love, but it happens to be true—nobody hates a dirty cop more than another cop. It's a personal affront, a profound insult, a hateful and treacherous act.

If it were up to me (which it is not), those who betray their oath of office and betray the public they have sworn to protect and serve would always receive the harshest penalties the law allows, and leave mercy to a higher authority.

✳   ✳   ✳

FOR THE most part, as I've already demonstrated, I conducted my investigations on my own. However, I did have a secret weapon, an ally who wasn't on the government payroll and wasn't included in any of my reports. It was Ava.

Take this one case: I was in New York on a special undercover assignment, doing business with a couple of Puerto Rican drug dealers. I was working in conjunction with Bureau of Narcotics agents stationed in the city.

Not every investigation proceeds like a bomb shot from a cannon. Instead, most require a lot of legwork, a lot of paper chasing, a lot of talking and waiting, and watching and waiting, and waiting and waiting, usually in the front seat of cars, or in a booth in a lousy coffee shop, or under a lamppost in the rain. During one of those extended, excruciatingly slow periods spent hunkered down with my New York counterparts, we did what men of all stripes usually do—we swapped war stories.

In the course of this can-you-top-this exchange, the New York agents told me about two SOBs the entire law enforcement structure in the city, from local to federal, cops to agents, had been after for years, to no avail. These two were major dope peddlers, operating under the protection of the mob, and they had somehow stayed out of the reach of the law.

We can't touch them, the boys from New York said. They're too smart, too cautious, too connected.

We were just shooting the breeze, but I seized on the story. It was the kind of challenge I pretty much couldn't resist.

"Give me that number," I said. "I'll take care of this."

Given that the agents didn't know me very well, it was not surprising that they hesitated, imagining that I might be kidding. Soon enough they realized I was serious, and after some hesitation, they scribbled the phone number on a piece of paper and handed it over. I tucked it away for later.

We finished the Puerto Rican case and I returned to Chicago. I pulled out that scrap of paper and started calling. I did it blind, without any informant, without an introduction.

It was hard to get something going. The bad guys were naturally suspicious, and a call from nowhere did not reassure them. Who are you? Who do you know? Who sent you? Who gave you this number? The usual questions, and maybe a few more, with a little extra edge.

I had an answer ready for every question. Even better, I had Ava, waiting in the wings.

The thing was, I used to give out my home phone number to all the dealers I was working with. Everyone knew prudent cops kept their private and professional lives absolutely split, separate, walled off from each other, for the sake of security. They lived at home and worked their cases from the office.

I couldn't operate that way. I worked day and night, aggressively, uncompromisingly. I had to give out my home number in order to accomplish everything I wanted to accomplish. And since I was offering up my home number to every jerk and malefactor and degenerate I met, I needed Ava to play a part in my multi-headed, never-ending performance, because I wasn't always home to field the calls.

Ava's role wasn't simply a matter of writing down a message. Oh no. Ava had to step up and act, and act as though my life depended on it, which, in fact, it did.

I worked so many cases at once, usually with a different fake name attached to each job, Ava had to keep a list by the phone to keep them all straight. If somebody asked for "Gino," Ava had to know that she was Gino's prostitute and answer accordingly. It wasn't a role her small-town upbringing had prepared her for, but it was one she figured out how to play like an honors graduate of the Lee Strasberg school of Method acting.

Her usual persona was that of "my woman, my broad," as they used to say, and she inhabited the part exceedingly well. Some lowlife would get Ava on the phone and give her information about a deal or a meeting to pass on to me, and other times I would have Ava pass messages back to the dealers.

My undercover work was so consistently hectic that sometimes Ava would play the game when she didn't have to. One day, this guy called and asked for "Johnny." Ava couldn't recall any alias by that name in my portfolio, but she went with it anyway. She said Johnny wasn't home and offered to take a message.

"Just tell him I'm waiting at the filling station," the guy said and hung up.

So far so good, except the reason Ava didn't remember my being Johnny was because I wasn't Johnny anytime, anywhere. The caller was just a guy looking for his friend. Ava says she still imagines the poor man standing at a filling station in the middle of nowhere, waiting for Johnny.

Getting back to the case, I was still working the two New Yorkers, trying to gain their confidence. Ava also spoke to them and helped ease their concerns. Most people will only go to so much trouble to finish anything, and that includes cops trying to make a case, especially when there are so many cases to be made. The truth was, most cops or agents would have forgotten these guys and moved on. I didn't forget, and I didn't stop. I kept going and eventually took the bad guys by surprise.

It took a few months, but we finally struck a deal for a kilo of heroin, in the days when a kilo was a substantial amount. As a topper, I convinced them to bring the heroin in person to Chicago. The two dealers drove to Illinois in their brand-new Chevrolet. I greeted them with handcuffs and a ride to jail. I took the drugs, and I took the Chevy.

The dealers flipped, meaning they cooperated in return for a reduced sentence, and the information they supplied resulted in the arrest of several major Mafia figures in New York.

And they said it couldn't be done.

* * *

IN ANOTHER case, I was negotiating with a bail bondsman for half a kilo of heroin when the jerk got himself arrested on a robbery charge. No slacker, the bondsman was also a central figure in a Chicago Municipal Court bail bond scandal soon thereafter. Stated another way, he was definitely wrong.

Cut to the not-too-distant future. I was strolling through the halls of the Illinois State Court when I happened to see the bondsman entering a courtroom. I quietly ducked in and discovered he was appearing before a judge on the robbery beef. I stayed to watch and found that the judge was about to let the guy off with probation.

Though this was just a coincidental encounter, I felt duty-bound to interrupt. I approached the bench and apprised the judge about the drug deal I had been brewing with the bondsman. My testimony led the judge to impose a one-to-ten-year sentence on this busy criminal.

* * *

SEE IF you can guess how this one ends.

I was working a dealer who was operating on a street corner not too far from my home. Angling to buy a sizable amount of heroin, I handed the dealer a down payment. He took the money and left, saying he'd soon return with the merchandise. About four hours later, I saw the dealer come sauntering down the avenue.

Very good, I thought to myself. Right on schedule.

However, fate in the form of a vigilant Chicago cop intervened. He spotted the dealer, who was already wanted, and arrested him on the spot. That might have been solid police work, but it seriously interfered with my investigation. As for the heroin I was supposed to be purchasing, it was lost because the dealer hadn't returned with the dope. Oh, he had gone out and picked up the heroin, and he had brought it back, but he hadn't brought it back all the way. He had hidden it close by, a standard procedure in this business.

And that wasn't good enough.

I sidled up to the arresting officer when the dealer was busy being handled by other cops and told him who I was. The cop didn't believe me. Not that I could completely blame him, since I was undercover and wasn't carrying official identification. Regardless, I persisted until I finally convinced the officer I was a fed. Once that hurdle had been conquered, I succinctly explained my improvised plan to him.

"Arrest me," I said. "Put me inside with him."

A simple and maybe even elegant solution, in its own rough, makeshift way. I would stick with this bum until I got what I was due.

I was handcuffed, driven away, and tossed into a holding tank along with my dealer and other slobs, including the rapists and murderers, the crooks and perverts, who normally walked the streets of Chicago.

I hung around my mark, and we verbally went at it for a while, taking turns accusing the other of causing this misfortune. Hey, that was the normal response of an individual (particularly the kind of individual who was actually guilty) suddenly facing an unanticipated prison term. Blame somebody else, anybody else. We shouted ourselves out before finally agreeing that it was just one of the hazards of our special occupation.

Once we were back on the same page, the rest was easy. I got the dealer to tell me where the dope was, the dope that I had already bought, the dope that was my evidence. Long story short, he had stashed it in a garbage can.

Now that I had the info, the trick was getting the word out without blowing my cover in front of all these lawbreakers and blowing my chances of making more deals. I couldn't walk up to the bars and announce that the jig was up. I had what I needed, but I had to figure out a way to get out.

I managed to slip a message to the police, instructing them to have one of my bureau comrades pose as a bail bondsman and get me sprung. That was the only way I could get out without arousing the dealer's suspicion. Unfortunately, it would take a day to set all that up, which meant that I would have to spend the night in jail.

When I was released in the morning, I went straight to the garbage can and grabbed the heroin.

Case closed.

But that didn't spell the end of the excitement, not on this morning after the night of February 20, 1960. In fact, the drug deal, the stint in jail, the bust—all that was the least of it.

I rushed straight from that garbage can to the hospital up the block, where Ava had given birth to my son, my firstborn, while I was in jail.

TURKEY

"NICKEL-BAG Joe" worked long and hard and got results—sometimes big results. Washington recognized and rewarded those results. I entered the bureau as a grade seven, in civil service terms. A year later, I had risen to grade nine and was then promoted to grade eleven, skipping grade ten, the only agent in bureau history to jump a level in promotion.

But a larger reward was in store for me, one I regarded as a very special and exciting honor. After four years in Chicago, I was to take on a new assignment.

And while I thought of it as an honor, others might have reasonably viewed it as a potential death sentence, spelling the end of either my career or the end of me.

*   *   *

TURKEY in 1961 was the hottest spot on earth as far as the drug business was concerned. Located between the East and the West, a nexus between Asia, Europe, and the Middle East, the country was the center of the global heroin trade at a time when the heroin trade had achieved a new height of vicious influence and reach. Turkey was the place where it all began, where the opium fields seemed to run on forever, where the legions of farmers harvested their crops and sold them to seemingly endless hordes of buyers. Those fields supplied the opium for the laboratories of the Corsican syndicate in Marseilles, which converted the raw material into morphine base and then heroin, which was shipped to America, primarily via Canada down to New York City. The New York end of the business was the focus of a terrific film, *The French Connection*.

This was no casual enterprise, but perhaps the most organized, continually successful criminal conspiracy in modern times. It was a conspiracy I would fight from the Near East to Europe, to the Middle East to Central America and South America, a battle I would wage on one front or another for the next eight years, culminating in the arrest of the mastermind in South America, a conclusion that will be revealed in due course.

The Bureau of Narcotics was responsible for stopping this deadly commerce, not to mention all the other drugs washing through our nation. Its 250 agents were arrayed against scores of drug cartels, thousands of criminal organizations, a numberless army of farmers and suppliers, dealers and mules, casual users and addicts, hit men and lawyers, and an ocean of drugs.

And so much of it began with Turkey, a land of mystery and intrigue, and so very far away and foreign, especially in 1961, especially to me, a kid from Springfield, Massachusetts. So what resources did the government of the United States, the most powerful government in the world, allocate to this critical, desperate battle? How many battalions of cops, how many shiploads of equipment, how much money, how much support?

You'll be looking at how much if you happen to look at my picture on the cover of this book. The bureau sent me. The bureau put me on a plane, dropped me off in Istanbul, and told me to get to work. Good luck, good-bye, keep in touch, and get the job done. I was one of the first half dozen bureau agents sent to work outside the United States, and I was solely responsible for not just Turkey, but for the entire Middle East.

I expect that most people assume that an American agent dispatched overseas is prepped and prepared in every manner possible. You would assume an American agent undergoes rigorous physical training and is outfitted with an assortment of the most advanced technological resources, from communications devices to weapons of every size and variety. You would assume an American agent is given a crash course in the language of the country in which he's going to be operating, along with courses in the history, culture, and politics of the region. You would assume an American agent would be handed a neatly typed list of contacts, high and low, official and civilian, with whom to work.

You might assume all that, and you'd be wrong. I wasn't provided with training or equipment or education or contacts. Nothing. And when I say nothing, I mean nothing.

Let me put it this way: Talking Turkey, I didn't know anything and I didn't know anybody. I had my trusty Smith & Wesson and a pathetically small roll of flash money. That was it. I had no support, no backup, no leads, and operating in a foreign nation, I also had no legal authority, power, or clout. I wasn't even officially sanctioned to carry a gun.

I was just a stranger in somebody else's country.

And it only got better. The Bureau of Narcotics was so starved for funds, and subsequently ran such a bare-bones organization, that my superiors refused to send my family with me. The bureau declared it did not have the money to put my wife and my baby on an airplane to Turkey. However, if I survived six months on the job—and survival in this assignment was both a literal and professional proposition—then perhaps the BN could scrape together the money for tickets for them. That was the deal, take it or leave it, though of course I didn't have the option of leaving it.

The fact was, it was far from certain that I could cut it. If I had been the type to sit down and calculate the odds, I might have become paralyzed by the enormity of the task, the paucity of my resources, the numbing isolation of my position.

Fortunately, I was not (and am not) a worrier. I get up and act, do what I can, and let the chips fall where they may. So I flew to Turkey and wasted not a moment getting down to business, doing it the only way I knew how, whether in Chicago or Istanbul. I walked the streets, I hung out in the seedier parts of town, I introduced myself to my Turkish counterparts. I tried to meet the local bad guys and make some contacts.

To say it wasn't easy is the understatement of the day. The Turkish cops weren't overwhelmed by the presence of some pushy foreigner in their midst. I understood how they felt; they had their own cases, their own priorities, their own careers, and they didn't really need to be worrying about some American riding into town with his own agenda—an agenda, by the way, neither the American nor the Turkish government seemed to care enough about to support in any substantive manner.

The criminals were even less impressed. Inherently suspicious, same as criminals everywhere, they weren't too eager to make a new friend, especially one who didn't speak their native tongue, who just walked through the door, looking to find narcotics for sale. For my part, I uncovered contacts in bars and clubs and on street corners and all the usual grimy places, but I didn't know which of these guys were reliable and knew what they were talking about. I didn't know who was dependable and the real deal, and who was a con man looking to rip me off. Nor did I know who was a homicidal maniac with a straight razor in his boot and a refrigerator filled with human heads, looking to add one more. I didn't know who was a waste of my time and who could lead me to the proverbial pot of gold.

It was all hit and miss, trial and error, guided by instinct and luck. A steep learning curve, straight up from zero. The only problem—well, one of the more dramatic problems—was that if you failed the course, you could die.

At this stage, I couldn't even think about making deals with the big boys at the top. As usual, I had to start pretty near the bottom, trying to get hooked into the mix, working my way up the drug ladder. I wasted time and money with one jerk or another, each claiming to be connected, tied into prime sources.

It wasn't working. I wasn't making the cases, and I was getting frustrated and angry. But I didn't have a lot of choices. There wasn't any other way to proceed. I had to keep looking and meeting and talking until I struck pay dirt. It wasn't fancy, it wasn't sophisticated, but that's what a lot of police work, especially undercover work, is all about.

But then, eventually, I started to connect. I started to get into the lowlife mix. I picked up a few Turkish phrases, and enough people knew at least some English that I could get by. I met one local, then two, then a few more informants and users and dealers. Small fry, maybe, but at least they were players, to one degree or another.

I was slowly building my network of bad guys, and I was getting acclimated to this very big, very different neighborhood. My sixth sense, my special policeman's nose and ear and eye, was back in fine style. I was negotiating and buying. I was beginning to break cases.

This change of fortune had a personal as well as professional impact on my life. As I neared the six-month deadline and I gained confidence and racked up some successes, I informed Washington that my son was going to celebrate his second birthday about a month before my trial period was up. I didn't mention this hoping for a gift from the agency. Rather, I mentioned it because a child under two flew for free, so if Ava and the baby hopped on that plane right away, the bureau would save the cost of a one-way ticket.

Just a reminder.

The speed with which the bureau jumped, you'd think Bob Hope wanted them for a USO show. Agents were immediately dispatched into the hills of Virginia to track down Ava and my son, who were off visiting relatives. They tracked them down and henceforth hustled them onto a plane and got my family to Turkey, just under the wire.

They moved so fast, Ava barely had time to pack. Not that she was bringing much with her: The bureau wouldn't pay to ship our furniture or hardly anything, for that matter. Still, both parties got what was most important to them—Washington saved its money, and I had my family.

Getting my family over early had a vital side benefit. It saved my life, literally.

I was scheduled to fly to Beirut that night. I had a big case going and needed to get to Lebanon. I hated to put off the flight—it wasn't in my nature—but I wouldn't have skipped my family's arrival in Turkey for anything.

We had a gala reception for Ava and baby at the airport. When I say "we," it's because I didn't show up alone. Indeed, a caravan of high-ranking representatives from the police and the military escorted me right onto the runway, bearing tremendous bouquets of flowers. It was a terrific welcome.

Lucky for me I was such a loyal family man. The flight I missed crashed into the mountains, killing all aboard. I got my family settled and took that same flight the next day. We flew over the wreckage of the downed turbojet.

That special set of unpleasant circumstances did not happen once to me, but twice. Gunplay isn't the only way to die.

Ava adjusted with remarkable ease to our new life. Istanbul might have been a big city, but it wasn't anything like Washington or Chicago. Nor did we live the way U.S. government employees lived in other postings, such as London or Paris. There was not much that was fancy about Istanbul, not in those days.

We lived in a small brick house in an American enclave located in the city, populated mainly by U.S. Army and embassy personnel. We didn't have a telephone in the house, which wasn't surprising since the neighborhood wasn't wired for phone service. Ava shopped at the army PX as well as local markets for food. Ava's friends were chiefly other Americans. Our son made a good friend, a little girl, who lived up the street.

Just like back home, Ava had to largely make her own way because I wasn't around much. I worked around the clock. I just came home to change clothes and get something decent to eat. I probably spent three out of four weeks in the boondocks, in the mountains of Turkey or Syria or Lebanon, in the border towns, in the valleys, in the fields, in the middle of nowhere surrounded by nothing but trouble and danger.

Like I've already indicated, this wasn't a fancy life. It was at least as hard on Ava as it was on me. But I loved it. I thought I was doing good work, important work, exciting work. One day I'm meeting with the president of Turkey, the next day I'm shooting it out with the bandits in the hinterlands.

I had my job, and Ava had hers, and I'm not sure which was more difficult. At least I had my mission, and that mission was the whole reason we were there. Ava had to find some normalcy in this place, for herself and for the baby, even though she was cut off from family and old friends, cut off from anything that was familiar and comforting, waiting for me to return from God knew where, God knew when, God knew how.

It wasn't always easy, but we did it together, in our own way. We were—we are—a family.

* * *

IT WAS a building process. I quickly understood that most of the action, the serious action, wasn't found in Istanbul, but in the fields that climbed the sides of the mountains and blanketed the valleys. That was where the poppy was cultivated and where the drug business began. That was the source, and just as with any sort of infection, if you attacked the source, you could wipe out the disease before it had the chance to spread.

Maybe because I had begun to prove to the Turkish police that I knew what I was doing, or maybe because I evidently wasn't going away, they started working with me, slowly but surely. I started off traveling around the countryside with one police officer, then we called on a couple of others, and it continued to grow. It was a little like Butch Cassidy and the Sundance Kid, the part when they began robbing banks in Bolivia and the Bolivians responded with a couple of cops, then more and more until it looked like the entire Bolivian army was involved. One major difference: Unlike in the movie, here in Turkey, the cops were the guys you were supposed to root for.

We started with villages close to Istanbul, villages and farms, mapping out the relationships among farmers and dealers and suppliers and shippers. We exhausted those and headed farther inland, where the bigger operators thrived. The task was enormous. One case only led to the next, and I soon found myself immersed at the front end of the international heroin trade.

We'd drive hundreds of miles into the mountains, risking my life and the lives of the Turkish cops and soldiers I brought along, just getting to the drugs. And the real danger was only beginning, because once we arrived, the waiting would begin—the waiting for the dealers to show up. We'd be holed up in the middle of nowhere, at night, in the dark. And let me tell you, you don't know how dark the night can be until you've gone 400 miles from the nearest gleam of electricity.

It was so dark that we'd only know somebody was coming when we'd hear the clanging of the bell hanging from the donkey that was ferrying the drugs in the far, far distance—because as dark as it was, it was just as quiet.

That clanging would get closer and closer until it was almost upon us. And we still didn't see anything or anybody, so we didn't know how many farmers and dealers were arrayed before us and how many weapons they were toting.

But it didn't matter in the end, because however many of them there were, I'd give the signal to leap out and grab the farmers and the drugs. The shooting would start, and the screams and curses, and we'd capture the opium as well as the farmers who didn't move fast enough to escape.

It was very exciting. I know that might sound a bit trite, but it was completely true. It was the height of adrenaline-rushing excitement when the moment came and the night erupted.

And then we'd immediately drive all the way back to Istanbul because we couldn't trust the local authorities in the mountains. I used to drive one, sometimes two nights without stopping, because hardly any of the Turks with whom I worked knew how to drive. I'd bring army K rations, which were hardly a delicacy, because I didn't want to eat the native, roadside cuisine. Inevitably, however, I'd wind up giving my K rations to the undernourished Turks, who craved the American army fare, and I'd eat whatever I could scrounge from the locals and hope I didn't get sick. I'd bring whiskey, which I'd also hand over to my Turkish compatriots, and drink raki, which tasted like Italian anisette.

I told you it wasn't London or Paris.

✳ ✳ ✳

I'D BEEN driving for I don't know how many hours, wrestling with the wheezing, aged truck I had rented a couple hundred miles ago. Up to now, the trek had been pretty much routine. I had driven to Ankara, the capital of Turkey, from my home in Istanbul in my government-issue 1957 Chevy, along the way picking up Commander Galip Labernas, my counterpart in the Turkish national police. He was an old pro, but his enthusiasm for crime busting had long ago evaporated and disappeared.

Labernas's lack of gusto in the performance of his task wasn't exactly an inspiration, but he wasn't corrupt, and he would do what was needed when called upon. In any event, I needed his official police powers. For the most part, the Turkish police were hardly models of law enforcement efficiency, being generally underpaid, undertrained, underequipped, and undermotivated. On the other hand, they were all I had. I had discovered that it was smart to work only with cops from either Istanbul or Ankara because the rural authorities were thoroughly bought and paid for by the local drug dealers and would give you away faster than you could spit.

From Ankara, Labernas and I had headed into rural Turkey, away from the bright lights—or any lights—and big cities. Of course, the further we journeyed from the main urban areas, the more difficult the roads became, until they were finally too much for my car, which was six years old and had been worn down traversing the rutted, dirt highways and byways of Turkey. But the heap was all the old Bureau of Narcotics could afford, so that was what I used, unless I managed to borrow the jeep from the U.S. Army colonel who lived next door.

I took the Chevy as far as it could go and then parked it in some village alongside the road and got the rusty truck.

I'd met the go-between who'd set up this transaction shortly after arriving in Turkey. He was a Lebanese "businessman" who was looking to score in the informer game. After striking out on several deals, he had begun to click, and I'd made a series of decent busts because of his efforts. This one was supposed to be big, maybe a half-ton of opium.

We drove all day and all night, not stopping to rest in one of the small hotels the road offered, twenty-five cents a bed, and all the bugs you can step over and on. I shared my whiskey and GI rations with Commander Labernas and kept spinning and shuddering along the narrow, rough mountain roads, used more by horses and donkeys than by lumbering, mechanized vehicles.

We always brought gum with us because rocks would puncture the gas tanks and we'd need something to cover up the holes. Gum wasn't exactly the recommended material, but it was the best we had, and it usually worked, at least temporarily.

Somewhere along the journey, we picked up about twenty soldiers from the paramilitary police and hid them in the back of the truck. We kept moving forward until, after two days and nights, we neared the town of Goceri.

It was as dark as night can be, and I proceeded slowly. We had almost reached the outskirts of the town when I spotted the signal, a flashlight blinking twice up ahead. I stopped the truck, got out with my own flashlight, and answered back. Identification established, I walked closer.

Back in Chicago, I had to spin out elaborate tales of my criminal background and intentions, proving myself to mobsters and killers, aware that the smallest slip could mean a quick death. Turkey was very different, much less sophisticated and suspicious, though no less dangerous. Most deals were set up by the go-between, and all the suppliers ever knew or cared about, particularly in the countryside, was that I was some foreigner—one day an Italian diplomat, the next a Dutch sailor—who had money and wanted to purchase opium. I would show up, flash the cash, and go from there. Simple—especially in theory.

Anyway, my Lebanese informer was waiting, along with one of the farmers/smugglers who had brought the opium. It was legal to grow opium in Turkey at the time. Refined, it provided the morphine base used for medicinal purposes all over the world. And the price paid for opium by drug smugglers was two or three times higher than the price the farmer could get from legitimate buyers. However, because the government regulated the crop, each farmer could divert only a few kilos from his lawful harvest and get away with it, and so it required a bunch of farmers to produce a take as sizable as half a ton.

On behalf of the supplier, the informer asked to see my money. I pulled out a thick roll of bills and waved it in front of their faces. Benjamin Franklin's face was on top, so the men could see I was loaded with $100 bills. Of course, the rest of the bills underneath the hundred on top were ones, because a lone hundred was all my pitiful Bureau of Narcotics budget could afford. Fortunately, I wasn't dealing with the cleverest of criminals, and the farmer didn't ask to count the money. He was satisfied.

"Where's the stuff?" I asked.

The Lebanese gave me directions down a side road, where I would find the opium and complete the transaction. I returned to my vehicle. The informer and the farmer went on ahead.

This was the hairy part. If the farmers or anybody else were planning to hold me up or kill me for my cash, it would be at the end of this road.

I cautiously headed down the bumpy lane. I had my headlights on high. Subtlety was not an issue: Any possible advantage to be gained by sneaking up on the farmers was no longer possible because the farmers certainly knew I was there. At this stage, my focus was on making sure I didn't careen off the road and plunge the truck off the mountain.

The headlights bounced off the bags of opium piled on the ground in the middle of the road, but even in the first flash off those burlap bags I recognized that this was no ordinary haul.

I halted the truck but didn't turn off the lights. I wanted to keep a little illumination on the scene. I glanced over at Labernas and nodded, a silent reminder to be ready.

I checked the .38 stuck in my waistband and stepped down.

I had never seen so much opium in any one place. It was collected in a huge mass of small and large bags, at least six feet wide and several feet high, with other sacks hanging off the sides of the pack animals that had transported them to this rendezvous. And it was not only the sheer quantity that was overwhelming, it was also the smell, the air suffused by that unmistakable musty odor.

All this opium brought one major complication. The more opium, the more farmers were required to contribute to the total, and every one of those farmers attended the transaction to ensure that he wasn't cheated out of his rightful share of the money. Standing before me were about twenty-five to thirty farmers, tough, bearded, mountain men, quiet and grim, armed with rifles and knives.

I glanced over to my Lebanese pal, who was grinning. He had known this was something special and had wanted to surprise me. Of course, if this had been a real deal instead of a buy-and-bust, I would never have had enough money, even if the BN had emptied its entire thin wallet into my bank account. Black market opium was going for $30 a kilo. Considering I was probably looking at a ton of it here, I would have needed a suitcase stuffed with hundreds, not just one measly bill plastered on top of a fake roll resting in my pocket.

The farmers were eyeing me, waiting for their money. They wouldn't wait long. The silence hung in the air. The moment had arrived. I sucked in some oxygen and shouted out the signal.

"Gel!"

Gel was Turkish for "come," and that yell was supposed to bring my Turkish partner and the troops crashing out of the truck and to center stage, guns at the ready.

Nothing happened. The farmers stared at me, confused. I shouted again, even louder. "Gel!"

Nothing. Not a damn peep. I was 408 miles from Istanbul, and that was where my backup might as well have been, for all the good it was doing me.

"GEL!"

I stood there, as alone as an undercover cop can be, facing the farmers, who thankfully still waited, confounded by this clearly crazy foreigner, evidently still anticipating their money.

I knew the farmers wouldn't stay frozen forever, so I did what came naturally: I attacked, which in this case meant pulling my gun and shouting, *"Interpol!"* (Almost everywhere, "Interpol" was the accepted, recognized shorthand for "foreign cop," and Lord knew shouting "United States Bureau of Narcotics!" would have been a meaningless jumble of sounds, not even words, to this crowd.)

So there we were, my six-shot revolver with the two-inch barrel and me, taking thirty-odd Turkish opium farmers into custody, which, I mention quite incidentally, I had no authority to do. I needed my Turkish compatriots to, first, make the bust official, and second, to save my life.

For some reason, the farmers didn't move. Perhaps they thought my performance was too funny to interrupt. Perhaps they thought it was too strange to take seriously. Perhaps they didn't know what the hell I was trying to do. I don't know. All I do know is that they didn't shoot me, and that was good for the moment.

On the other side of the ledger, maybe my Turkish allies were waiting to see if the farmers would quickly kill me, thereby closing the case and rendering their participation in this potentially ugly situation unnecessary. Maybe I had survived long enough for the cavalry to wake up and get its act together. Whichever, all of a sudden, the troops started leaping out of the back of my truck. The soldiers didn't believe in quietly flanking the enemy and taking prisoners, because they emerged from the back of the truck screaming unintelligibly and wildly firing their weapons in the air. This utterly stupid barrage only served to spook the farmers, most of whom instantly turned and fled with their animals into the night.

One farmer just a few feet away raised a rifle and pointed it at me, and there was nothing I could do. He had me dead. But either his rifle jammed or he simply didn't fire, because nothing happened. And then other bodies got in the way, the action shifted, and it was over.

The farmers were vanishing, which, upon reflection, was preferable to them deciding en masse to shoot it out with the soldiers, with me in the middle. At that instant, however, with my adrenaline pumping, I was furious that people were escaping. I saw a donkey getting away with probably a hundred kilos strapped to his back, and I fired at him. Maybe because he was fading into the darkness, or maybe because a revolver with a two-inch barrel is accurate only at a distance the length of the average living room, or maybe because I'm a lousy shot, the donkey got away without a scratch.

Most of the farmers/smugglers also melted away into the night. Pursuit was impossible. These were their mountains and valleys, and they knew every rock and path and hole. If my gang of outsiders had stepped out of the headlights and into the dark, we would have been swallowed and scattered and lost.

Nevertheless, we rounded up a handful of the farmers and somehow managed not to get anyone killed on either side. I didn't reprimand my Turkish allies. I figured there was really no point; you accepted the way things were or you asked for a new assignment somewhere else.

Anyway, I had something more interesting to do. This was my first opportunity to take a good long look at the catch. This was big, unbelievably big. I had never heard of anybody snatching so much opium before.

To a cop, all that confiscated opium was a beautiful sight.

It wasn't too smart to spend a lot of time standing around congratulating ourselves. We were deep in hostile territory, and the farmers could conceivably organize themselves into an ambush. I helped the troops load the opium and the prisoners into the truck, and away we went. Same as on the trip out, I drove pretty much straight through, and two days later I was back in Istanbul. The prisoners were led away, and the opium was weighed. The haul was an extraordinary one ton plus, the largest seizure ever made in Turkey. The case received worldwide publicity. Even so, I could not help thinking about that donkey and the hundred kilos that got away.

I went home, took a shower, and went back out to make the next buy and the next bust. It was early morning when I left the house.

✳   ✳   ✳

I WAS up in the mountains with a contingent of Turkish cops, approaching Afyon. It had been a typically rough ride, even with my army colonel's jeep, but then, they were all rough rides.

It was around 10 p.m., and the deal was about to go down. Seven Turks approached, as per arrangement, and delivered 224 kilos of opium via horse and wagon. I had my borrowed jeep and a truck. As per usual, the national policemen were concealed inside the truck.

I gave the signal, and the policemen came tumbling out. The seven Turks chose to neither surrender nor flee. They pulled their weapons, a gun battle erupted, and two of the Turkish dealers were killed.

It was ugly, but that was the way it went. We were playing for keeps, all of us. It wasn't an accident that everybody, bad guys and good guys together, on that lonely road outside of Afyon on that pitch-black night, was armed and ready.

Nonetheless, the Turkish governor of the region had not been properly forewarned and advised of my investigation. The governor didn't like this slight and decided to show us who was the boss. This was a case of local politics, and I had inadvertently stepped into it.

The governor started to make noises about foreigners and interference and murder and anything else he could dream up. He intended to use me, along with five Turkish cops, to cause trouble. Considering his important and very public position (compared with my politically sensitive, somewhat murky status), he had the potential to do so.

The governor didn't get to play his petty game for long. Between his political betters back in Istanbul and the American ambassador, pressure was applied from both sides. The governor crumbled. The charges were dropped, and the press didn't get a chance to smear the story all over the front pages.

I can't say I lost much sleep over the whole affair. It's not that I was glad the dealers had been killed. I wasn't. But it happened, and more often than on that one occasion.

Nobody was embarrassed. I returned to work.

That wasn't hard to do, because I had never stopped.

✳   ✳   ✳

I SPENT over three years in Turkey, fighting throughout the Near and Middle East. I operated on my own and with whatever allies I could find, and I relied on my own discretion and judgment. I received the Exceptional Service Award from the general director of the Turkish National Police, a Special Service Award from the U.S. Treasury Department, as well as a Superior Performance Award from Treasury. (Awards and commendations are one of the prime currencies of success for those in government service. In the course of my career, I've garnered a score of such citations and decorations, including the Excellence of Performance Award from the DEA, the Extraordinary Service Award from the Office of Special Investigations of the U.S. Air Force, a Special Award of Honor from the International Narcotics Officers Association, awards from police departments in Baltimore, San Antonio, and Arizona, and on and on.)

While I enjoyed unprecedented and perhaps even extraordinary success, it was no cut-and-dried business. I had my false leads, dead ends, wasted efforts. I spent a fair amount of time cultivating a semi-famous Turkish actor who claimed to be in with big-time drug dealers. In my undercover guise, I accompanied him on trips into the mountains and wined and dined him at the Hilton Hotel in Istanbul, even letting him take a spin on the dance floor with Ava.

But it was a waste of time. He was all talk and no action. All that talk added up to nothing.

Hey, in this business, you had to kiss a lot of fast-talking, con-artist frogs to find a drug-dealing prince, to coin a phrase.

Regardless, this was an instance where different government agencies, working independently of one another—from the Bureau of Narcotics in Turkey and the region, represented by me, at the start of the heroin pipeline, to the NYPD, represented by a handful of dedicated cops at the final, receiving end of the enterprise—bore down and did not let up and halted the heroin trade. Let me repeat that: We halted the Turkey-to-France-to-the-U.S. connection, no two ways about it, and kept it under control as long as we kept on the pressure.

Yes, other gangs and other routes took its place, and opium from the so-called Golden Triangle, primarily the Southeast Asian countries of Burma, Laos, Vietnam, and Thailand, would quickly emerge as a giant problem, especially as the Vietnam War intensified and American troops flooded into the region.

Still, rather obviously, if we could stop the flow of heroin in one place, why not another and another and another? Today, Afghanistan is the foremost producer of opium, a trade controlled by our bitter enemies, the Taliban and Al Qaeda. As of this writing, the United States has 27,000 troops in that country, along with air bases, intelligence assets, and other resources. During 2006, our government spent more than $420 million combating Afghan narcotics. Nonetheless, according to a report released by the inspectors general of the U.S. State and Defense departments, 2.9 million Afghans were involved in cultivation, equivalent to an eighth of the population, and acreage devoted to poppy cultivation in 2006 was about 59 percent higher than in 2005. What's the problem? Evidently, the United States would like to focus on eradication—destroying the poppy fields—while the Afghans and also our British allies would prefer to concentrate on long-term crop substitution.

Without going into policy matters or tactical details, in a country that we liberated from terrorists and fundamentalists, a country now given a chance to build a decent, reasonable, fairer government and thus create the opportunity for a better life for its people, a country where we have spent $23 billion on reconstruction since our 2001 invasion, is it too much to state that we should have no hesitation and no opposition in demanding that we immediately intensify the effort to starve our enemies and protect our citizens by stopping the export of opium, by whatever means necessary?

We stopped the Turkish drug trade with far fewer resources and different though just-as-difficult circumstances than we have in Afghanistan today—we stopped it essentially with one man, working with whomever would help. If we did it once, we can do it again. Assuming we, as a nation, really want to—and that's a question that has yet to be decided.

BACK HOME

I COMPLETED my tour of duty and came back home, a welcome respite, especially for my family, from the inconveniences of foreign service. We were reunited with all the people and things we loved so much: family, friends, phones, paved roads, pizza, cheeseburgers, television, and everything else you can think of that makes America so American.

The year was 1964, and I was special agent-in-charge in San Antonio, Texas, with jurisdiction from the Texas border with Mexico up to Waco. The drug trade between the United States and Mexico was heating up, and the southern border—Texas, New Mexico, Arizona, California—was wide open. Just like it still is, by the way.

The shutdown of the Canadian/New York end of the French Connection meant that heroin and other drugs were increasingly rerouted through Latin America and Mexico into the United States. And so the war continued, fought on another front.

I worked closely with the Texas Department of Public Safety, the Bexar County Sheriff's Department, the San Antonio PD's narcotics squad, and local law enforcement in towns throughout Texas, but fought with U.S. Customs, which had about 300 agents, with primary jurisdiction for the border. Customs guarded its prerogative jealously, and that made for turf battles that obstructed the mission.

But that was the way it always goes—you take the good with the bad.

Case: A two-month investigation led to the arrest of a San Antonio man and the seizure of $100,000 worth of heroin.

Case: Five men and women were arrested after a raid by federal, state, and local officers uncovered a large quantity of marijuana and barbiturates.

Case: Four and a half ounces of heroin, valued at $35,000, was grabbed, and two men and a woman were charged with illegally importing and selling a narcotic.

Case: Fourteen were arrested in a multiagency raid that also netted a sizable amount of illegal drugs. It was the fourth large-scale raid in ten months in San Antonio, resulting in the capture of dozens of drug suspects.

Case: I personally led the raiding party that confiscated half a million dollars' worth of pure heroin and an abundant quantity of procaine, a synthetic cocaine, as well as a tall stack of $20 bills, in the biggest drug haul in the city's history.

And that was just the beginning.

Case: I didn't have enough agents to work all the cases we had going, so even though I was a supervisor, a boss, I went back undercover. In that guise, I met a Mexican dealer in San Antonio, purchased a sample of heroin, and arranged to buy a considerably larger amount. Cutting to the chase, I enticed the dealer to personally deliver the heroin in front of the federal building that housed the Bureau of Narcotics. When the dealer showed up, I came downstairs, arrested him, and brought him right up to my office.

Case: In a somewhat similar instance, I bought heroin several times from another Mexican national, entering into negotiations for a much greater purchase. A few days later, before the deal could be consummated, I was walking through the lobby of the very same federal building when I spotted the Mexican. He was filling out a civil service application for a job at a military base.

The dealer saw me and smiled. "Hey, man," he said, "you work here?"

Even though my undercover identity hadn't been blown, this was too close for comfort.

"Yes, I do," I said. "And you're under arrest."

Case: Posing as an Italian drug dealer from Chicago, I traveled to Ciudad Acuña, a small city in Mexico. My target was a fugitive from America, and the Bureau of Narcotics wanted him back. I tracked him, made contact, initiated negotiations, and agreed on a deal, quickly leading to his capture by the Mexican federal police and a trip back to the United States.

Case: I assisted my Mexican colleagues in another situation involving a couple of other dealers. Still playing the role of the Chicago drug dealer, I made the approach and was soon accepting delivery of twenty ounces of heroin. The *federales* were on the scene, ready to round up the pair.

One of the panicked dealers made a run for it. He didn't have a chance. The cops had him in their sights and were about to shoot.

I jumped up and tackled the dealer, who had come to his senses and proceeded to hug me, thanking me for saving his life. Then I turned him over to the Mexicans, still in one piece.

Case: Drugs were running rampant through the high schools and colleges. We received word that a trio of high school students, including the son of a local police chief, was selling marijuana by bulk throughout the city. Though I was thirty-five years old, I took the direct approach, without benefit of an informant, and briefly went undercover at the group's high school. Before long, I had purchased several pounds of pot. All of the boys were eighteen years old at the time of their arrest—no longer juveniles facing juvenile penalties, but full-fledged adults facing adult consequences.

✳   ✳   ✳

THE DRUG war kept expanding, and more and more cops and agents and agencies were thrown into the breach. In San Antonio, the Bureau of Narcotics, which led the federal government's end of the fight, was part of the Treasury Department. But the narcotics bureau was not the sole federal agency in town. In 1966, the Bureau of Drug Abuse Control was formed under the jurisdiction of the Food and Drug Administration, which was itself a component of the Department of Health, Education, and Welfare (HEW). The Bureau of Narcotics focused on what were regarded as "hard narcotics," such as heroin, morphine, and other opium derivatives, as well as marijuana. This new agency was charged with pursuing LSD, barbiturates, mescaline, amphetamines, and peyote-type drugs. Three hundred agents were recruited for HEW's latest bureaucratic addition, many of whom were narcotics bureau veterans.

President Lyndon Johnson soon realized that this split authority didn't make any sense. He had the Bureau of Narcotics, which by this time was reorganized as the Bureau of Narcotics and Dangerous

Drugs (BNDD), absorb the Bureau of Drug Abuse Control. This merger, as logical as it was, would lead to some problems as agents and administrators vied for position and power. The two directors of the individual agencies became associate directors of the new bureau, and an outsider, John Ingersoll, the police chief of Charlotte, North Carolina, was brought in as the boss. As you might imagine, that set the stage for intrigue on a scale that would do a Greek tragedy proud. I always tried my best to stay out of the fray, and on this occasion I succeeded. I would not always be so lucky, as you will soon see.

Speaking of bureaucratic infighting, the Bureau of Narcotics and the Federal Bureau of Investigation had always had something of an adversarial relationship, embodied by the legendary founders of the two agencies, Harry Anslinger of the BN and J. Edgar Hoover of the FBI. Part of the fundamental and quite bitter dispute between the departments resulted from Hoover's decades-long insistence that the Mafia did not exist, that organized crime was a fiction. Anslinger knew better because the mob was deeply involved in drugs. Hoover had his own political reasons for denying the existence of the Mafia, such as his overriding interest in pursuing Communists and other subversives. Regardless of his motivations, Hoover's intransigence, which forced a draining, wasteful battle between the agencies, inevitably hurt the national effort in the drug war.

The failure of the federal government and its many agencies to work together and tackle this problem in the most efficient manner possible only made the situation worse, which, in convoluted government-think, only benefited both agencies, allowing them to further validate their existences and increase their budgets and power. In brief, the government's very incompetence was the justification for giving that same government more taxpayer money to do the job at which it had already failed.

✶　✶　✶

I **WAS** named special agent-in-charge in Washington, D.C. The assignment only lasted eight months; not long, but long enough to make my usual number of cases.

I initiated an investigation into reports that a bureau deputy director based in Baltimore had gone bad. This fellow had joined us from HEW's Bureau of Drug Abuse Control, and he had become something of a rival, for really no sensible reason—just bureaucratic careerism at play. I had solid information that he was selling heroin out of his office. Because of the intra-agency tension the merger had created, my investigation had to be handled with the utmost discretion. The probe was classified as a secret mission by Commissioner Henry Giordano. Eventually, confronted with the evidence, the deputy director caved, flipped, and implicated his confederates, some of whom were also agents.

In another case, I was posing as the owner of a Pittsburgh pizza joint that specialized in selling "pizza over the counter and marijuana under the counter," to quote a man known as "Big Joe." Big Joe and his buddy, "Little Joe," were happy to supply the Pittsburgh restaurateur with forty-five pounds of pot for $4,000 in cash.

Nothing out of the ordinary, not in the drug business. Not so far.

I first met the boys in a Georgetown eatery where they had established something of a reputation in the D.C. drug community. The boys were aged twenty-one and twenty. The younger man—Little Joe—was the son of a fairly prominent Virginia public official.

One of my informants introduced us, and I played the role of the eager buyer. I responded, as my newfound pals would expect an out-of-town wholesaler to respond, with enthusiasm. We arranged to exchange the merchandise for the money. I'd done it a thousand times before, and with guys a lot smarter and tougher than these two. These boys were nothing—small-time, small-fry, maybe one step above amateurs.

So one dark May night, I drove up in a shiny red Cadillac (which we had seized from the drug dealer and used to present the right front) and picked up both Joes. I told them I had brought their money, four grand cached in a paper bag locked in the truck, so they were happy. I forgot to mention that along with the dough, I had stashed a fellow agent in that big trunk. I also forgot to mention that a second car of agents was following us.

We cruised into Virginia. It was nearing 2 a.m. The road was deserted.

Business as usual.

The Joes told me "a man driving a milk truck" had the dope, and we were meeting up with him at a lookout point on the George Washington Parkway just below Dolly Madison Boulevard.

Okay.

When we reached the spot, nobody was there. No milk truck, no milkman. Little Joe got out of the car and walked to a trash can to see if the supplier had left a message. He returned with directions to drive toward the town of Vienna.

Okay. Drug deals aren't planned in a lawyer's office. (Well, *most* drug deals aren't planned in a lawyer's office.) Schedules aren't fixed. Things change. Problems arise. People adapt.

We drove on. We left the main road and turned onto a dirt path, which was some unsuspecting soul's lonely driveway. I spotted my backup off to the side of the road, sitting in a car, angling in to park close by.

The Joes told me to stop the car. The driveway was very isolated, very dark, and very quiet.

I had seen this movie before, and it was not a comedy.

I said I was tired of this runaround and was heading back to Washington. However, before I could turn the car around, both Joes pulled out handguns, pointed them at me, and announced that they wanted the money. There was no marijuana, they told me. Surprise!

Big Joe demanded the keys so he could get the paper bag and the loot out of the trunk. Little Joe stuck the gun into the back of my neck. I handed Big Joe the keys, and he opened his door and stepped out. I knew I couldn't let him open that trunk. The agent hiding there wouldn't have a chance.

Little Joe ordered me to place my hands on the steering wheel. His gun was starting to dig a hole in my neck. It was time to act.

I told him I was a federal agent and used my best command voice to order him to hand over his weapons and tell Big Joe to come back. My words caused Little Joe to pause and consider. That was all the opening I needed, because I had no intention of waiting for his decision. I whirled around and reached for the gun. I grabbed it, but Little Joe managed to hold on. We struggled for several moments, and then I lost my grip.

A bullet passed by my head and smashed through the windshield as I lunged for the door handle, and then more bullets ripped into my seat. I managed to push the door open, and as I fell out of the car and on my knees, I heard several more shots whistle past.

As I pulled my Smith & Wesson .38 with the two-inch barrel from my inside jacket pocket, I quickly calculated that Little Joe's pistol was empty. I turned toward the rear of the Caddy, because my first concern was for my fellow agent still locked in the trunk.

Big Joe was ready. His handgun was aimed at me, and he pulled the trigger.

Nothing happened—the gun misfired. But that didn't mean the weapon would necessarily continue to misfire.

I had definitely had enough. It's personal when they start shooting point-blank at you, whether it's at the back of your head or the front.

I returned fire before Big Joe could clear his gun and start banging away. I shot at Big Joe six times and missed. In my defense, I was to the side of the trunk and Big Joe was behind it, and I had to shoot high to make certain I didn't strike the car and hit my fellow agent.

On the other hand, I never was the best shot, as I might have previously mentioned.

Bang, bang, bang, bang, bang, bang. I should have hit the son of a bitch at least once. But it was not to be: Six shots and I was done. I was out of bullets.

Where the hell was my backup? Where the hell was that second car? They had to have heard those shots.

I didn't drop my gun. I didn't put it down, because even though I knew I was essentially unarmed, I could see that the bad guys didn't know it. So I kept pointing my two-incher at both Joes, Big and Little, and returned to my command voice.

Surrender, I ordered in a harsh tone. You are surrounded. Other agents are moving in. You are surrounded. Surrender. Give up.

I kept talking because as long as somebody talks, and somebody listens, nobody shoots. It's really true. Most people have to stop and think before they can pull the trigger and fire. The two actions seem to be incompatible. I'll leave it to you to consider whatever larger lessons might be lurking there.

The pair of Joes hesitated. Mexican standoff. Bluff and counterbluff.

The agent in the trunk, hearing me shout that the area was surrounded by feds, started to yell. I kept talking. Sometimes the Joes, confused, panicked, half-rabid, threatened to kill the agent still locked in the trunk; sometimes they threatened to kill me. I just kept talking. I talked for twenty unbelievably long minutes.

Eventually, the Joes calmed down just enough to lose their nerve, realizing they didn't have the stomach to keep going, to slug it out to the death. They were more scared idiots than hard-core killers, and they must have figured they had no way out, no guaranteed, clean way out, unless they wanted to keep shooting and getting shot at, and maybe get themselves killed—assuming I had bullets, of course.

I took their guns, handcuffed them, and got my buddy out of the Caddy's trunk. The poor guy was so angry at what happened—angry at the two Joes, angry at the missing backup, just plain angry—that he fired two shots into the air in a furious attempt to alert the backup.

Astonishingly, after everything that had already occurred, his action worked. The agents arrived a few moments later, in a hurry. (I later learned that the agents in the backup vehicle had inexplicably rolled up their windows and were listening to the radio, which explained how they managed to miss the entire shoot-out. Later in his career, one of those agents would become fairly well known as the head of the New York office. When he retired and wrote his memoirs, I seem to recall that he somehow omitted this incident from the tome.)

Examining the car the next day, I discovered just how close I had come to my final showdown. The red Cadillac was punctured by bullet holes through the windshield, the dashboard, all over. One was especially interesting. You see, the Caddy was equipped with every luxury extra its former owner could buy, and that included a pull-down tray attached to the back of the front seats, similar to those found in an airplane. The trays were constructed of steel, apparently heavy-duty steel, because I found serious dents in the tray where bullets had struck and been deflected. Without that tray, those bullets would have ripped through the seat and struck me right in the back.

God, I loved that car.

The Joes were convicted of assaulting a federal agent. Each received a five-year sentence.

I received a nice letter of commendation from U.S. Attorney Ramsey Clark, and a $500 cash award.

Case closed. Next.

✳   ✳   ✳

MY NEXT assignment was as the deputy regional director of the Maryland Region, based in Baltimore. The BNDD, as you might recall, had been shifted from Treasury to the Justice Department, and I worked pretty much directly for Deputy Attorney General

Richard Kleindienst. It was during the Nixon administration, and the President was cracking down on drugs, leading to Operation Intercept along the Mexican border.

I was stationed in Long Beach, California, and was constantly on the go, monitoring events, talking to the troops, checking on results. As detailed earlier, Operation Intercept came and went, but it showed, once again, just like in Turkey, that the battle was not hopeless, not when it's conducted with all-out vigor and tenacity.

And the battle had to be fought on all fronts, which was a lesson that was thrust in my face over and over back in Baltimore, where, between my border responsibilities, I was still working cases.

Case: A twenty-eight-year-old third-grade teacher at a parochial school was arrested with five ounces of cocaine in her purse, with a potential street value of $90,000.

Case: In a house in a quiet upper-income neighborhood, we discovered $35,000 worth of marijuana. I spent six months undercover to reach this moment. The story began, as it usually did, on the street, negotiating with small-time pushers, and gradually led to larger and larger purchases, with bigger and bigger dealers, culminating in an invitation to walk through the door of this two-story frame house and get down to the real dealing. After examining the merchandise, I managed to sidle up to a window and signal the police waiting outside to raid the place. Seconds later, it was all over. Five men were taken into custody.

Mundane cases they were—at least more mundane when compared to international intrigue in Turkey or Mexico—but the inevitable result of a war fought globally, with consequences, along with pain and suffering, that reached everywhere.

✳   ✳   ✳

FOUR MONTHS after Operation Intercept was abruptly shut down, I was appointed the regional director for Mexico and Central and South America. I was thirty-eight years old and the youngest regional director in the bureau's history. It had taken all my diplomatic skills (and maybe a little more) to survive the considerable political fallout from Operation Intercept, but here I was, taking on one big job.

It was an interesting time to assume such an important position. Many Mexican officials, as well as ordinary citizens, were still angry about the operation. As the *Baltimore Sun* reported, "The Mexican press, which does not venture far beyond the bounds of government policy, reacted as if Mr. Nixon and Mr. Mitchell were telling the whole world that all Mexicans were smugglers and defilers of American youth."

Happy or not, I was headquartered in Mexico City and had to find a way to work with the Mexicans. Just as Turkey had been the center of the drug war in the early sixties, so Latin America was rapidly emerging as the nexus for the worldwide drug conspiracy in the seventies, giving me the distinction of being the only U.S. narcotics enforcement agent to not only serve but also supervise in the two hottest places in the world for drugs.

Once again, Ava had to pack up the house and kids and move. You might recall that our son was almost two years old when we moved to Turkey. Eight years later, we had a baby girl, who was now the two-year-old in the family.

Once again, Ava would be left largely on her own to handle the family as I took on this daunting task. I had some specifics in mind and some ideas how to achieve those goals. My first objective was resurrecting and reinventing Operation Intercept.

Never mind the political uproar the operation had created and the resistance I was guaranteed to encounter from Washington. In addition, anyone who has ever worked for the government knows that nothing is more difficult than restarting a program. The normal vicious bureaucratic infighting over credit and control is magnified a thousandfold when the program has a history and a specific agency has a stake in that history.

No matter. I had a twist on the original plan that I believed would succeed, and I was determined to see it through. I embarked on a round of lobbying and pushing and promoting and some late-night drinking to convince the attorney general, the deputy attorney general, and others holding the highest ranks in the American government that Operation Intercept needed to be reborn as Operation Cooperation, a name chosen for its friendly, encompassing spirit. Spirit aside, where Intercept concentrated solely on the border, Cooperation was intended to strike deep into Mexico. More than anything else, Intercept and Cooperation resembled one another in the uproar each was guaranteed to create throughout Mexico.

I threw in something of a bone to ease the pain for the politicians—I included Canada in the plan so it didn't look like we were picking on Mexico. Of course, Canada and our northern border wasn't an issue then, but politics demanded we look evenhanded. (This was a time before the terms "politically correct" and "racial profiling" were in vogue, so "evenhanded" will have to do.) I scheduled in two meetings every month: one down on the Mexican border with my fellow American feds and our Mexican counterparts, and a duplicate meeting up on the Canadian border.

Eventually, the big bosses came around to my proposal. Kleindienst used to travel quite often to Mexico, and we'd talk for hours, outlining new strategies and reviewing the progress of plans already underway. His support, and the support of President Nixon, showed me how invaluable real leadership is in any fight. Our ambassador in Mexico—for once—was neither contemptuously obstructionist nor aggressively troublesome. Nevertheless, in line with his State Department lineage and bureaucratic priorities, he was also not overly interested in stirring up diplomatic problems with excessive talk about dynamic drug enforcement.

However, once it became clear that the President of the United States had made the drug war a priority, regularly dispatching the number-two man at Justice and other officials to Mexico City to meet with me, then the ambassador and his staff fell in step with the program. The same applied to the CIA, which had a strong presence in the region and never hesitated to assert its self-appointed authority over any issue. Without the President behind me, I would have wasted a ludicrous amount of time waging war with the spy agency. With the President's backing, the CIA and the ambassador, not to mention Customs, the FBI, and the rest, had to acknowledge my primacy in the drug war.

In short, when the dust settled, nobody was willing to mess with my agents or with me. And that meant I could do my job without having to constantly look over my shoulder.

One example: A Panamanian air traffic controller was being paid off to help drug-transport planes sneak past radar checks into the United States. Naturally, I wanted to nail him, but I had no authority as long as he stayed out of the Canal Zone, which was American territory on Panamanian soil. I learned that the man had one weakness (apart from being corrupt): He loved playing softball, and he especially loved playing in a game that was regularly held in the Canal Zone at the military base with American soldiers. And that's how we nabbed him, luring him onto the base with the promise of softball. We got him and locked him up and quickly shipped him back to the United States via unmarked jet to stand trial for international drug trafficking.

I received a fair measure of political heat for the arrest and plane ride. The Panamanian government was more than a bit upset, which of course upset the American ambassador. The air traffic controller was close to the Panamanian leader, General Manuel Noriega, and other Panamanian officials. It was an awkward situation from a diplomatic viewpoint—good police work from the law enforcement perspective. And in this instance, the priorities of law enforcement won out.

That's how it rolled when I had Washington behind me. Nobody dared get too seriously in my way, and the job got done.

Operation Cooperation was immediately successful. American agents, money, and technology helped Mexican police track down marijuana fields, heroin shipments, and drug laboratories. Virtually every week brought a new achievement, another victory.

Senator Charles Percy of Illinois had been "deeply disturbed" by Operation Intercept. The success of Operation Cooperation made just as powerful an impact on him. In fact, the esteemed Republican senator felt moved to insert a newspaper article into the Congressional Record that listed some of our accomplishments:

> In Tijuana, officials of both countries ran down a dope ring that had been supplying heroin, cocaine, and marijuana for the past fifteen years. In San Antonio, the former head of the Mexican secret service and his accomplices were picked up with marijuana valued by police at forty-four million. Close to three thousand pounds of marijuana was taken, and eighteen persons were picked up in a raid on a ranch in the state of Michoacan. Three barge loads, about eight thousand pounds, were seized on the California coast after their trip from Mexico—all this and more, in May alone.

The drug trade was changing. The violence was accelerating. The Mafia used to control the drug traffic. Its bosses and soldiers were always tough, frequently brutal, and sometimes murderous, but even the Mafia, despite its central psychotic disposition, had its boundaries. For one, it had rules against killing police or reporters or family members of even their bitterest enemies.

However, the mob was under serious assault by law enforcement. Overseas, we had broken the Turkish connection and damaged the European link with the drug trade. All this had happened just as both the narcotics markets and profits exploded. Such a market violation upsets basic economic imperatives and so cannot exist for long. Thus, as the Mafia's control weakened, others rushed to fill the breach.

Entrepreneurs throughout Latin America were among the first to take advantage of this opportunity. The drugs that had been shipped through Canada and New York were now moving through South America and Panama. I fought in Mexico and throughout Central America, and then expanded the fight south. I opened an office in Buenos Aires because the routing for drugs used to come through Argentina and Paraguay, then into Panama and north to Miami. When Miami got hot, the drugs started coming in across Mexico in increasing quantities. French heroin, called white powder for its purity, was often routed to Chicago and New York. Mexican heroin, or brown heroin, was easy to find throughout the southwestern states.

The Mafia's relatively restrained rules about murder were summarily tossed out by the Latin drug rings. The Colombian drug dealers, in particular, rapidly established well-deserved reputations as killers who would torture and murder not only their rivals and enemies, but also their parents and wives and children and friends.

The Mexicans were no slouches either when it came to violence. The war between the dealers and police could be ugly and bloody. Mexico resembled Turkey in several respects—the terrain was rough, the cops were underpaid, the people were poor, the government was sometimes ineffective and corrupt, the drugs were abundant, and ever more so, the danger was real.

Not every bust made the papers.

I was running an investigation into a fairly sizable drug ring. We had progressed to the point where I had two undercover American agents and three Mexican federal police officers ready to make a large marijuana buy. They were carrying a nice bundle of cash, driving deep into the mountains, approximately a hundred miles outside of Acapulco.

Unfortunately, my agents deviated from my instructions not to veer far from the main road. My information and my experience told me that trouble was brewing. The local cops, who more closely resembled a gang of security guards for hire than a legally authorized and directed police unit, could not be trusted.

No matter. When my agents did exactly what they were told not to do and were lured off the road, the ambush was sprung. The deal went bad, the shooting started. Way up in the mountains, far from supervisory oversight or intervention, the local police were no good. They were compromised and corrupted, and they were out to kill my men and steal the cash.

Two of our Mexican officers, federales, were critically wounded. The American agents returned fire and killed five of the attackers.

Somehow, the agents and federales escaped. But that was not the end, not by any measure. We couldn't leave it at that. No damn way. Not the Mexican government, and not this American official.

Not long after, I accompanied a contingent from the Mexican army that headed into the mountains. It didn't take us long to locate the surviving members of the village police unit that had attacked the agents. A ferocious gun battle erupted. Several of the bad guys were killed and many others were captured. The Mexicans dealt summarily with the murderous cops.

I know I often refer to the fight against drugs as a "battle" and a "war." After reading some of these stories, perhaps you have a better understanding why.

✹　✹　✹

THE PROBLEM of corruption is a matter of money, mortality, and morality. It destroys lives and souls. It tears apart families and governments.

And with so much money floating through the drug world—so much easy, available, untraceable money—corruption is pernicious and pervasive.

For most honest people confronted with evidence of corruption on the part of a colleague or business associate, the impulse is to turn him in or simply turn away. This impulse, however expressed, this repulsion, is not only entirely normal, it is healthy.

It is also a luxury.

As an agent or administrator in the field, that luxury is not an option. The job has to get done. The locals have to be consulted and considered. The politicos and generals and cops have to be wooed and won over. They're either with you or against you. If they're against you, you're dead. If they're with you—well, that can mean many things. But at least you're not dead.

I had to deal with Manuel Noriega. In the early seventies, he was chief of military intelligence of the Panamanian National Guard and the power behind the country's leader, and his personal mentor, General Omar Torrijos. Torrijos would later die when his plane exploded in midair, courtesy of a bomb most likely planted by Lieutenant Colonel Noriega, clearing the way for Noriega to seize complete control of Panama.

I had to go down into the bunker that served as his headquarters and let him know what we were doing, more or less, and consult with him on strategy and resources and schedules. I had to work with him even though I knew the stories about payoffs and dirty dealing and the entire range of brutal, criminal corruption that began with Noriega and filtered down, throughout his coterie of aides and ministers and flunkies, throughout the National Guard that was the backbone of his power.

The BNDD knew that Noriega was involved with drug dealers, murderers, and every other type of scum it was possible to find in Latin America. He was not the passive sort, either, but dispatched pilots and others to facilitate drug transport into the

United States. We also knew one more thing—that Noriega was on the CIA payroll and had been for years. He was considered a vital part of the war between democracy and communism raging throughout Latin America, assisting those we supported fighting in Nicaragua and El Salvador. Noriega played both sides: He would secretly fly in weapons to the contras, on behalf of the CIA, and fly out drugs, destined for the States, for Columbia's notorious Medellin cartel. He established what a U.S. Senate subcommittee investigating our relationship with Noriega would call our hemisphere's first "narcokeptocracy."

*　*　*

THE PANAMANIAN government wasn't that dissimilar from other governments with which I dealt. That was the name of the game—dealing. You either dealt with the powers that be or you didn't, and if you chose the latter path, then you might as well have packed up and gone home. And we couldn't afford to not be there, not with the havoc that drugs were causing back home.

I wouldn't claim that the Panamanians or the Mexicans or the Colombians or any of the others were always straight with us, or were always gung ho to pursue the bad guys, or were interested in making every case. But we had no choice because the locals were playing on their own turf, and we were there to play. And play we did.

The American government cannot reform every corrupt or inept regime and society around the world. Of course, considering that our own government is hardly infallible, let alone incorruptible, it would be presumptuous to think that we could. Regardless, we have to protect our borders and our people to the best of our abilities, even if that means sometimes dealing with those who do not come close to matching ordinary standards of decency and honesty.

In our drug war, the boundaries we establish and abide by are those of our own values. So we must act whenever we can, whenever we have a chance of achieving success, whenever we can thwart the flow of drugs into our nation, whenever we can accomplish our goals without compromising our basic values.

Those standards and values determine the limits of our own official tolerance. Some governments are beyond the pale of conduct of any kind. Paraguay assuredly came close to that line, practically fudging those boundaries.

It all went back to Turkey and the French Connection, and the massive, international drug/criminal/subversive organization that arose out of that conspiracy. (I include subversive because many of the people involved in drugs in South America were also involved in insurgent groups and activities.)

As the moviegoers among you will recall, at the end of the film *The French Connection*, the mastermind behind the organization got away clean, disappearing into thin air off the New York docks. And while I am not inclined to call upon a Hollywood movie for factual verification, and the facts in that otherwise fine film were more than a little skewed—in particular, overstating the significance of the New York link for the movie's dramatic purposes—the general notion of a mastermind who escaped was true.

I had fought this mastermind and his organization in Turkey and was about to fight this same man again. The final chapter in this saga was about to be written.

After all these years, I had tracked down Auguste Ricord. He was a nasty piece of work: Il Comandante, as he was nicknamed, was a World War II French war criminal who had collaborated with the Gestapo after the Nazis conquered France. (Finally, a moment in this book when invoking the Nazis is actually appropriate.) A member of the Carlingue (the French Gestapo), he had taken part of the funds stolen by the Carlingue during the war to build drug laboratories around Marseilles. When the Turkey-to-New York route was shut down, Ricord shifted his operation to Paraguay. South America was a favorite destination of Nazis on the run, and Paraguay welcomed them with open arms. General Alfredo Stroessner, yet another Juan Perón wannabe (i.e., another brutal, greedy dictator with an oversized view of his petty regime) ruled for forty-five horrid years, building palaces and monuments to himself while the people starved. He not only granted Paraguayan citizenship to Josef Mengele, the maniacal "doctor" who performed unspeakable experiments on concentration camp inmates, but was rumored to be a close friend of the Angel of Death.

In such a place, Ricord found a home. Presiding over his reconstituted drug network from a nightclub in Asunción, Paraguay's capital, Ricord worked with American Mafia drug kingpin Santo Trafficante, Jr., to smuggle heroin from Paraguay to New York. In short order, he had smuggled $145 million worth of heroin into our country with the active cooperation of the Paraguayan government, which provided everything from passports to planes to a landing strip for those planes.

Unlike other drug lords, and definitely unlike members of the Paraguayan government, Ricord maintained a low profile. He lived simply, quietly, trying not to attract attention. (This was in sharp contrast to General Andres Rodriguez, the father-in-law of Stroessner's coke-addled son, Freddy, and a trusted confederate until he overthrew Stroessner and took power. Rodriguez's home was an astonishing, obscene replica of Versailles, built with the money he had earned from his dealings with Ricord. In fact, Rodriguez provided the transport planes I mentioned, and the landing strip was located on his ranch. In a startling move, undoubtedly unprecedented in its unselfish decency in the Paraguayan story, *El Presidente* Rodriguez would institute political, legal, and economic reforms that would lead to the first truly free elections in that country's history and help establish a democracy.)

Ricord quietly went about his day and his business, doing without his own knockoff historic palace, or private zoo, or army of bodyguards. He was smart, and he was connected across South

America. Scores of politicos, bureaucrats, soldiers, cops, and others were all neatly and regularly paid off, allowing him to run the biggest smuggling ring in the country and operate around the globe. Paraguay was a strange and isolated country, landlocked by geography, cut off by the character of its bizarre, forbidding state.

Regardless, it was a country, so the State Department had an ambassador and an embassy planted in Asunción. And, as usual, the U.S. ambassador's first priority was protecting his bit of turf. Having American drug agents messing around in his little patch was decidedly not on his program.

As per protocol, I informed the ambassador of my investigation, and the ambassador told me I couldn't work operationally on the ground or with the local police. You see, even in a nation that corrupt, the ambassador knew there are always enough cops, local and federal, who believe in what they do and want to do what is right, enough good cops around for me to assemble a team and make some noise. And noise was just what he wanted to avoid.

"Of course I can operate," I replied.

So now we were in the middle of a bureaucratic jurisdictional dispute, intragovernment variety. When faced with such a problem, the only solution is to go to the top as quickly as possible. I called Dick Kleindienst.

The U.S. deputy attorney general immediately grasped the situation and set it right. In no time, the ambassador got the word—cooperate. I didn't have such optimistic plans for the ambassador and me. I just wanted him to stay out of the way. After that, the rest was no problem.

It had to be fast and covert. An unmarked government 707 was flown from the United States to Paraguay, landing in the middle of the night. I had my agents on the ground and a handful of honest local cops. The son of a bitch might have been smart, but he was easy pickings. Auguste Ricord was captured and hustled aboard the jet, which flew directly to Dallas, allowing us to forgo extradition problems between the two nations.

Ricord stood trial and was convicted. After almost a decade, my personal battle with the vicious, murderous organization known the world over as the French Connection, a battle I had waged from the bottom to the very top, beginning in the mountains of Turkey and ending in an airport outside Asunción, Paraguay, was finally over.

*　　*　　*

IT WAS time for Washington to screw up our efforts in the drug war again by reorganizing the BNDD into the Drug Enforcement Administration (DEA). The blood was in the water as jockeying for the most important jobs, the most impressive offices, and the most glamorous postings began in earnest.

Once again, I wasn't interested in politicking, I was a working agent, not a political animal. Not that it mattered this go-round, because it was my turn to get caught in the infighting. As you must have noted by now, I've ruffled more than a few feathers in pursuit of doing my job. I didn't suffer fools, politicians, or bureaucrats (or any blending of the three) gladly, and I didn't hesitate to run over anybody who stood between my objective and me.

Sure, I was good at my job, but combine that with my—how shall we say?—naturally outgoing personality and the two together made me a more attractive target in this typically ugly situation. And because D.C. turf battles are all about screwing with whatever already is, no matter the negative consequences, as long as it embarrassed or upset your enemies, I was dead in the crosshairs.

I was transferred to Washington, D.C., and given an office large enough to hold a basketball game, complete with spectators. The office came equipped with a combination lock on the door. The lock was a leftover from the previous occupant, who had been in charge of intelligence for the bureau.

I was designated section chief, Office of Intelligence, with responsibility for Turkey, which, in government terms, made perfect sense, as I had just spent almost a decade about as far from Turkey as you could get. I had no staff, no resources, and no one really expected or cared if I did anything approaching actual work.

Some people in my position would have surveyed the scene and decided their official careers were over, but that attitude wasn't part of my genetic code. I hadn't been fired—I had been too successful and was too valuable for that—but I had been put on ice. It was crap. I marched into the new administrator's office and told him exactly that, no-holds-barred and in definitely colorful language. I also told him I would be busting dealers and traffickers at the agency, whatever they wanted to call it, long after he had been booted out from his exalted standing.

My Washington exile lasted exactly one year, from July 1973 to July 1974. The wheel of fortune spun again and new bosses and new priorities emerged, and I was reassigned, back to a real job, back in the real world.

I was named deputy regional director for the Massachusetts Region, based in Boston. And while I might have been away from the field for a year, nothing had changed, not the bad guys and their motives and actions, nor our motives and actions in response.

Case: I discovered that two former federal narcotics agents were selling drugs and government secrets to drug traffickers, including the routes of U.S. military air patrols along the Mexican border. Most treacherously, the ex-feds supplied the names and identities of informants to the dealers, instantly placing the lives of these confidential sources in grave danger. When one of these turncoats was arrested in Washington, he was carrying a printout from a DEA computer with informant names and other invaluable information on it. The men charged between $500 and $2,000 per name, sometimes providing a photo as well. Not very much money for a person's life.

Case: Seven people were rounded up in Holyoke, Massachusetts, and another three in Chicago, in the course of breaking a million-dollar drug ring. Eleven pounds of heroin was grabbed, with a dealer-to-dealer value of $150,000 and a street value of more than $1 million.

Case: A second-year offensive tackle for the New England Patriots was arrested for selling cocaine on two occasions to an undercover agent. His capture was a small though highly publicized piece of our smashing a major international cocaine ring.

Case: Three people were seized in a luxury apartment complex, along with a half pound of cocaine and an ounce of heroin. As a bonus, $100,000 in stolen gems was also recovered.

☀   ☀   ☀

I WAS transferred to Phoenix in 1978, as the special agent-in-charge of Arizona. This was a job I wanted and a job I pushed hard to get. I had a couple of reasons.

First, Arizona was emerging as a vital spot in the drug war. As Latin American cartels took control of much of the international drug business, the always-porous border between Mexico and the United States became busier and more dangerous as the key trans-shipment point. And while we tend to think of Latin America in terms of the cocaine trade, the cartels were increasingly interested in diversifying, in pushing any product that had a market. For example, with the upsurge in heroin use, heroin labs were starting to be discovered in Latin America.

When I came to Arizona, the drug consumer could find available any narcotic that suited his taste or purpose. Lysergic acid diethylamide—LSD—was experiencing a dramatic surge in popularity. Heroin, marijuana, and amphetamines were all in abundance, soon followed by crack, angel dust, crystal meth, and anything else that could be grown, mixed, manufactured, ingested, inhaled, injected, bought, and sold.

Despite all the contenders, cocaine reigned as number one, and it maintains its hold on top position in the drug universe to this day. Cocaine emerged in the seventies as the most lucrative business in the United States, bigger than cars, computers, or clothes. At times, it seemed as if everybody wanted in. Everybody, of course, who was willing to step over the line and try for that easy money—laws, risks, and consequences be damned.

Case: Three men were arrested and $1 million in drugs was confiscated in Mesa. The largest component of the haul was 800,000 Valium tablets.

Case: A twenty-five-member federal and state task force raided a ranch house in the desert outside Camp Verde. The ranch contained a sophisticated drug laboratory, as well as numerous weapons, guard dogs, and communications equipment. Two men were arrested.

Case: A long-time supervisor for the Phoenix Country Club, who oversaw functions at the prestigious club, was arrested and charged with acting as a major importer of drugs from Mexico. Club members were quoted as being "completely shocked" by the arrest.

Case: Three men were taken into custody at a private residence located on the grounds of the exclusive McCormick Ranch in Scottsdale. A lab was discovered inside, with the capacity to manufacture four pounds of methamphetamine every forty-eight hours. One pound of the stuff had a street value of $100,000.

Case: A Phoenix hairstylist was charged with possession of cocaine with intent to distribute, and in quantity sufficient to earn her being held on a bond of $5 million. The arrest was part of a DEA investigation into a cocaine ring with ties in California, Iowa, Missouri, and Florida.

Case: A man was arrested in a Phoenix hotel room with five pounds of cocaine worth $500,000 on the street. Nothing unusual there, nothing that didn't happen far too frequently. What rendered this arrest deserving of note was that the man was the former head of the Phoenix office of the Arizona Criminal Intelligence System Agency, an official state bureau that acted as a clearinghouse for information on drugs and drug dealers in Arizona. He had worked for the agency for almost six years and had been dismissed a month before his arrest for unspecified "administrative reasons."

Case: Fifty-three people, including two Phoenix firemen, were indicted by a federal grand jury. All were suspects in a major cocaine ring based in Phoenix and stretching across seven states. More than a hundred DEA agents and local police units moved out at predawn in Phoenix as part of a coordinated effort to catch drug traffickers in Arizona, California, Florida, Hawaii, Iowa, Kansas, and Missouri. In addition to the firefighters, occupations of the traffickers ranged from clerk to stockbroker, janitor to lawyer.

Not long after the raid, one of the kingpins of the organization was also charged with conspiring to murder witnesses in the case after he approached fellow inmates in the Maricopa County jail, seeking to recruit hit men. His offer for the elimination of potential witnesses was $4,000 per murder.

✳   ✳   ✳

IN 1979, I initiated an investigation that eventually led to the largest heroin case ever made in Arizona and the second-largest in the United States. An Iranian national living in our country on a resident alien visa, and claiming to be an unemployed musician, was arrested with approximately twelve pounds of heroin. This was not brown heroin from Mexico or even the white variety from Turkey and France. No, this was heroin from the Golden Crescent of Afghanistan, Pakistan, and Iran, processed in Iranian laboratories, marking its first appearance in Arizona. This heroin was so pure that its street value was at least $20 million.

But that seizure was not the end of it. The drugs had been transported from Iran to Kuwait, and then flown by suitcase to Phoenix. Dubbed "the Kuwait Connection" by the media, this was not an instance of an individual acting alone; rather, it was a major conspiracy, with links to many gangs and perhaps even governments. In addition, this case was occurring at the same time that the fundamentalist regime of Ayatollah Khomeini was holding American citizens hostage in our embassy in Tehran, and American anger against Iran was running hot. The political dimensions could not be ignored.

Of the twelve original defendants, including the ringleader and his wife, nine were Iranian. They were clearly associated with a Middle Eastern gang that might very well have been connected to Khomeini's fiercely anti-American government. The radical Islamic state was short of cash, having effectively cut itself off from most of the rest of the world. The drug trade was a fast way to make a lot of money while striking a blow against its supposed enemies in the bargain.

The ringleader was let out on bail and arrested a few months later carrying another suitcase with $1.75 million in heroin stashed inside. Four more confederates were arrested, two of them Iranian.

The real questions were: How much heroin had slipped into the country before the conspiracy was uncovered? How many others who were part of the organization remained hidden throughout the country, and precisely what rank did the captured defendants occupy in the ring's hierarchy? And, most tantalizing and surely most dangerous of all, how deeply involved was the Iranian government in the smuggling operation?

I have made the point more than once that drugs must be fought at every level. This case illustrates that point. Drug cartels conspire with governments (as well as banks, airlines, and every other useful institution) to achieve their objectives. Sometimes, partners in these illicit ventures have different goals in mind, which may or may not overlap. In this instance, the traffickers might have been only interested in making as much as money as they could, while the ayatollahs might have been interested in both making money and inflicting harm on the United States. Having said that, in this case, it was more likely they were all tied together, greedy and religious at the same time, working together to cause maximum, profitable damage.

When the stakes are this high, the methods employed by the bad guys can be nothing less than brutal and cruel. It is imperative that we recognize these enemies for who and what they are and respond accordingly.

* * *

THERE WAS another reason I wanted to get transferred to Arizona (remember, there was a second reason), and that was because I was starting to think about the end of my federal career. It had been a long run, over three decades, and it had been a good run, too. I had traveled the world and encountered some of the best people, and probably even more of the worst people, on the planet. I had done a job that I regarded as important and necessary: important for protecting society, necessary for building a better one.

But I was also ready for a change. The Bureau of Narcotics that I had known was a virtually intimate group of a handful of agents operating semi-independently, relying on their own wits and skills. Now it had grown into the DEA, a mammoth bureaucracy divided into layers upon layers of divisions and offices, with over 5,000 special agents, an even greater number of support staff, and a budget of $2.415 billion in 2006. I bet the current DEA has more secretaries on staff than the Bureau of Narcotics had agents when I first joined up, when our 1957 budget was barely $6 million.

In so many ways, the modern DEA is eminently more capable, more sophisticated, and more powerful than the old BN, and its agents better trained, equipped, and supported—though, even so, the success rate of the DEA is no better, and perhaps significantly less, than what we achieved in the old days. A reasonable estimate is that back in those old days about 10 percent of the drugs heading into the United States were stopped; today, the projected percentage is—you guessed it—10 percent. And back then, we did stop some extremely virulent organizations and routes, from Turkey to Paraguay to Mexico.

We weren't fancy, but we were good.

I wasn't the only one ready for a change. I had led Ava and the kids around the world, going wherever the bureau sent me. They had had many remarkable experiences, seen many amazing places, lived a life unlike anything most people could even imagine. However, they deserved a permanent home, preferably in a nice, safe neighborhood in their own country. I had been everywhere, and I knew Arizona would be a wonderful last stop for my family.

I lobbied for Arizona, as did others, you can be sure, and was awarded the posting. I served for four years, then retired. I was still a relatively young man, fifty years old, and decided to try the business world. I opened a travel agency with my wife. We had a unique appreciation of both travel and foreign destinations, and the business was a success.

Still, I can't say I found it satisfying. After fighting the international drug trade, going head-to-head with the world's most dangerous criminals, and experiencing gunplay on a regular basis, booking plane tickets for family vacations didn't quite measure up.

I needed a new challenge, and I had a good one in mind.

I announced I was running for the Republican nomination for sheriff. I had never been involved in politics before but knew what had to be done. I spoke before any group that would have me. I raised a small amount of money for posters, mailers, and other expenses. I shook hands and gave a handful of interviews.

The officeholder at the time had received a serious black eye for botching the 1991 mass murder investigation known as the Buddhist temple murders. Two high school boys had slaughtered six monks and three other people, and the crime had gained international publicity—the bad kind of publicity, the kind no politician, community, or state wants. The pressure was on to solve the case.

Unfortunately, the sheriff had initially arrested the wrong people and subsequently paid out $4 million in settlements. He had embarrassed himself, the sheriff's office, and the state of Arizona in mishandling the case.

The sheriff was also a Republican, and I was confident I could take him in the primary. Still, it's never a sure thing when you take on an incumbent, but I took the nomination by four percentage points, by far the smallest margin of victory I would ever experience in my new career. The general election was a walkover, and just like that, I was the new sheriff of Maricopa County.

I had run enormous operations on behalf of the government of the United States. I had been in charge of dozens of agents spread over entire continents. I had not only managed and survived, but I had triumphed. With that background, I was confident I could handle this new position, this new responsibility.

I would win and achieve my goals, but it wasn't a day at the beach, especially in a county without any beachfront property. I would learn a lot, especially how different it is to be an elected official as opposed to an appointed officer, and how that not only changed your perspective but your fundamental ability to do your job, to be creative and bold and direct, and responsive to both the people and your own conscience.

I thought I would like the job. I thought I would appreciate the work and feel good about serving the community. I was right, and I was wrong. I did like the job. What I didn't realize was how much I would love it.

MEDIA MATTERS

IT'S TIME TO talk about the media. It's a topic I couldn't avoid even if I wanted to . . . not that I want to. Despite the gun battles, the record drug seizures, the international wheeling and dealing, my relationship to the media has created as much controversy and as much confusion as any action I've taken in my career. So let's take this one-sided opportunity to clear up any misunderstanding, once and for all.

Through all of my four terms in office, my relationship with the media has been both complicated and surprisingly predictable. The number of separate media outlets that have covered "the Sheriff Joe story" reaches well over 2,000. I've been interviewed thousands upon thousands of time, in every format imaginable, from neighborhood papers to local radio shows to major periodicals to national television programs to borderless websites. From *The Today Show* in the morning to *Lou Dobbs Tonight* in the afternoon to *60 Minutes* in the evening to *Nightline* late at night, I've been covered up and down, right to left, *by* the right and the left and those allegedly neutral. TV crews from Britain to Korea, Germany to Japan, have produced one-hour specials about my office and about me, and we have been the subject of numerous television series, not only in this country but overseas as well. Everything we do has been covered, from the tents and our version of punishment (for a thirteen-part reality show in England), to our efforts on behalf of animals (for an Animal Planet series), to numerous stories on the long-running program *America's Most Wanted*. I've been questioned, lectured, hectored, insulted, profiled, paneled, praised, and promoted.

I can count on one hand the recognizable programs on which I have not appeared, and try as I might, I'm not sure I can imagine a scenario in which Oprah Winfrey would invite me on her show.

My relationship with the media was and remains something of a love-hate situation, a bond that is necessary though sometimes ridiculous, sometimes twisted, and definitely, frequently contentious. As an elected official, it is imperative that I keep the public informed as to what I am thinking and what my office is doing. The right to feel safe within your home and in your community, to live free from fear, is the most basic right of any individual—and the most fundamental responsibility of government.

At the same time, the press has its own responsibility, which is, first, to shine a light on what's happening in government, and second, to act as the public's watchdog and investigate what that light reveals and what might be hiding in the darker corners.

Of course, while that is all absolutely true, it is also true that the media, in all their many forms, from television to print to radio to the Internet, are also many-headed businesses, competing first with each other and then with other forms of information, entertainment, and communication. And that ceaseless, ruthless competition colors how the various organs of the media see certain people and events, and what they do in response.

And that reality has affected the press coverage of me, and thus the press coverage of the Maricopa County Sheriff's Office, because that coverage has changed, and Lord knows I haven't. I haven't changed how I speak to the public, the politicians, or the press, and I haven't changed trying to be as aggressive and as innovative as possible, no matter how controversial those moves prove to be.

* * *

IN THE OLD days, going back a dozen years or more, when I first took office, the media were relentless. They really believed they were going to get me. They were going to catch me saying something so outrageous that I would lose the support of the people, or they were going to catch me doing something so horrific or bizarre or inhumane that my days as sheriff would be numbered. Not that most of them cared enough about what I was doing to object on political or philosophical grounds. No, "getting" me was merely a doorway to a higher profile and better job for the individual reporter and increased ratings and ad sales for TV stations and newspapers. The journalists came at me smiling the way vultures and sharks open their mouths, with ravenously wide, unlaughing grins, before devouring their prey. I understood from the start that in the eyes of too many journalists, this was all a show and we were all bit actors in their personally directed dramas, ultimately starring themselves. It might astonish you how often a reporter would try to pound me, accuse me of some preposterous offense, or trick me into some absurd admission—unsuccessfully, of course—the process dragging on for ten minutes, thirty minutes, an hour, and then, with the camera off or the pen down, that same belligerent reporter would smile and become another person, friendly and laughing, as though we're all in on the joke.

Prime example: Back in those old, relentless media days, a correspondent for an NBC newsmagazine show called *Now* (since deceased) came to town to do a profile of me. Despite NBC's stellar reputation as a bastion of honest journalism, the reporter arrived with a list of assumptions he not only intended to prove, but hammer home to the audience. He called posse members "brown-shirted," a vivid reference to Nazi Party members, and if anybody happened to miss the comparison, he neatly boxed his feelings into an unequivocal context: "If this graduation of brown-shirted posse members smacks of fascism, it doesn't bother the sheriff."

There are insults and then there are insults, and then there's being compared to the Nazis. And all this high-minded First Amendment venom was being directed at volunteers who spend their time, effort, and some money, too, patrolling their neighborhoods to make sure that the people who live there stay safe. Wow.

Whether that line of reasoning was more obnoxious or stupid was up for discussion, but it was hardly the only outrage perpetrated during that NBC visit. In fact, it was not my prime motivation in bringing up the interview out of the thousands of interviews I've done. I've chosen to highlight that network story because of what happened next.

You see, the NBC reporter and I tramped through all the usual hot-button issues—the jail, the posse, the chain gang, on and on—and then the man asked the predictable closer, after a proper introduction for the benefit of the audience: "Sheriff Joe has such a high profile that people who follow politics in these parts think he's running for something. The statehouse?"

Even though that sounded like a question, it wasn't. Instead, the reporter turned to me and said, "The big rap on you, Sheriff, is that you're sort of a media hog."

You'd think I was the one who had called the reporter, asked him to fly to Phoenix all the way from New York, asked him to show up and discover what a thousand reporters had discovered before him so that he could be the one to warn the world about the wild sheriff in the Wild West.

So I gave him the overtly obvious answer. "You know," I said, "you came to me, I didn't go to you."

"True," NBC's ace correspondent admitted. "I guess what I'm asking here—are you running for something?"

I laughed and shook my head. There was, of course, only one very simple, very direct answer. "No."

The son of a—I mean, the distinguished correspondent—didn't believe me. "You can tell me. Come on, Joe, you can tell me."

I thought I just had, but his patronizing manner said the message hadn't gotten through, and I basically addressed that. "Even if I told you no, you would never believe me."

"That's probably true."

"They keep saying, 'You're doing this for political reasons.' I just got elected!"

None of this moved him off his high perch. "Joe," he insisted, as though he had a right to insist on anything, "I want to hear a Sherman-like statement: 'I don't want to be governor. I'm not ever going to run for governor.' Repeat after me."

(Putting into perspective his obnoxious tone, I cannot help but note that correspondents routinely treat the most awful dictators and other miscreants with the utmost respect and outright deference. In fact, my comment at the time to one and all seems singularly relevant today, and I quote: "I wasn't sure why Saddam Hussein rated more courtesy than the sheriff of Maricopa County . . .")

Anyway, I played along and responded, "I do not want to be the governor. I want to be the sheriff. The sheriff is the best job in this country."

You'd think that would do it, assuming you're a normal person of normal intelligence, but that wasn't good enough for Mister NBC. "I will never run for governor," he intoned, as if stating a pledge.

"I will never run for governor," I repeated.

Like a hungry dog, the reporter was ready to leap. "I will—"

The words caught in his throat. From dog back to human being, the news had finally gotten through to him. "You said it." He seemed victorious, like he had gotten some concession from me, which was nonsense, pure and simple. I loved my job, and continue to love my job, and that is that.

By the way, the NBC guy reverted to form in his closing statement. "In a country that is frightened and angry about crime, Joe Arpaio, cocky and controversial, is a hero. Though he works in seeming disregard of the Constitution, his constituents love him. He's scoring big with the voters, and despite his protests, his next shot may be for the statehouse."

It's been over thirteen years since that NBC story. I'm gearing up for another election campaign to win another four-year term in the same job.

(Incidentally, at a certain point, can you reasonably say you've fulfilled an electoral, or nonelectoral, pledge? After so many years, is it sensible, is it smart, to be absolutely restricted in action, to be unable to respond as events and priorities change? Hey, George Washington returned home after winning the Revolutionary War, done with public life, until he was called back into service by an insistent nation. And, by the way, this is not an announcement of a run for governor or any other position on my part. Just an interesting question worth pondering.)

I checked and learned that the reporter retired a few years ago. Do you think if someone stopped him and asked, he would say he made a mistake in how he reported on me? Do you think if you requested that he review the interview and look at the record, and somehow he agreed to do so, he would care?

In truth, I can't say that the reporter truly believed any of the over-the-top crap he spewed, with comparisons to the Nazis and so on. Perhaps I should say I can't believe he believed any of that at all. But I am sure he pitched a certain story to his bosses back in New York about this lunatic, right-wing, protofascist sheriff out west, and that was the story they bought, and that was the story he was going to tell, no matter what the facts showed, no matter what he learned. In other words, he was acting no differently from a film director who follows a script to construct the story he wants to present on the screen.

That's showbiz, which is what the news biz has become, to an extent that ultimately cannot be healthy for America.

* * *

THOSE CONFRONTATIONAL encounters are, in any event, pretty much a thing of the past (which is not to say that the news biz is any less a new form of entertainment, only that the focus has shifted). Maybe it's because I've survived so long and with such public support that I've either exhausted the media's energy to crank up the self-righteous machinery, or maybe, and more likely, they've just seen the futility and lack of public appreciation for their contrary posturing. Maybe it has nothing to do with me, but rather that the whole country has shifted to a more conservative way of thinking and has taken the press, willingly or not, along with it.

It is hard to imagine a national talk show host ten years ago say-ing to me what talk show host Glenn Beck of CNN declared on his program: "I've had many people tell me today that you're an American hero, and I appreciate the work you're doing. Thank you, sir."

Not that I think there's anything wrong with what Beck said, inci-dentally. But it's decidedly different from the way it used to be.

The leading television talk show host a decade ago was a fellow named Phil Donahue. *The Phil Donahue Show* was a true pioneer in the format back then, although today it is largely forgotten, and Phil himself has faded into the pale shadow of yesterday, his name, unbelievably to me, unknown to the vast majority of young people. Regardless, in his day, no show was more important or popular, or more cutting-edge, entertaining, and interesting, than *Donahue*.

I had my Donahue moment about two years into my first term when I was invited on his program to discuss Tent City Jail, which was new enough to be a media phenomenon. (Of course, what I didn't realize was that the media, from Arizona to Australia, would still be covering the tents a dozen years later with the excitement of Columbus discovering America.) This was a televised test by fire— or at least that's how Phil and his producers probably intended it to be, although the outcome was somewhat different.

"Sheriff Joe Arpaio of Maricopa County, Arizona," Phil began his introduction. "Proud Maricopa County of which Phoenix is the county seat. You're the sheriff. Boy, you take no prisoners."

"Oh," I said, "I take a lot of them. I need more."

"Yeah," Phil said. He had a crew shooting from inside the tents. "Sheriff, how many people are in this prison facility?"

"Phil, it's a jail. I don't have the prisons, I have the jails." It's a common mistake, confusing the two terms, though less excusable for a TV host with a large staff conducting research and preparing a conversation on the matter.

"Oh, okay," Phil said. "Prison is a state facility, jail is county?"

"That's correct." I related how I had gotten the tents for free from the federal government, as opposed to spending hundreds of millions of taxpayer dollars to build new hard facilities.

Phil wasn't impressed by the economics. "And it's 120 degrees in these tents in the desert of Arizona in the heat of the summer," he scolded, his voice rising. "That's cruel and unusual punishment, Sheriff."

"Well, our servicemen and women went to Saudi Arabia," I replied, referring to Operations Desert Shield and Desert Storm. "They lived in tents in the desert, and they didn't even commit a crime. So I don't call that cruel and unusual punishment."

The audience applauded enthusiastically, which showed Phil his crowd wasn't with him on this subject. Still, that was pretty much how it started, and Phil did not let up or alter his appreciation of my tent innovation.

"Those are Korean War tents?" he asked.

"Some have holes in them," I said, "but it never rains in Phoenix anyway."

"But one of the problems is that they never breathe," Donahue persevered, his anxiety escalating. "That's that old-fashioned water-proofing. I mean, there's no air in there!"

"There's air in there," I said. "I haven't lost anyone. There've been no problems in the tents with the inmates."

I proceeded to explain to an alternatively shocked and appalled Phil how I had taken away coffee and TV, except for the Disney Channel, the Weather Channel, and a couple others; eliminated movies; served donated, green bologna; and generally made jail into an unpleasant experience—an experience that anybody with a brain wouldn't want to repeat. (Of course, we've made the whole jail experience even more "minimalist" since then, but that's another story.)

Then Phil and I talked about the chain gang, and in case you couldn't have guessed, if Donahue was starting to sweat over the green bologna, he was practically apoplectic about the chain gang.

I detailed how they wore orange uniforms and cleaned up the streets of Phoenix.

"And to those who would say this is arcane," Phil began, warming up, "it's medieval, you're cruel, we do have protections. Prisoners are people. I mean, it's true, they should be incarcerated, pay their price, do the crime, pay the time. But Sheriff, we're going back to the eighteenth century, the seventeenth century, here."

So it went, me talking about my programs, Phil not liking them, the audience—*his* audience—firmly on my side. Finally, it was time for the big finish, Donahue style.

"When you start canceling hot lunches," said Phil, "and feeding your prisoners bologna sandwiches, and you're getting a standing ovation from an angry, frightened community that's just put another lock on their door, when you take away TV and *Playboy*, when you juvenile your prison population, you convey the notion somehow that the prisoners really aren't human beings, and we don't have to bring to them any kind of due process, and screw the Bill of Rights."

And that wasn't all.

"And more and more cops start to play more and more cowboy. And the anger builds, the divisions build, the walls between the prisoners and the guards build, and pretty soon somebody says something to somebody else and ka-boom! And you've got some real hardworking public servants in Maricopa County held hostage."

Wait—more still.

"And I want to tell you something," Phil told the world and me, "like it or not, if that happens, and I pray it doesn't, Sheriff, because I'm here to tell you that I don't have all the answers. But one of the first things you're going to do is restore hot lunches to get those guards out, you're going to restore *Playboy* magazine, you're going to restore CNN and television. This is all a rootin', tootin', shootin', short-lived effort to prove that you're tough . . ."

Hey, I can talk. In fact, I can go on and on, and on occasion I have. No doubt. But Donahue more than showed what he was made of, verbally speaking, and with neither shame nor hesitation. So it was my turn.

"Who said I'm going to restore it? You're telling me I'm going to restore it. I'm not going to restore it. First of all, we haven't had any problem. We haven't had any riots. We've had three or four problems with 150,000 people coming through my system—150,000 a year. We run the most efficient jail system in the country. Our meals are down to thirty cents a meal per inmate. We send our inmates out to pick fruits and vegetables. I even have 48,000 corn dogs free of charge from New York that I feed the inmates. I haven't had the problems."

(Note: Since that time, we've considerably improved on those numbers; meals are now down to fifteen cents per inmate, served only twice a day. Not the direction I imagine Phil thought we should be heading.)

A couple of other people said their pieces, and then Donahue moved in for another attempt at a kill shot.

"They're gonna rise up," Phil darkly predicted. "I mean, I heard about you, Sheriff. Charles Dickens wrote about you in those schools."

Just as the NBC newsmagazine reporter vowed I'd run for governor, and I didn't, Donahue guaranteed the prison revolution would force me to return cable news and naked centerfolds, and I haven't.

And, let us not forget, both shows have been swept into television's waste bin of failed and forgotten misdeeds of popular culture. Not that I'm claiming any credit, but let's not forget that it is also true that every presidential candidate who has visited the tents has lost. Coincidence?

Back to the main point, the days of rough-and-tumble, give-and-take media altercations seem to be mainly gone, and after sometimes enjoying and sometimes enduring endless rounds of interviews and stories, domestic and foreign, in print and on radio and television, I think I'm a pretty fair judge. Oh, you can appear on a cable news show and participate in a shouting match, but that's not actually news. That's a cable network with twenty-four hours to fill, unlimited lists of "experts" at hand, and not enough actual news (or, more accurately, not enough journalists to cover the actual news), and a small, bored audience to stimulate. Hence, toss a couple of know-it-alls into the mix who are willing to play the game, shrieking at each other on cue, and presto!—instant TV.

No, I have to say, it's generally feel-good interviews these days. Not that I miss aggressively obnoxious questioning. Not at all, and have no fear, there's still enough of that to go around to remind me of the old days. But it certainly isn't like the old days, not in intensity.

* * *

LET ME give you a more typical example of what the news business has become, through the lens of a high-profile story in which I found myself involved as a result of my belief that I had something to contribute to the case.

But I'm getting ahead of myself.

It started with this professional celebrity, or person famous for being famous, or whatever the hell she does or is, this skinny girl named Paris Hilton. As we all know, in nauseating detail, this Hilton character found herself in some trouble, owing to driving drunk, getting arrested, then getting her driver's license suspended, then getting caught driving with that suspended license, then getting caught speeding, still on her suspended license. The judge took particular umbrage as her misdeeds piled up and sentenced her to actual jail time, like she was a normal miscreant, not a privileged, protected VIP.

Well, given her wealth and fame, that jail sentence caused quite an uproar, and—oh yeah, we all know too much about it already, so I'll make it quick—the sheriff in Los Angeles, Lee Baca, let her go with undue haste, well short of even a reasonably small percentage of her total sentence. His rationale veered between Hilton's allegedly delicate mental state (as though anybody feels good about going to jail) and the overcrowding that plagued his jail system.

Those reasons didn't exactly cut it with a public fed up with celebrity bad behavior (at least some celebrities' bad behavior). The outcry was enormous and ferocious, and that wasn't much of a surprise, for this was clearly a case of preferential treatment on so many levels, in and out of jail.

A lightbulb went off in my head, as it does with perhaps startling frequency, and I saw a solution to Sheriff Baca's problem, a solution that was elegant in its simplicity. If L.A. couldn't find room in its hoosegow for one scrawny socialite, then I'd take her off its hands and put her in the tents. Perfect: Justice would be served, Baca would be off the hook, the Tent City Jail would receive a nice round of publicity promoting our efforts to provide effective low-cost incarceration, and Hilton might get the chance to see what life is like on the chain gang. A win for everybody.

I phoned Lee Baca, whom I have long regarded as a friend, and told him my idea. He sounded interested and said he'd consider it.

The press had already gotten wind of my proposal and was calling. Hey, it was a good idea, and I'm not the type to hide my good ideas (maybe also my okay ideas) under a bushel. I announced my intention to the world and the world came knocking.

Naturally, most people assumed I was doing it just for the PR value. And, as we return to the topic of the media, that's why I was heading out to the tents. I was waiting in a small room with cinder-block walls, filled with scratched metal desks close together, a couple of old computers, and a handful of deputies and detention officers—the jailhouse version of a green room. On the other side of the door, you could hear the sound of meals being served, our famous cheap-and-yet-filling, officially nutritious meals.

The door opened and a Special Response Team (SRT) entered, three men and one woman, dressed all in black, including body armor and shin guards. They were all very fit and very strong, including the young woman. SRT was tasked with handling problems the detention officers on duty couldn't handle, especially physical clashes among the prisoners or between the prisoners and the guards. They were definitely an imposing group, and intimidation helped end a lot of arguments before they got too far.

When the clock on the wall read quarter to five, we got up and left the makeshift green room. In the heat of an Arizona summer afternoon, there was no point in heading outside until absolutely necessary. Now it was necessary because the show started in fifteen minutes. One show would be followed by another, each an hour in length. A lot of sweat would be shed today in service of the television gods.

So we strode through the dining area on the women's side. (It will surprise no one that the men and women are segregated in every building and in every setting.) The women whooped and hollered a bit, and a bunch crowded around, holding out the postcards we provided to them so that they could write notes home, requesting my autograph. The postcards had scenes of the tents and the inmates and came in three varieties with different sayings: "Crime Never Pays." "Keep America Beautiful." "Hello from Sunny Arizona!"

As usual, I obliged as best as I could, all the while still moving. TV waits for no mortal.

We stepped outdoors and into the yard where the tents were lined up, one after another, their poles sunk into concrete pads, the sides of the tents pulled up to let in any breeze—assuming a breeze could be found within a hundred miles. Surrounding the tents were reams of barbed wire and corrugated fence.

The women who weren't out on the chain gang or on another work detail were either in the dining area eating, or walking through the yard, or lying on their bunks, reading, talking, dozing, or just sweating.

The locals were there, their camera crews off to the side, not getting in the way of the network lights and cables and camera. A chair was waiting for me, set up between two tents. I sat down and the soundman clipped the mike to my shirt. I turned around and looked at the inmates who had gathered around, about twenty women, most of them giggling, ready for their close-up.

"Stand close, ladies," I instructed. "And don't talk when we're on. Unless I turn around—then you can say 'Boo!'"

I quizzed the women while waiting for the show to get underway. "Anybody go through Alpha?"

Alpha, as you might recall, was our very successful drug program. One woman raised her hand. "I did," she said. "And I didn't even want to smoke cigarettes anymore."

"Good for you," I said.

One woman revealed she had done time in both federal prison (and with Martha Stewart, no less) and my tents.

"Which is better?" I asked, immediately realizing I didn't know which answer I'd prefer. "Don't answer that."

The cameraman raised his hand, signaling it was time. I looked at the lens, picturing Larry King on the other end.

It was a panel with too many people, too many lawyers and social commentators and showbiz types, everybody eager to get in his two cents on this pressing issue. The cherry on the top was that the sound wasn't very good, crackly and hard to hear. The problem was supposedly on the other end, back in Atlanta, but it didn't matter. Bad was bad. An hour of that and then we went right into *Nancy Grace*, where the sound was better, though the situation was the same regarding the crowded field. Two hours of one person talking over another, nobody saying anything too interesting and certainly nothing too important. And all the while, the ladies behind me persevered, finding out precisely how glamorous this television stuff really was.

After that CNN segment wrapped, the local stations jumped in, getting their one-minute pieces for their evening news shows. The basic theme I used for every show was the same. "I could put all these gals under house arrest," I said, indicating the women behind me, in response to repeated questions concerning whether I'd alleviate jail crowding by sending the convicted home. "I'll never do it. No excuse for overcrowding."

That theme was the reason for doing these interviews from the jail, surrounded by inmates.

By the end, I was tired of listening to some people coddling poor Paris as though she were the victim. "It's kind of bizarre," I grumbled to one of the locals. "Who is she? She's a nothing."

My incidental involvement with the Paris Hilton case kept the media coming in a continual stream, local and national. Phoenix anchor John Hook, another guy I've known a long time and whom I like to think of as a friend, started off fairly boldly, at least boldly in this watered-down media environment. But of course he had covered me for years, so he had some idea as to what was what—or maybe it's more accurate to say, so he liked to think.

"You get in the middle of this Paris Hilton business," Hook began, "saying you'll take her if Los Angeles won't make her serve her full sentence, knowing full well they'll never release her."

You can't let an interviewer get away with that. "How do you know that? Why would you say that?"

"Why would they?" John said. "And how would her attorney ever agree to that?"

"What, come to our Tent City?"

"They would never, in a million years, agree to that."

"I didn't speak to her attorney," I said, "I spoke to the sheriff, Lee Baca, and talked to the head of the jails. I talked to both of these guys. I told them, if you have a problem, I'll take her. They didn't say no. They didn't say no."

Hook was not done. "But why inject yourself in the middle of the Paris Hilton thing, other than to get headlines?" He had been around here long enough to know that was a perfect setup line.

"To get headlines," I repeated, amused. "Do I need her to get headlines? I don't need her to get headlines. I can get headlines with pink underwear and everything else."

"And you have," he responded, chuckling, sort of acknowledging I had scored with that one. "You have. All right, you were serious."

"Of course."

"You would have taken her," John said, stating the obvious.

"You know why I wanted her here?" I said quickly, gathering some steam of my own. "To live in the tents, to maybe be on the female chain gang? I wanted her to do a favor for the Maricopa County people here, and [for people] across the nation, to show if you violate [the laws of] the nation, you're going to be in a tough jail system."

It wasn't that different with the nationals, from tone to questions. The truth is, the days of Walter Cronkite are over. It used to be that reporters would maintain a stiff upper lip and professional manner no matter what. Today, the emphasis is on communicating and connecting, on being in league with the audience, on being in on the joke, so to speak. That's the game for everyone, from local anchors to network hosts. Thus, anytime a TV personage can take a subject in the headlines and play with it, attempting to reach out to the audience in a human as opposed to a journalistic manner— assuming the audience likes it when the reporter or host drops his serious mask and shows himself to be one of the guys, with an easy laugh or convivial smile—he goes for it.

That's why there are more local anchors and feature reporters and talk show hosts than investigative journalists. That's why a city the size of Phoenix does not have one serious television commentator anymore.

*　*　*

GLENN BECK replayed my interview about Paris Hilton on his weekend review show. "One of my favorite interviews of the week," he said by way of introducing the segment.

"She actually would work on the chain gang if she were with you?" Beck said, with a big smile. "You're the only one in America that has a chain gang left, right?"

"We're the only ones in the history of the world who put females on a chain gang. I'm an equal opportunity guy," I said, "so we don't treat women differently because they're in a jail system."

Beck was flat-out laughing. "I've got to tell you, Sheriff, and I mean this with all due respect, man. I love you, I'd vote for you—how did you get elected? Nobody says these things, or does these things."

"You mean, how do I keep getting reelected?"

Beck was relishing his disbelief. "How do you keep your job in today's America? How do you keep your job?"

"Well, just use common sense. Not afraid to talk to you, or the media, tell it like it is. And I'm elected. Who's going to fire me?"

"Okay," he said. "So now you have her working possibly on a chain gang. But is it true that she would also be burying dead bodies?"

"My chain gang," I said, "men, and women, and juveniles, every Thursday they go to the county cemetery and bury the indigent. Yes."

Beck shook his head. "I have to tell you, man, I'm just . . . I wouldn't want to commit a crime in your neighborhood. I just don't want to commit it. So how do you think she's going to fare in, you know, a regular jail? I mean, it will make her more famous."

"I'm sure she'll be treated properly in L.A. county. But I run a different jail system."

"Let me ask you an honest question," Glenn said. "Do you really seriously think that this was real, or is this just a publicity thing for you?"

How many times do you think, by this time, I'd already answered that question? "No, I'm spreading the word," I replied. "If you get caught, whether you're rich, or whatever, you should do the time. I'm trying to send a word to Maricopa County, plus the country. I'm hoping that she does what she was sentenced and does the time. Just because she's rich and famous, it doesn't matter. . . . I've talked to journalists from all over the world. I keep saying, this is not the Hilton Hotel."

Beck had a good closer. "When you stay at the Hilton, generally, you don't have to bury the dead."

And then there was MSNBC.

"Nice to see you today, Sheriff," said Contessa Brewer, and then we got into it.

"We have 2,000 [inmates] in the tents," I said, "and can take one more. I called the sheriff and offered to help him out."

"And what was his reaction?"

"Well," I said, "he appreciated it. Let's see what happens on his end. Remember, we did have a famous singer arrested for DUI here in Arizona." I was discreetly referring to Diana Ross, arrested in Tucson in 2002, convicted in 2004, of driving under the influence. "Guess what? The judge on the East Coast let her do her time on the East Coast. So there's a precedent that's already been set."

"Do you think Paris Hilton would be the kind of person who'd want to take you up on your offer?" asked Contessa. "Because, on the one hand, she would get to wear pink, but on the other hand, tents have high humidity; it might really play with her hair."

Glenn Beck had also mentioned that she might like to wear pink, and others had mentioned our singular attire.

"We'd make her wear striped uniforms," I said. "I guess you'd worry about looking fat." Contessa had to agree with that.

"Wouldn't it be nice," I said, "if she were on a chain gang, to send everybody a deterrent? You don't drink and drive. And you don't get any special favors just because of jail overcrowding."

"Do you really get upset," Brewer wondered, "about people who drive on suspended licenses and think it's no big deal?"

"I think it's very important. The stats show that the majority of young people in that age group who get killed are killed in traffic accidents."

Contessa had a nice send-off. "Sheriff Joe, you always have a way of putting things into words that make it easy for the rest of us to understand. I appreciate that, sir."

And so it went, interview after interview, day after day, until the Hilton thing blew over and we were on to the next hot topic.

Was it worth it, to dive into the Paris Hilton circus? Apart from the sheer fun of watching the media spin on their collective head like a thousand tops in search of anything they could keep feeding a public insatiably interested in the story, it provided me a forum to discuss things that were more important and deserved discussion, from jail overcrowding, to equal treatment for all inmates, to the consequences of driving while under the influence, to flouting the law no matter who you were. Does anyone believe I would have been accorded such a wide-reaching forum to talk about any of these issues without wrapping it around the flimsy figure of a silly celebutante? Even I, with all my media contacts and media experience, don't think so.

Listen, I won't claim it's always this easy. Right here at home, our very own daily newspaper, the *Arizona Republic*, does whatever it can to avoid reporting on anything my office does. And the local rag, the Phoenix *New Times*, is the exception that proves the rule, with a modus operandi that appears to have been summed up by its owner in an interview in *New York* magazine: "Our papers have butt-violated every goddamn politician who ever came down the pike!"

In the summer of 2004, the rag published my home address in an article on its website, violating a state law that prohibits revealing just that information on the Internet regarding any peace officer. In case anyone missed the point, around Christmas 2006, the same rag splashed my address across its cover.

Though the paper made a point on its pages to deny the possibility that this could prove dangerous to either myself or to my family, the paper's protestations only proved that was a ridiculous, self-serving assertion. Of course, printing my address held that potential, whether we're talking about the organized assassination plot revealed in Chapter One, or a lone nut seized by an impulse to go out and do harm, destination now in hand, ripped from the rag's cover.

Of course, the paper's illegitimate act in revealing my address had nothing to do with journalism and everything to do with a vindictive pettiness that would be insufferable in a child and is absolutely unacceptable, legally and ethically, in an adult, and almost impossible to contemplate in a corporation, where such a deed would require the agreement and participation of more than one individual and at least part of the editorial staff, all together implementing a considered policy decision.

But that's why *New Times* is a rag, a free giveaway, filled with ads for escort services and prostitutes or, as the rag itself calls such offers, "adult entertainment." If the *New Times* ever possessed any claim to pursuing actual journalism, it long ago dissipated both its legitimacy and, for the most part, any hope of gaining either influence or an audience.

Any discussion of the media must discuss speed. The time for reflection is finished, the ability to get the news (or what appears to be the news) on the air or on the Web immediately trumps any attempt at reason or discretion or objectivity. Being first is what counts. Sometimes it seems it's the only thing that counts.

A small example: Not long ago, coming on the heels of Atlanta Falcons quarterback Michael Vick's guilty plea in a dogfighting scheme, my deputies investigated a tip left on my animal-abuse hotline and raided the home of Earl Simmons, aka rapper DMX, who, according to what I've been told, was a big star a few years ago but had more recently seen his fame fade as he fell into relative obscurity. Celeb or not, a dozen pit bulls were found on his property, badly undernourished and otherwise abused. Also discovered were the corpses of three other dogs, a sizable cache of weapons, and some illegal narcotics. As of this writing, the disposition of the case is far from resolved, but I get angry thinking about the kind of person who would choose to abuse an animal. The fact that I *was* angry prompted me to drive to Simmons's house in New River and see what was what for myself.

As you might imagine, I knew what was happening pretty much as the raid went down. New River is a town outside of Phoenix, to the northwest. It's a good drive, and before I could get there (and I didn't waste too much time) the media was already on the story. A local television station carried a short segment about it, which triggered MSNBC to run with it, both on cable TV and on the Internet. Within minutes, the few known details were being covered that same afternoon on the Web by the *Boston Herald, International Herald Tribune,* Dateline France, E! Online, MTV, TMZ, Reuters, *Arizona Republic,* and many others. Every local and major national television outlet jumped on the story before the day was over.

But legitimate news organizations and their websites were not the only ones to alert the world. Others websites interested in the tale included The Gay Socialites, based in New York, the self-proclaimed "#1 source for everything that's gay with a healthy helping of celebrity scoop!" The Actress Archives, also from New York, and at least four sites from the U.K., including Monsters and Critics, Showbiz Spy, *K9 Magazine,* and Contactmusic.com, and a host of others elsewhere, were on it.

That wasn't the end of it, but only the beginning, as website after website—hundreds in all, large and small and smaller—followed up with their own versions of the story, or just reprinted what was already out there.

For better or worse, DMX wasn't as famous as Paris Hilton or as dangerous as Charles Manson, but his story circled the globe in a virtual flash. In this instance, the handful of reported facts were reported correctly, although they could have just as easily been reported incorrectly (as they frequently are) and still receive equivalent international play. And that doesn't even count the stories that are simply made up, invented for malicious or political or some other such reason. The conspiracy theories that abound on the Internet regarding the "real" perpetrators of 9/11 are prime and horrific examples. Google "9/11 conspiracy" and you'll be rewarded with over 4 million separate hits explaining how the Bush administration, or rogue elements within the U.S. military/intelligence

community, or the Israelis, or somebody other than Islamic terrorists actually committed the crime. As moronic as these notions are,
their influence is undeniable. Extraordinarily, more than a third of
Americans believe our government either assisted in the attack or
did nothing to stop it. If that's true here, you can imagine the per-
centages overseas. Just one example: Only 3 percent of Pakistanis
believe Al Qaeda had something to do with the events of 9/11.
While you can't simply blame the Internet and television for people's prejudices, stupidity, and ignorance, it is certain that when we
can readily find the rumors and lies that feed our beliefs, those
beliefs are reinforced and hardened into absolute certainties.

That's a dangerous reality and far beyond my ability, or perhaps
anybody's ability, to change. Nonetheless, it is the way it is, and God
help us all.

＊　　＊　　＊

SO THAT'S the state of the media, from where I sit. I referred to the
Paris Hilton event as a "circus," and so we have it: a world of bread
and circuses, just like in Roman days. Only in place of the Roman
gladiators, the powers that be are attempting to pacify the people
using the Hilton business and other celebrity nonsense, as well as car
chases, apartment fires, sports, and any freak, deadly or pathetic,
willing or forced to perform for the cameras. My goal, my job, is to
get my message out in between the jokers and bloodshed. I bet more
people know me from the pink underwear business rather than any
of my other policy initiatives, which is fine, because the pink boxers
both saved taxpayer money and made an important point, opening
the door to discussing other programs and issues. And so whatever
works, whatever gains me a forum to carry the discussion about law
and order to the widest audience possible, works for me.

Yes, to answer the question so many people ask. Yes, I enjoy the
press and its attention. It's interesting and amusing to bat ideas back

and forth with all sorts of reporters and interviewers. It's also part of my job, to serve the public not in secrecy but in the public arena.

Truth be told, it amazes me that others in public service don't adopt my philosophy, if not my precise manner, of dealing with the media. It amazes me how many run when they see a microphone, or even try to cover up facts and events that no one in his right mind would think about covering up, because there's nothing to hide, until that microphone appears and causes their brains to lock and their instincts to go haywire. An open door and reasonable transparency (reasonable to the extent that the mission of the organization isn't compromised) is the best friend of any public official. Democracy depends upon honesty and collaboration, the direct involvement of an informed public working with its chosen government representatives. So when I see a congressperson or state senator or mayor or president avoid the media, as either a right or a necessity, I am dumbstruck.

It's that simple. Do I think the press wants to get me in print or on camera because of my charm and good looks? Well, maybe Ava would think so, but the real reason is because I'm good copy and good video, and that reality is just another tool, and a key tool, to help me accomplish so much. Actually, if you think about it, the media are so consequential to my success that you could consider the entire industry one of my most valuable partners in pursuing my goals and thriving in my post.

That's a description I don't believe will find a lot of fans inside the media. But that's the way it goes.

POLITICS, AS USUAL

THE DAY TENT City Jail opened was a landmark occasion. The inmates were there, the media was there, and that meant the politicians were there. A crew from French television, a writer from a Norwegian magazine, Senator Phil Gramm from Texas (who was running for President), the list was long and noteworthy.

It was time to start, and who better to make the introductions but Arizona's own, Senator John McCain. He offered some gracious words on my behalf, calling me "the best known and most popular politician in America, and the most popular sheriff in America, and a man who has revolutionized the office."

We got along just fine for several years. Why wouldn't we? We were both Republicans, both veterans, both elected officials, both regarded as tough on a lot of issues. It wasn't like we were buddies or had any deep, personal relationship, but we cooperated when the occasion arose, and that was sufficient.

All that was about to change. It was 1999, and McCain called. He said he was going to run for President, and he wanted my endorsement. I wasn't ready to settle on a candidate just yet but did say, as things stood right then, that I would probably support him.

That was that. I didn't hear again from McCain. He didn't call before he announced for President, and he didn't call me after.

A year went by.

In the meantime, George W. Bush came to town. He was then the governor of Texas, and he was running for President, too. He wanted to meet, and we did. After my time in Texas with the DEA, I was particularly interested in what he had to say about Mexico and illegal immigration, and its effect on American workers and small businesses.

I liked Bush. I liked that he seemed to understand how American businesses profited on the backs of cheap labor, and how that cheap labor also hurt the opportunity of our own workers to compete and earn a reasonable wage. I also liked that he expressed compassion for the illegals and the desperate situation that brought them to the United States. (Later on, we would see that when it came to illegal immigration, Bush's compassion interfered with his ability to effectively do his job. My compassion didn't. Of course, considering how events have turned out in Iraq, a debate over "compassion" rings a bit hollow.)

The governor asked for my endorsement, and I gave it to him. We shook hands.

Word immediately got out that I was going to endorse Bush, and the phone rang. It was John McCain. You're the greatest, he told me, in an unusual, to say the least, expression of enthusiasm. I need you. I need your help. You can't do it. You can't endorse Bush.

I explained that the deed was done. Bush had asked, I had agreed. We had shaken hands. I had given my word.

McCain pressed, but it was pointless. I didn't feel bad about having to turn him down. The senator might have been able to secure my endorsement if he had communicated with me in the course of the year and we could have talked more about the issues, perhaps come to a meeting of the minds, but that hadn't happened. Why, I couldn't say. Maybe McCain thought that as Arizona's own candidate, he possessed some divine call on all local loyalties. Maybe he had originally calculated I held no value to his campaign and then belatedly changed his mind. Whatever, he was wrong.

The senator did not take my position with good humor. He has a reputation for holding a grudge (not to mention an angry, bitter temper that's regularly directed at staffers and others around him), and he quickly developed a world-class doozy against me. Whatever relationship we had previously had was over, finished, gone.

The situation did not improve with Bush's election. In fact, on a presidential visit to Arizona, when both the senator and I were on hand to greet Bush, McCain consciously turned his back on both the President and myself when we shook hands. I not only remember it well, I have the photograph to prove it.

McCain took his shot at revenge in 2004 when I was up for reelection. The timing probably seemed perfect to him: He was working his way into the good graces of President Bush by not only toeing the party line but pushing himself out front as one of the administration's champions. McCain was secure in his Senate seat, and he was the darling of much of the media, even the liberal media, which had anointed him the conservative it was okay to love. He had already been declared the front-runner for the Republican presidential nomination in 2008, practically the presumptive nominee.

Yours truly, on the other hand, was confronting almost the opposite situation. I was already on the outs with much of the local Republican Party hierarchy because I was never under the party's thumb, blindly following the party line simply because it was the party line. My relationship with the local party structure really took a turn for the worse when I defended Janet Napolitano, the Arizona attorney general and former U.S. attorney, during her bruising 2002 race for governor. I had worked with Janet during her tenure as state attorney general and also as the federal prosecutor in Arizona, and I respected and liked her. Nonetheless, I would not have gotten involved in her race if her opponent hadn't launched a vicious, personal attack, claiming that she was "soft on child molesters" and, as if that obscene and ludicrous charge wasn't bad enough, also implying that she had some personal reason for giving these monsters an alleged free pass.

That might have been the way the game is played, politics as usual, but I couldn't stand it, and I wouldn't stand by and do nothing. This sort of underhanded assault capsulated the core of what was wrong with American politics, and fortunately I was in position to act—or, more precisely, counteract these scurrilous claims.

It made no difference to me that Janet was a Democrat. The fundamental wrongness of this situation was more important than political affiliation.

I appeared in a TV commercial sticking up for Janet's character and career.

> *This is Sheriff Joe Arpaio with an urgent message. Janet Napolitano has been attacked with the most vicious TV ad in Arizona history. The ad is outrageous and untrue. As U.S. attorney, she was the number-one prosecutor of child molesters in the nation. As our attorney general, Janet Napolitano has stood with law enforcement to protect our families.*
>
> *This is Joe Arpaio. Join me in rejecting the attacks against Janet Napolitano.*

You'll take note that I never endorsed Janet for governor. That wasn't the point of the ad. It was a matter of principle, not politics. Regardless, some local Republican Party types didn't see it that way.

They were incensed that I came to the assistance of the Democratic candidate. And when Janet won by fewer than 9,000 votes and my ad was credited by some commentators and analysts for making the difference in the outcome, well, fuel was definitely added to the partisan fire.

All this set the stage for McCain to gain his revenge. He endorsed a candidate running against me in the Republican primary, a candidate who was both personally and professionally unqualified, with a history more than a little strange and undeniably sordid. And then the Maricopa County Republican Executive Guidance Committee, a fancy name for a bunch of county GOP leaders, voted seventeen to eleven to support that same opponent. Interestingly, the county chairman mentioned before the vote that a "confidential source" had pledged $250,000 to the county Republican bank account—a very substantial sum to a local organization—on the condition that my opponent received its endorsement. Not that that should influence anyone's vote, the chairman added, because, as he later told an interviewer, "I would never put the party, while I'm its leader, in a position where it could appear that we had been bought."

Buying a politician . . . no one's ever heard of that happening, right?

Blood was in the water, and the piling on commenced. The *Arizona Republic*, never a fan, threw its editorial support to my opponent. Unions I had tangled with, in defense of my deputies, now saw their chance to carve out a new slice of power and rushed to the side of my opponent.

McCain egged them all on. To the outside observer, not to mention a number of people inside Arizona's political crowd, it seemed a bit weird, almost unseemly, that a United States senator would get so involved in a county race for sheriff. But then this wasn't an ordinary county race, because, to be simply honest, I'm not your ordinary cop, and McCain is definitely not your ordinary senator. The distinction, at least as far as I see it, is that I'm different in a positive, pioneering, constructive way, whereas McCain is noteworthy

for his always-ready anger and his bitterly unforgiving nature—
except when it's politically expedient. That allowance for expediency
was evident virtually since the day McCain lost the 2000 presidential race, when he determined that, despite the personal savaging he
had suffered at the hands of Bush operatives during the South
Carolina primary, victory in 2008 meant cozying up to President
Bush and his allies in the "mainstream" Republican Party—cozying
up to the same people who had denounced McCain as "the fag candidate" because he had met with the Log Cabin Republicans, the gay
Republican group; claimed that his adopted daughter from
Bangladesh was actually his own illegitimate black child; and even
dug up some Vietnam veteran to stand beside a smiling Bush and the
television cameras and allege that the authentic war hero was not a
war hero but instead a man who "came home and forgot us."

Still, McCain wanted to be President, and so he somehow put
aside whatever pride he possessed and has been one of Bush's biggest
cheerleaders ever since. The immediate result was that McCain
stunned and lost some of his old supporters, who didn't appreciate
this political deathbed conversion. He even forfeited his standing as
the liberals' favorite conservative. Maybe the gambit will work and
maybe it won't; as these words are written, the campaign is still on
and the jury is still out.

The fate of McCain's 2008 presidential campaign is not relevant
here. In truth, I can't say I'm too concerned whether McCain takes
the big prize or fades forever from the national scene. The real point
is that McCain forgave Bush because his ambition could not afford
his anger, no matter how righteous, while I remained high on his hit
list, year after year, because his ambition was not adversely affected
by his well-celebrated anger, and so he could let that demon out to
play and run free.

So they went after me, guns blazing, confidence high. The real
key for McCain and his fellow plotters was that this was a primary,
not the general election, and that meant voter turnout would be low

and in part dependent upon the party mechanism getting the most committed Republicans to go to the polls. That meant the county leaders and similar types had a larger hand than usual in the outcome.

And in case anyone wondered about McCain's devotion to this angry cause, he recorded a message—and not a pro-Arpaio message—that about 100,000 voters heard when they picked up their ringing phones.

And then it was time to vote.

When it was all said and done, I won the primary, and quite handily, too. My margin of victory was eleven percentage points— a landslide by anyone else's count, though not as large as I've gotten on other occasions, and not much compared to my general election margin of twenty-six points, but hey, a win is a win, and a big win is that much sweeter.

The whole McCain tale, costarring the local Republican Party, is symptomatic of what politics is increasingly all about, and not coincidentally, it illustrates exactly what is wrong with politics. Petty, mean, unfair, unprincipled: I make sure to count my fingers after shaking hands with a politico, just to check that none are missing.

That's why I hesitate when people ask me if I'm a politician. Yes, I'm an elected official. Yes, I'm a public servant. Yes, I'm proud of my job and my responsibility. But no, I don't like to think of myself as a politician.

I told the McCain story not because it was so unusual, but because it was so typical. Not the specific set of facts, but the motivation and reasoning and emotion underlying the actions, the manner of dealing with people and problems and issues in general, the way in which the world is viewed, the way business, political business, is conducted—that was typical.

For years, I had to contend with the local county attorney, again a fellow Republican, and again somebody with a quick temper, shaky ego, and perpetually jealous, unsatisfied spirit. It made absolutely no sense that the county attorney and the sheriff would not cooperate in almost every instance. Damn, all you had to do to know that is watch any episode of *Law and Order.* The cops open the show by tracking down and arresting the bad guys, and the prosecutors take over and take them to court and send them away.

Hell, if TV can figure that out, you'd think an actual county attorney could do the same. But no, this particular politician tried to get in my way time and time again, in actions both petty and large. The bottom line was this: He had big dreams, far grander than his present position, dreams of becoming governor, and he resented the publicity I received. His resentment morphed into an unyielding urge to criticize MCSO and me to anyone who would listen. And it was ugly and nasty and unproductive. It certainly never did him any good.

When he finally left office (to the remorse of precious few), the new county attorney and I quickly established a more normal relationship, and our offices have worked together smoothly ever since.

You just have to read Shakespeare or Homer or the Bible to understand that envy and insecurity and fear and hate are some of the darker instincts and emotions that drive humanity. Politicians are nothing if not human, and they're not necessarily the noblest examples of the species. Whatever base motivation you can imagine, whatever childish, stupid, selfish impulse you can think up, you can rely on politicians to lead the parade, and that goes from the humble county attorney to a U.S. senator and beyond.

And speaking of United States senators, here's an epilogue of sorts to the McCain story. The day after I won that 2004 election, he was walking through an airport when he ran into an old friend of mine, a guy I have known ever since we joined the army on the same day. Being my friend, the guy went on and on about what a great job I was doing. With my presence on the public scene ensured for another four years, and perhaps with his own extravagant ambitions in mind, evidently figuring it was better to switch than fight, McCain did not miss a beat.

"Oh, yes," he said enthusiastically. "What a great guy."

And still the story doesn't end there, for one night, my home phone rang. The good senator was ready to formally open his 2008 presidential campaign, and as astonishing as it might sound to the very young and very innocent, McCain was back, once again requesting a meeting. I wasn't surprised, because that's what politicians are all about, doing whatever is good for their ambitions at that moment. Shame is not part of their vocabulary.

McCain dismissed the past with a throwaway line. "That's just politics." It was time to start over, time for a new day and a new campaign. I was reminded of what they say in the mob when they're about to do something really bad, even to a friend: "It's not personal, it's just business."

McCain didn't come out and ask for my endorsement; he talked around it. He didn't ask and I didn't offer.

The truth was, even with everything that had happened, if I had thought McCain would have made the best President, whether in 2000 or 2008, I would have offered my endorsement. But I liked Bush in 2000 and preferred him to McCain and the other Republican candidates, and that's how I felt about former Massachusetts Governor Mitt Romney in 2008.

In all my campaigns, I've never asked for anyone's endorsement. I never felt I needed it, never felt it was important, because I preferred to go straight to the people and let my own words and my own ideas and my own record speak for themselves.

I don't really consider myself a professional politician, and the feeling might be reciprocated by those very same politicos. Oh, now they need me, or think they do. They want to get their photos taken with me, they want to stand shoulder to shoulder on television, they want encouragement and support. (Not that my support is necessarily a guarantee of success: Four presidential candidates have toured the tents—McCain, Gramm, Senator Bob Dole of Kansas, and Governor Pete Wilson of California—and none gained the prize. I was the honorary chair for the Mitt Romney for President campaign in Arizona. Romney's a fine man, a smart administrator, a successful governor . . . but you should have stayed away from the tents, Mitt, at least until the votes were in.)

And as much as they want whatever they want from me, it's all for show. Do you know how many politicians have asked my opinion about illegal immigration? Not one. Not one has asked what a guy who worked both sides of the border for more than a decade—first running the DEA office in Texas, then heading up the Mexico and Central and South America operation from Mexico City, and then back on our side of the line, working out of Arizona—might have to say about the debate. No one has asked a guy who's the only local official doing anything about stopping illegals what he might have to contribute to the discussion.

It's not like they don't ask advice because they're lining up to attack me. Oh no, they don't do that at all. They say nice things and then they go back to Washington or their own states. And they do nothing.

I already said that the news business has become show business—how far behind (or maybe far ahead) is the political business?

Otto von Bismarck, the nineteenth-century Prussian statesman, declared that politics is the art of the possible. That's supposed to mean that ideology and principles are all well and good, even important and ennobling, but actually accomplishing something in the face of competing factions, conflicting priorities, and limited resources and time, and still getting something done—if even just part of what you wanted done—that is the true art of politics.

No one can accuse contemporary politicians of not compromising in pursuit of objectives. However, compromise today seems to be more about every congressperson ensuring that he gets a piece of the taxpayers' pie to fund his district's or state's useless project or some such other thing, rather than taking brave and principled stands. Politics might be the art of the possible, but that doesn't have to mean being small and shallow and self-interested and, when you add it up, cowardly. That certainly wasn't what Bismarck had in mind, or he wouldn't have managed, through political maneuvering and war, to create a unified German nation. Now, I'm not suggesting we resort to similar tactics (although you can make a pretty good case that's exactly what we've been doing lately, only with far less success than Bismarck), but you get the idea.

By the measure of my own career, I know that to honestly and effectively enforce the law and protect the public and the public interest frequently means transcending the limits of any officer's purview, transcending the bounds of any department's jurisdiction, and transcending the specific definition of law enforcement itself. This is not to say, before anyone gets alarmed, that a cop has either the right or responsibility to break the law or his oath. Not at all. What I am saying is that some problems cannot be solved by law enforcement itself, but by law enforcement working with political entities and forces. You can arrest dealers on the corner, and Lord knows I put truckloads of them in jail, but you're not going to stop drug dealing at its source without the government stepping up and insisting that it get done, by whatever means necessary, government to government. Money laundering, weapons sales, immigration, prostitution rings, pedophile groups, Internet scams—we have to fight on the street and in the halls of government.

It's no different from the new reality that business faces: competing with Chinese manufacturers or outsourcing production to Bangladesh, the media instantly broadcasting through the Web or television to the entire world, or medicine having to contend in every small town and neighborhood with diseases that can originate anywhere on the planet.

We are all connected, and few matters can be understood in isolation. In the end, political decisions must be made on what are traditional law enforcement issues. But we can't always wait for the politicians to stand up and act and do what's right. Their deliberate inaction has forced me to take the lead. That is the essence of what has happened with illegal immigration. I have had no choice, as an elected official sworn to uphold the law, but to stop waiting and do whatever is right and practical and principled. I guess that's one of the beauties of a nation-state with so many levels of separate and overlapping government—if the feds don't get it done, maybe the state will, and if not the state, then the locals. And if Maricopa County can help show the way, then so be it.

That's why, despite all the negative things I've had to say about politics and politicians in general, about the often tiresome, often tawdry business, I'm still on duty, still preparing to run for another term. And don't you doubt it, assuming all goes well, I'll run for another term after that. Hey, age is just a state of mind . . . isn't that what they say?

I'll keep running because I believe in what I do. I'll keep running because as imperfect as the system is, as much crap as I have to accept as part of the game, it's still the only game in town.

THE MORE THINGS STAY THE SAME, THE MORE THEY BETTER CHANGE

NEW ZEALAND came to visit. Well, not all of New Zealand, but it's starting to feel that way. I had Channel One in the office a week ago, and somebody else from what I guess was Down Under's Down Under, and now Channel Three was here. Actually, Channel Three (what happened to Channel Two?) was following this poor guy whose wife was murdered by someone who had been sent to jail literally over a hundred times and was still let out to kill. The widower had been sponsored by an anti-crime group that was looking to tighten New Zealand's evidently relaxed laws regarding the disposition of bad guys. They had brought him to Phoenix, with their own documentary crew in tow, which was being followed by the Channel Three crew, which in turn had attracted a freelance photographer to capture the whole traveling circus.

I didn't know that much about New Zealand, but I did know this many visitors had to lighten the Auckland morning commute. The documentary crew filmed for a while as I talked to the victim and also the politicians, who wanted me to fly to New Zealand and explain to their countrymen all the good work I've been doing and how they could do the same. I thanked them but declined, explaining I was a full-time sheriff—overtime, really—and wasn't flying God knew how many miles one-way (okay, 6,776 miles) to the other side of the planet and taking that much time away from my job.

Still, it was nice of them to stop by for a chat. And then it was on to the next visitor . . . because there was always somebody next.

✳   ✳   ✳

A PHOTOGRAPH popped up on the Internet. Somebody had taken my face and stuck it on a body of a guy in a Ku Klux Klan sheet. And that guy—me—was holding a noose before the head of a man who was evidently Hispanic. The caption read, "Arpio (sic) new political career KKK." The badly doctored photo could be found on the website of a pro-immigration group, the very same group whose leader, Elias Bermudez, was named by the Yuma PD's confidential source as a key participant in the assassination plot we were still investigating, the plot that had forced my office to expend time and resources to take appropriate precautions, just in case.

Even so, this incident would have come and gone without anybody noticing, because Bermudez's site wasn't exactly an Internet hot spot. The fly in that ointment was that Bermudez was aware of his site's limitations and didn't wait for the world to discover the photo, but e-mailed it to news organizations, politicians, and assorted friends. I suppose he thought it was going to be a big winner for him. He was wrong.

Was I surprised that Bermudez was taking part in this tawdry photo business? No, just as I wasn't surprised he was trying to have it both ways on this occasion, because that's what self-righteous, self-serving people do. I know, because when you hang around politicians and reporters long enough, well, you get to know a lot about supremely self-interested types. When the picture first appeared, he had defended it, acknowledging that it had been his decision to place it on his group's website. Quickly, however, as Bermudez belatedly recognized that both media and public reaction to the photo was extremely negative, he had a change of heart—kind of a deathbed conversion.

I agreed to appear with him on the local NBC news outlet because I was angry and wanted the truth on the record. I got to start the segment: "We have a little history, he and I, and I think the picture will become clearer, as time goes, regarding his activities. . . . [On another occasion], he accused me of being associated with the Third Reich, Germany, where they were encouraging people to report the Jews, and now he's putting out this vicious piece of garbage to the whole world," I said.

Bermudez did his little dance, attempting to appeal to the vast majority of the audience who found this stunt wrong at best, disgusting more likely. "I want to let the public know that resending that picture through the Internet was truly a stupidity on my part," he said.

Grammar aside, as always, he kept an eye on his core constituency, because without them, he had nothing. So, after a brief apology, he added, "It is actually the true feelings through the eyes of the Hispanic community."

I rejected his apology. "He's very good at saying something and then he backtracks when he looks at what the public opinion is."

He was ridiculous, and his words and actions only proved that, incident after incident.

The Nazi analogy, as obscene and nonsensical as anything could be, reared its ugly head again, because what's a pro–illegal immigrant press conference without invoking Nazis? At such a press conference, which was called to protest my illegal immigrant hotline, an actual Arizona state senator by the name of Ben Miranda stated, "It certainly brings back memories, to some people, of the thirties in Germany, the era in Germany when many civil rights were violated."

Is that the proper term for concentration camps these days? How about genocide? Maybe *Kristallnacht?*

Another genius made his own contribution at the press gathering, calling the Nazis back for an encore, declaring, "It is a throwback to the Third Reich where people were trained to call and report and put the word out on Jews."

The bottom line: The immigration agitator, the alleged state senator, and any and all other rabble-rousers could pull all the stunts they wanted, or shout all their hateful claims, but none of it was going to stop me from doing my job.

I was doing precisely that, my job, when I announced that I was banning illegal immigrants from visiting inmates in my jails. It seemed obvious enough—we didn't allow convicted felons to do any visiting, so why would we allow known illegal aliens (emphasis on illegal) that privilege? If we did run across any illegals, we'd arrest them. Case closed. Or, more accurately, new case opened.

What transpired next typified the difficulty of dealing with this issue. The office put together a form that every visitor had to fill out. It had different boxes to check, one denoting the visitor was born in the United States, the other box for naturalized citizens. The latter category asked for the number and date of the person's naturalization certificate, as well as numbers and dates of his passport or passports.

This was wrong on a couple of counts. One, naturalized citizens weren't likely to walk around with their naturalization papers on them, as though we were living in 1960s Soviet Union or, for a final Nazi reference, 1930s Germany. And two, it was simply wrong to differentiate between native-born and naturalized Americans, who (apart from the opportunity to run for president) are equal under the law.

The problem quickly came to light when a court interpreter, who is a naturalized citizen, was refused entry to the jail. I immediately changed the policy, declaring my deep respect for those who come here legally—like my mother and father who came from Italy—went through the system, and became naturalized. At the same time, I also announced we would continue to enforce the policy against any illegals visiting the jails, and we would require identification from everyone, which we would run through the computer.

The process isn't perfect, and we have to keep refining it, making sure to be both fair and efficient. Mistakes have been made, and will surely continue to be made, from the local to the federal level. It's regrettable and unavoidable because this is a difficult, evolving crisis that forces us to be flexible and responsive, to try new tactics and strategies, disregarding those that don't work and pushing those that do. It's a little like war, where events compel reaction and the battlefield is an ever-changing landscape.

One more way this situation is a little like war: The casualties are starting to mount, and the antagonists are becoming better armed, with automatic weapons, rocket-propelled grenades, and an arsenal of high-tech equipment. They use those weapons against one another and law enforcement, government agents, journalists, politicians, and anyone else who stands in their way.

While I shifted one policy, I stood fast on another. Representatives from an organization called the New Sanctuary Movement came to visit me in my office. They brought a letter, signed by ninety members of the clergy, that called my illegal immigration hotline "unconscionable," with "an intolerable potential to intimidate and ostracize one particular group" and "incite neighbor against neighbor."

The New Sanctuary Movement's handsome website reveals it to be quite an impressive group, with buttons leading to pages detailing news coverage on the group; pages listing the names and addresses of theological allies from California to Oregon to Arizona to Colorado to Texas to Kansas to Illinois to Wisconsin to Washington, D.C., to New York; pages recounting the many actions the group and its friends have taken; pages with information on how to join and organize and help, complete with "tool kits" filled with legal forms and media management and educational handbooks and commentaries. The site proclaims its mission is to protect the "basic common rights" of immigrants, opposing "the violation of these rights under current immigration policy." These common rights include "1) livelihood; 2) family unity; and 3) physical and emotional safety," rights that exist "regardless of national origin."

Carefully consider those last words—"regardless of national origin." That's an amazing statement, because if national origin is not the key determinant in how we decide how to deal with immigration, if it is relegated to a secondary position, it is being pushed into instant irrelevance. If that is so, then citizenship has no meaning, and borders have no meaning, and being American (or Mexican or Italian or Japanese) has no meaning. Are we prepared to give up our sovereignty? Are we willing to give up our national identity? Are we ready to throw away the American idea?

Consider the words of President Felipe Calderón of Mexico, in his annual formal address to his nation: "I have said that Mexico does not stop at its border, that whenever there is a Mexican, there is Mexico. And, for this reason, the government action on behalf of our countrymen is guided by principles, for the defense and protection of their rights."

Wow. Now that's a showstopper. What the man was doing was essentially declaring war (presumably the nonviolent variety) on the United States by asserting that the millions of Mexicans who illegally reside north of the border constitute a legitimate and successful invasion, a *de facto* annexation of American territory that the Mexican state has not only the right but the obligation to defend.

Did the man really mean it? Time for a rhetorical question: Do you think any politician means anything he's saying when he's addressing his angry, unemployed, poor nation? So maybe he meant it literally, or maybe it was just a dramatic flourish for the impressionable audience. Either way, it was a pretty amazing statement for any president of any country to make, especially *that* country, which is so dependent upon *this* country.

We've allowed that kind of brazen and bizarre talk. We've set the stage where such talk is almost inevitable by not insisting that the sanctity of America's borders is not open for discussion or debate.

Back to my meeting with members of the New Sanctuary Movement: A reverend from Tucson told the press she was surprised that I agreed to meet with the group. I could not imagine why; I've never hid from my critics, the media, or the public. We met for a good hour, and I listened while they explained their objection to the hotline. I had heard objections before, which I earlier related within these pages. I asked them to give the hotline a chance. It would not be employed to unfairly target anyone. Its sole purpose was to help law enforcement do its job. I saw no compelling reason to close the hotline.

The meeting ended. The spokesperson for the group told the press the encounter had been "productive." Glad to hear they felt that way. The hotline remained in operation.

✳   ✳   ✳

ACROSS THE country, the issue of illegal immigration has been gaining more serious attention because of events that have shocked and horrified the public. Far from Arizona and the border, an illegal alien from Peru was arrested for the execution-style murder of three young men, ages eighteen to twenty, in a Newark, New Jersey, playground on August 4, 2007. Apart from the pointless and utterly cold-blooded nature of the crime—the victims forced to kneel against a wall and then shot in the head—it additionally shocked and angered the nation that the suspect had already been arrested several times and had been released each time instead of being held and/or deported. Two of his three arrests were on sexual assault charges: He was accused of raping a five-year-old girl in his care. Somehow, even though he was in this country illegally, he was released on bail on all three occasions.

The arresting police never reported the suspect's immigration status to anyone else in the federal government, including U.S. Immigration and Customs Enforcement (ICE), which maintains an office in the area that acts as a liaison with local police. Nor did the New Jersey prosecutors alert the feds.

Adding insult to injury, the Newark Municipal Council had previously adopted a nonbinding resolution that committed the city to being a "sanctuary" for immigrants. The mayor of Newark, while expressing frustration that this particular suspect had been let out on bail, continued to firmly argue against involving city police in immigration matters, saying such a role would hurt law enforcement's relationship with what he called "the most marginalized and vulnerable people within our community."

To my mind, and to increasing numbers of Americans, the proper "relationship" between law enforcement and those breaking the law should be one securely bound by handcuffs.

Newark is far from the only place experiencing a disturbing surge in violence and crime. Sometimes the stories are hard to believe: In Laredo, Texas, teenager Rosalio Reta was stopped in his $70,000 luxury sedan, earned from his work as a hit man for the Gulf cartel. Though American born, Reta was a frequent visitor to Mexico, walking across the border from Laredo even at a very young age, and soon he became enamored of the high life of the drug gangs. When all of thirteen years old, he began working for the cartel.

Now seventeen, sentenced to forty years for murder, and facing another trial for another murder, the young man told of being part of a "cell" of young enforcers that murdered rivals and tracked members of the cartel's own ranks, working both sides of the border. Reta was part of Los Zetas, the murderous organization that has been growing virtually unchecked inside Mexico in size and power for several years. It was the organization that was linked to the assassination conspiracy against me. A former Zetas gunman, serving time on a federal illegal weapons conviction, explained how the group, on behalf of the cartel, had set up three teams of operatives in Laredo so that they could perform different jobs, from the more mundane, such as purchasing vehicles for drug transportation, to its particular expertise, killing anybody in its way.

The orders would come from a cartel commander in Nuevo Laredo, Mexico, right across the border.

While Reta was not an illegal immigrant, the confluence of illegal immigration, drugs, kidnapping, rape, murder, and probably any other immoral and illicit activity you can imagine, can only flourish because of the American inability to protect our borders. To date, that inability has been the result of official disinterest, prompted by political cowardice, intellectual dishonesty, and cheap labor.

Slowly, the government has started to acknowledge the growing danger to America. The majority staff of the Subcommittee on Investigations of the House Committee on Homeland Security investigated "the triple threat" of illegal immigration, drug smuggling, and violence on domestic security. The report they released sounded more than a few alarms. Some of their conclusions:

> Mexican drug cartels operating along the Southwest border are more sophisticated and dangerous than any other organized criminal enterprise. The Mexican cartels, and the smuggling rings and gangs they leverage, wield substantial control over the routes into the United States and pose substantial challenges to U.S. law enforcement to secure the Southwest border. The cartels operate along the border with military-grade weapons, technology, and intelligence and their own respective paramilitary enforcers.

In addition, human smugglers coordinate with the drug cartels, paying a fee to use the cartels' safe smuggling routes into the United States. There are also indications the cartels may be moving to diversify their criminal enterprises to include the increasingly lucrative human smuggling trade.

Moreover, U.S. law enforcement has established that there is increasing coordination between Mexican drug cartels, human smuggling networks, and U.S.-based gangs. The cartels use street and prison gangs located in the United States as their distribution networks. In the United States, the gang members operate as surrogates and enforcers for the cartels.

Murders and kidnappings on the both sides of the border have significantly increased in recent years. The violence along the U.S.-Mexican border has increased so dramatically, the United States ambassador to Mexico, Tony Garza . . . has issued an unprecedented number of diplomatic notes to the Mexican government and threat advisories to U.S. citizens traveling to Mexico. During August 2005, the ambassador closed the U.S. consulate in Nuevo Laredo for one week in order to assess security.

This new generation of sophisticated and violent cartels, along the Southwest border, is presenting significant challenges to U.S. law enforcement. These criminal syndicates have unlimited money to buy the most advanced weapons and technology available. The cartels monitor the movements and communications of law enforcement and use that intelligence to enable the criminals to transport their cargo accordingly.

In addition to the criminal activities and violence of the cartels on our Southwest border, there is an ever-present threat of terrorist infiltration over the Southwest border. Data indicates that there are hundreds of illegal aliens apprehended entering the United States each year who are from countries known to support and sponsor terrorism.

You can't get much stronger and more definite than that, and coming directly from the United States Congress, that's quite a punch. Of course, the assessment was written by the Republicans, who formed the majority at that time. The minority Democrats attacked the report as "irresponsible," not to mention "inflammatory, uncorroborated, and partisan." Before anyone gets too excited about which party stood where on the issue, I am ready to bet that if the Democrats had written that report, the Republicans would have been the ones condemning it. That's how they do things in Washington. Not always . . . but usually.

One more fact: That report was released back in October 2006. If you haven't already heard about it—and the odds are you haven't—that's because the report, and all its testimony, facts, and conclusions, barely caused a ripple in the media or with the public. It came and it went, and that was the end of that.

So here we are.

On August 15, 2007, the Border Patrol's chief patrol agent for the Laredo sector declared at a town hall that "the Border Patrol is not equipped to stop illegal immigrants." He also noted that drug trafficking was not on the agency's list of priorities. "The Border Patrol's mission is not to do any of those things," he said. Instead, the man continued, the BP's mission is to keep the country safe from terrorists and terrorist weapons. If and when the day comes when terrorists cross the border, the chief patrol agent averred, the agency will be ready.

The BP's man statement caused an uproar, at least a small uproar, among those who paid attention to these matters. By this stage, it didn't seem possible that anyone at Border Patrol, let alone a ranking officer, could not have a better understanding of what was at stake. But there it was.

At the same time, we were making progress on other fronts. Twenty-six local law enforcement agencies have signed formal agreements with the federal government to deputize corrections officers to check the immigration status of prisoners. Similarly, state legislatures have not been waiting for the feds to figure out what it needs doing, and they have been passing bills at the state level to deal with the issue as they see fit.

Arkansas passed a new law prohibiting state agencies from contracting with businesses that hire illegal immigrants. Oregon banned anyone who wasn't a lawyer from performing immigration consulting work. Louisiana barred the state from issuing driver's licenses to foreigners until criminal background checks have been conducted.

From January to November 2007, forty-six states passed 244 new immigration laws, according to the National Conference of State Legislatures, more than double the eighty-four laws approved in all of 2006.

Here in Arizona, the legislature passed a bill requiring employers to use a new federal database to avoid hiring illegal immigrants. However, Illinois passed its own law, preventing businesses from utilizing that same database, contending that it contained too many errors.

And in the better-late-than-never category: In the wake of the Newark mass murders, New Jersey's attorney general ordered local law enforcement to inquire about the immigration status of criminal suspects and to alert the feds when they believe someone under arrest is in the country illegally. On the other hand, the Essex County prosecutor—one of several offices in the state that did not check into the immigration status of the alleged murderer—did not (as of this writing) back down from her position of only notifying immigration officials upon conviction.

✳   ✳   ✳

WHILE IT is crucial that the states do whatever they believe is right to protect their territories and their citizens, it is also crucial for the federal government to not only contribute to the exponentially expanding fight, but lead it, with all the resources at its command.

Of course, I'm not waiting for the feds or anybody else to win this battle. The truth is there's no winning, not in the traditional sense, because the battle never ends. Crime, in virtually any form, is not something that will ever disappear, not as long as human nature remains the same as it has forever, driven by both our finer qualities of compassion and love and sacrifice, and also by greed, selfishness, stupidity, jealousy, and violence. We will not stop crime, whether we are talking about human smuggling or drugs or even terrorism, and all the other more mundane offenses, but we can control it. We can control our borders. We can control who comes through our airports and what goods enter through our ports. We can control what happens on our streets. We can control what happens in our schoolyards. We can control how vulnerable we are in our power plants, water systems, and other essential services. We can control how prepared we are to respond to an attack or disaster of any kind. We can control how much money and manpower we put into protecting our neighborhoods and our nation.

More than forty illegals, men, women and children, were recently discovered in a drop house in a quiet neighborhood in west Phoenix. Three suspected coyotes were among those nabbed. The locale was discovered when one of the illegals escaped the house and ran to a neighbor, who called the police. The Mexicans had been held against their will by the coyotes, who were demanding ransom payments from their relatives back home. They had been held for four days with little food or water in a small house, the air-conditioning turned off.

This was just one lone drop house of so, so many in Phoenix and throughout Maricopa County. Rents are cheap, and housing is available for short-term leases, so each gang can have dozens of houses at its command. My deputies know the locations of many potential drop houses, properties sitting empty, but we don't have the resources to indefinitely stake out each one, waiting for a load to appear and make use of it.

The human smuggling business might be brutal and inhumane, but it's not rocket science. The profits are so enormous, the risks so minimal, that losing one drop house, or one drop house per day, will not stop the smugglers. By fighting here and there, in piecemeal fashion, we are playing catch-up in a game that will never end. Once again, the answer is clear: Get to the border and shut it down.

The conspiracy that I wrote about in Chapter One remains an open case. Nobody's taken a shot, but the investigators aren't convinced it won't happen. Often, in this kind of unpleasant business, you never know what's real and what isn't until you find a plan, a gun, even a body—or they find you first.

Do I think it's possible? You might as well ask me if I think it's possible that millions of Mexicans are encouraged by their own government to leave their homes and land and risk their lives to come across the border in the hope of finding happier lives, rather than that government taking responsibility for improving the lot of its people. Is it possible that political opportunists on both sides of the border use the misery of these men, women, and children to push their own ambitions and agendas? Is it possible that Mexican drug cartels are permitted to terrorize border towns and corrupt government officials and murder police officers? Is it possible that 2,000 Mexican soldiers and cops and criminals are allowed to coalesce into a modern-day Murder, Inc., that is not only responsible for the deaths of perhaps thousands, but also threatens the existence of the Mexican state? Finally, and, for our purposes, perhaps most significantly, is it possible that the government of the United States continues to tolerate the borders of our country remaining undefended and dangerously vulnerable?

Given that all that is not only possible but simply, shockingly true, then I have to say yes, it is certainly possible that among those profiting in one way or another in the havoc and horror that is engulfing Arizona and the entire Southwest, there are people who would plot, without hesitation, to kill one more cop.

Regardless, I know that for many people, this business of illegal immigrants and drug traffickers and hit men and kidnappers and endless victims simply doesn't make sense in their own reality, where Mexicans and other Hispanics trim their trees and build their homes and raise their children. Can it really be that bad, that ominous, that dangerous? Can't we just keep going along as we have been and leave it at that?

It's always an option to only see the trimmed trees and new homes and coddled children, and hope that someone will fix whatever problems might be lurking out there and everything will be okay. It's always an option unless you are crossing the border or defending it, unless you are transporting drugs or fighting them, unless you are a Maricopa County deputy sheriff and forced to deal with the villains and victims of this reality, unless you are called to the middle of nowhere, on the west side of the county, on a dirt road in the desert, where three dead bodies are waiting.

Three men are stretched out across the road. They're all lined up parallel to one another, as though positioned for execution. Two are lying facedown, and the third man is on his back. It rained in the early morning hours, so their clothes are wet and splattered with dirt.

They have all been shot in the head. They are seventeen, twenty, and twenty-two years old—more boys than men.

One fellow's arms are bent at the elbows and his hands are tucked under his chest, while his legs are extended straight out. Little divots are etched into the ground around the toes of his shoes, as though his feet were moving back and forth, trying to get away, right before he died. A large pool of blood is drying around the top of his skull. He has been shot four times from the neck up. Three shots came from the back, one from the front, perhaps implying he spun around during the attack, catching one of the rounds in his right cheek. A fifth bullet entered and exited through his left foot, an injury probably suffered while he was already down.

He is wearing jeans and a jacket with a picture of a smiling Winnie the Pooh embroidered on the back. Underneath the smiling face are the words, *The sort of bear who's always here.*

He has $63.70 in his pocket.

The other two corpses are in no better shape. They are soaked in blood, their faces ripped apart, chunks of flesh gouged out, bits of their brains and bodies tossed on the ground. Shells from two 9-millimeter guns and a .45-caliber surround the victims.

It doesn't take long for my detectives to discover what happened. Long story short, it revolves around a drug deal and an unpaid debt by one of the young men, owed to another group of young men— two of whom are related through marriage of the common-law kind. All six young men, killers and deceased, are Mexican, and all are illegal. There are wives and girlfriends and children involved. The wives and girlfriends are also illegal; the children, one now an orphan, are American by birth.

The killers escape back to Mexico. They are not in jail for long, as they pay off the proper authorities and get out. We learn of this episode and hasten to inform the local cops of the homicides, and they rearrest the men. While it's no surprise that our request for extradition is denied, it is a little surprising that the murderers remain in custody, unable to buy their way out of jail a second time. Evidently, the Mexicans take the murder of their own seriously. The killers are tried, convicted, and dropped down into the dark hole that is the Mexican prison system.

Illegal immigration tied to drugs and tied to murder. Each of those facts led to other facts. Each of those acts was the product of so many other illegal acts and dangerous actors. Nothing that affects so many people can exist in isolation, can be kept separated from touching, directly or indirectly, all of us.

Crime does not cure itself. Crime does not go away of its own accord. Crime is an insatiable parasite, feeding off its host—society—until there is nothing left to take, corrupt, or destroy.

This is a fight we must win, or we shall all lose. This is a fight worth fighting. It is a fight I am proud to have been part of for most of my life. It is a fight I will continue to be part of, for as long as the people of Maricopa County place their faith in me to serve as their sheriff.

INDEX